High Hopes

Also by Harvey Aronson

THE DEFENSE NEVER RESTS
THE KILLING OF JOEY GALLO
ESTABLISHMENT OF INNOCENCE
DEAL

HIGH HOPES

The Amityville Murders____

Gerard Sullivan and Harvey Aronson

Coward, McCann & Geoghegan New York

Copyright © 1981 by Gerard Sullivan and Harvey Aronson.

All rights reserved. This book, or parts thereof, may not
be reproduced in any form without permission in writing from
the publisher. Published on the same day in Canada by
Academic Press Canada Limited, Toronto.

Library of Congress Cataloging in Publication Data

Sullivan, Gerard.
  High hopes.

  1. De Feo, Ronnie. 2. Crime and criminals—New
York (State)—Biography. 1. Aronson, Harvey, joint
author. II. Title. III. Title: Amityville murders.
HV6248.D33S94   364.1′523′0924   [B]   80-25054
ISBN 0-698-11076-5

PRINTED IN THE UNITED STATES OF AMERICA

For Betty, Kim and Jill, whose patience meant everything.

Contents

Prologue

THE CALL that brings the case to official notice is logged by the Suffolk County Police Department at 6:35 P.M. on November 13, 1974. As the caller comes on the line, he is talking to somebody nearby. "Hey . . . hey," he is asking. "What's the number here?" In the background, a dog is barking.

Then the 911 operator comes on. A young woman, she is obviously trained to go by the book.

Operator: "Suffolk County Police. May I help you?"

Man: "Hah?"

Operator: This is Suffolk County Police. May I help you?"

Man: "We have a shooting here. Uh, DeFeo." (He asks somebody on his end of the line for "the name of the street." The dog's bark continues to dominate the background.)

Operator: "Sir, what is your name?"

Man: "Joey Yeswit."

Operator: "Can you spell that?"

Man: "Yeah. Y-E-S-W-I-T."

Operator: "Y-E-S-W . . ."

Man: "Hah?"

Operator: "Y-E-S . . ."

Man: "Y-E-S-W-I-T."

Operator: ". . . W-I-T. Your phone number?"

Man: "I don't even know if it's here. There's, uh, I don't have a phone number here." (He's right to be puzzled—there is no number on the instrument he is using.)

Operator: "Okay, where you calling from?"

Man: "It's in Amityville. Call up the Amityville Police, and it's right off, uh . . ." (Again, he queries somebody nearby. "What's the name of the street here? What's the name of the street, Billy?")

Man: (Back on the line after a pause metered by the dog's barking.) "Ocean Avenue in Amityville."

Operator: "Austin?"

Man: (Emphasizing the syllables.) "Ocean Avenue. What the . . .?"

Operator: "Ocean . . . Avenue? Offa where?"

Man: "It's right off Merrick Road. Ocean Avenue."

Operator: "Merrick Poad. What's . . . what's the problem, Sir?"

Man: "It's a shooting!"

Operator: "There's a shooting. Anybody hurt?"

Man: "Hah?"

Operator: "Anybody hurt?"

Man: "Yeah, it's uh, uh—everybody's dead."

Operator: "Whattaya mean, everybody's *dead*?"

Man: "I don't know what happened. Kid come running in the bar. He says everybody in the family was killed, and we came down here."

Operator: "Hold on a second, Sir." (Her agitation evident as she asks a police officer to take over the call. "There's a guy here, he says there's been a shooting and everybody's *dead*.")

10

Police Officer: "Hello."

Man: "Hello."

Police Officer: "What's your name?"

Man: "My name is Joe Yeswit."

Police Officer: "George Edwards?"

Man: "Joe Yeswit."

Police Officer: "How do you spell it?"

Man: "What? I just . . . How many times do I have to tell you? Y-E-S-W-I-T."

Police Officer: "Where're you at?"

Man: "I'm in Ocean Avenue. I don't know the name of the street. The guy . . ."

Police Officer: "What number?"

Man: "I don't have a number here. There's no number on the phone."

Police Officer: "What number on the house?"

Man: "I don't even know that."

Police Officer: "Where're you at? Ocean Avenue and what?"

Man: "In Amityville. Call up the Amityville Police and have someone come down here. They know the family."

Police Officer: "Amityville."

Man: "Yeah. Amityville."

Police Officer: "Okay. Now, tell me what's wrong."

Man: "I don't know. Guy come running in the bar. Guy come running in the bar and said there—his mother and father are shot. We ran down to his house and everybody in the house is shot. I don't know how long, you know. So, uh . . ."

Police Officer: "Uh, what's the add . . . what's the address of the house?"

Man: "Uh, hold on. Let me go look up the number. All right. Hold on." (He drops the phone. There are background voices, but they are unintelligible. And the dog is still barking.)

Man: (Returning after a few seconds.) "Hello. Hello?"

Police Officer: "Yes."

Man: "One-twelve Ocean Avenue, Amityville."

11

Police Officer: "One-what?"

Man: "One-twelve Ocean Avenue, Amityville."

Police Officer: "Is that Amityville or North Amityville?"

Man: "Amityville. Right on . . . south of Merrick Road."

Police Officer: "Is it right in the village limits?"

Man: "No, it's uh . . . you know where the high school is?"

Police Officer: "Yeah."

Man: "It's in the village limits, yeah."

Police Officer: "Yeah. That's the village limits, right?"

Man: "Yeah."

Police Officer: "Eh, okay, what's your phone number?"

Man: (Calmly repeating his previous answer to the same question.) "I don't even have one. There's no number on the phone."

Police Officer: "All right, where're you calling from? Public phone?"

Man: "No, I'm calling right from the house, because I don't see a number on the phone."

Police Officer: "You're at the house itself?"

Man: "Yeah."

Police Officer: "How many bodies are there?"

Man: "I think, uh, I don't know—uh, I think they said four."

Police Officer: "There's four?"

Man: "Yeah."

Police Officer: "Okay, what's your name again—Yeswit?"

Man: "Joey Yeswit."

Police Officer: "What's your first name?"

Man: "Joe. Joe."

Police Officer: "Joe."

Man: "Joseph."

Police Officer: "Where do you live, Joe?"

Man: "I live in Lindenhurst."

Police Officer: "Whereabouts?"

Man: "Uh, Forty-eighth Street."

Police Officer: "Forty-eighth Street?"

Man: "Yeah."

Police Officer: "What number?"

Man: "Uh, three-forty."

Police Officer: "Three-forty. What's your phone number at home, Joe?"

Man: "Uh." (He gives the number.)

Police Officer: (Repeats the number.) "All right, you stay right there at the house, and I'll call the Amityville Village P.D. and they'll come down."

Man: "Okay."

Police Officer: "Okay."

Man: "Bye, bye."

The caller hangs up the phone. After almost four minutes, he has gotten his message across. He has made only one mistake. There are not four bodies in the house.

There are six.

PART ONE

Crime and Arrest_____

1

THERE WERE EIGHT SHOTS, but no one in the neighboring homes on Ocean Avenue in Amityville heard them. The best explanation anyone could give for this was that the three-story home muffled sound like a castle. At 3:02 A.M. that Wednesday, November 13, 1974, a fifteen-year-old boy two doors away was awakened by a barking dog. The teen-ager, John Nemeth, checked his clock and walked to the south window of his attic bedroom. He tried to peer past the vacant house next door to the DeFeo home at 112 Ocean Avenue, from which the barking seemed to be coming. The barking was incessant. It was sufficiently irritating so that the teen-ager, who would have to get up for school in a few hours, thought about calling the police.

He got as far as the steps leading downstairs before deciding he was better off going back to bed. John was sure the malefactor was the DeFeos' gray-and-white English sheepdog.

He knew the dog's bark and had even petted it a few times. Usually, the dog was taken in at night, and it had never awakened him before. When he looked out the attic window, the boy's view was blocked by the empty house next to him and the winter-thin branches of beech and oak trees as well as by smaller evergreens. But he was almost certain from the volume and direction of the barking that the sheepdog was outside— tied up by the north stoop where it was often kept during the day near a shed for garbage cans that was attached to the house. Number 112 was unusual in that it was built sideways to the street. Whereas the other even-numbered homes on Ocean Avenue faced the street on the west and a canal on the east, the DeFeo residence faced south and north to adjacent houses. The front entrance was on the south with a paved driveway running alongside.

The dog's voice scratched the night. It was not the animal's regular bark. "That night it was howling, like," John Nemeth would testify almost a year later. The dog howled steadily for fifteen minutes. It stopped, but started again a minute later. This time, the howling went on for five minutes. Then Ocean Avenue was silent. There was just the canal, the Amityville River, lapping along the bulkheads as it mirrored the night south to the Great South Bay.

Shortly before 3:45 A.M., a barmaid drove south on Ocean Avenue. The barmaid, Deborah Cosentino, worked at the Chatterbox Bar and Grill, a few blocks west of Ocean on Merrick Road—the latter artery a once-major route that still winds through the South Shore of Long Island, pocked by gas stations, small businesses, bars and eating places. It is similar to other of the Island's fading and bangled highways except for the boatyards that signal its proximity to the bay. As it runs through the village of Amityville, Long Island (population 10,700), Merrick Road is a dividing line. On the north of Merrick Road, there are hospitals, a movie house, offices and a bustling shopping area. On the south, quiet streets such as Ocean Avenue meander to the water in a pleasant cadence measured by large old homes—many of them Dutch Colonial and Victorian, white-shingled and fronted by neat lawns and long-settled maples and elms. Along Ocean Avenue, the backs of the homes are fringed by green yards reaching to docks and boathouses. The canal widens as it approaches the bay, the bulkheaded shoreline ridged like a house key.

Ms. Cosentino would remember closing up the Chatterbox at 3:30 A.M.. She decided to have a nightcap at Henry's, a neighborhood bar that was located between Pizza T and Sportackular, Inc., in a small shopping area on the southwest corner of Merrick and Ocean. But Henry's was also closed and so she turned right on Ocean Avenue to go home. If she had not decided to stop at Henry's, she would have taken a different route.

It was still quiet on Ocean Avenue, the street shadowed by the large trees. Ms. Cosentino was driving between 40 and 50 miles an hour but she couldn't help noticing the house at number 112, where Ronald and Louise DeFeo lived with their five children: Ronald, Jr., twenty-three; Dawn, eighteen; Allison, thirteen; Mark, eleven; and John, nine. Lights at the front and rear of the house went on automatically after dark, and normally the place stood out because of a brightly lit shrine on the lawn facing the street. The shrine, one of several on the property, showed St. Joseph holding the Christ child. In front of them, three angels, each about ten inches high, kneeled in adoration. Ronald DeFeo, Sr., had been seen on the front lawn saying his rosary beads in front of the shrine. And not much more than a year before, it had been the center of a neighborhood scene. Ronald, Jr., had accused John Nemeth's little sister of throwing stones at the statues. When Mrs. Nemeth reported the child's denial, Ronald, Jr., became furious and started shouting at her. They were in the DeFeo driveway with Ronald, Jr., hollering that if Mrs. Nemeth wasn't a lady, he'd punch her in the nose. What's more, he had a lot of connections and she'd better watch her step. And if her husband came over later, he'd punch him in the nose, too. As passing motorists slowed down to see what was happening, the young man followed the woman to her house while continuing to yell at her. Mrs. Nemeth was surprised—she and Mrs. DeFeo had been friendly, and she had never found Ronald, Jr., to be anything but polite.

But the shrine was not what caught Deborah Cosentino's attention as she drove down the street. Set against the shadowed block like an electric torch, the DeFeo home blazed with light. All three floors were illuminated—every room seemed to be lit up. The house was dark-shingled with white trim, and the small, fan-shaped windows atop the Ocean Avenue side glared at the street like the eyes of an ebony jack-o'-lantern.

The barmaid glanced to the left as she passed. She knew Ronald DeFeo, Jr., from high school and as a customer at the Chatterbox. They had never dated, but she had been in the DeFeo home a couple of times. Ronnie seemed pleasant enough—generally, he was a nice person. But he could be a violent drunk. A couple of times when he was into booze, she had seen him throw bar stools and break pool cues.

Attracted by the lights, Ms. Cosentino wondered if Ronnie were home. She looked for his car in the driveway, but didn't spot it. She would remember his car as an aqua Wildcat, although he actually drove a blue Electra. Nevertheless, the only car she noticed as she went by was a station wagon. She would remember that afterwards. She would also remember how she felt about all the lights being on in the house. "It just seemed kind of strange at that hour of the night."

At 7 A.M., John Nemeth went outside to wait for his school bus. The bus stop was directly across the street from the DeFeo house. He noticed two cars parked in the driveway—a green station wagon and a red LeSabre. He did not see a third car.

Nor did he see the sheepdog outside. And there was no barking. If something had disturbed the animal, it was over.

2

SOMETIME BETWEEN 3:30 A.M. and 4:40 A.M. that November 13th, Ronald Joseph DeFeo, Jr., took a shower and trimmed his beard. He had to be careful near his lip, which was still slightly swollen from a fight with his father two days before. Ronald was five-eight, about one hundred and seventy-five pounds, hairy-chested and huskily built without looking like someone who had weighed two hundred and fifty pounds as a teen-ager. The face that stared back at him from the mirror was fair-complexioned with long, curving brows, wide-set brown eyes, a broad, straight nose and a spade-shaped beard that connected to a mustache and sideburns. His brown hair was collar-length, worn over his ears and brushed to the right side without a part. His most arresting feature was his eyes. He was adept at direct stares, and he could grin by relying on his eyes and barely moving his lips.

Satisfied with his appearance, Ronald left the bathroom,

which was one of three in the house, not counting the lavatory in the kitchen. The bathroom was on the third floor where he and his oldest sister, Dawn, slept. Dawn's room was on the east side of the house toward the canal; Ronald's was the west bedroom facing the street. The floor of the young man's room was covered with a gray, white and blue shag rug, and the walls were brightly papered in red-and-blue polka dots on a white background. At the head of his bed, the polka-dot motif changed into mock road signs and posterlike drawings, the latter including a nude blonde whose lower torso was blanketed by the legend: "NOT NOW, DARLING." The night table contained a clock radio, an alarm clock, a Princess phone and a lamp whose base was made of a Galliano bottle in the guise of a Napoleonic soldier but whose shade was surmounted by a peace sign. A leather jacket was draped neatly over his desk chair, and he had left two pennies and a dime sprawled near a pack of matches and a large ashtray on the desk blotter, which was bordered by a marble pen stand and the model of a fully rigged galleon. The room registered Ronald's habits and interests from the cigarette stubs in the ashtray to the overflowing toolbox in an open storage closet. Ronnie enjoyed the water—his father had given him a four-thousand-dollar speedboat when he was fourteen—and a large painting above his desk showed a three-masted sailing ship breasting surging white-caps. Tapes were stacked in a metal unit near the room's entrance, and a dusty gun rack rode the wall above them. The rack contained a .22-caliber rifle and a shotgun. A .22-caliber pellet rifle leaned against a nearby corner. And there was more. Across the room, two gun cartons stood next to an old-fashioned steam radiator. The labels showed that both boxes had contained seven-shot Marlin rifles. One was a .22-caliber semi-automatic. The other was a .35-caliber carbine.

Ronnie, or Butch, as he was known to friends, put on his usual work outfit: brown boots, a pair of blue dungarees and a blue cotton shirt. Lettering inside the shirt identified both the

22

wearer and his place of employment. "BRIG-BUTCH," it said; the "BRIG" stood for the Brigante-Karl Buick Agency on Coney Island Avenue in Brooklyn, which was owned by Ronnie's maternal grandfather, Michael Brigante. On days when Ronnie was going to work—especially when he wasn't driving in with his father, who was the firm's service manager—it was not unusual for him to leave early to avoid the traffic buildup on the Southern State Parkway. If the agency was closed when he arrived, he could catch a little extra sleep in his car or have breakfast at a nearby luncheonette. This particular morning, he had some errands to do first.

As was often the case, Ronnie couldn't find his car keys. With Dawn driving to school every day, the car situation had become complicated—there were four drivers and three cars in the family, and keys were frequently misappropriated or mislaid. Ronnie decided to look around in the kitchen, and started down the red-carpeted stairs to the first floor. On the way, he passed a series of gold-framed oil paintings. They were all family portraits, their very existence a testament to the good life in suburbia. One showed his sisters as children nestling side by side with a book in their laps, and their dark hair caressing their party dresses. Another depicted his brothers kneeling in a meadow. Mark held a toy dog in his right hand, and his left arm was on John's shoulder. A third painting was of Ronnie and his father. Done in warm brown tones, the portrait showed Ronnie holding a wine glass, which his father was filling from a decanter. The elder DeFeo stood squat and powerful, a broad-faced man working at holding his half-smile. His sleeve was rolled back and his left forearm looked massive against the flask. Both men were looking straight ahead—if there really had been wine in the container, the father would have been spilling it all over his son's knees.

Downstairs, Ronnie spotted a set of keys on a hallway radiator. They were not his but included a key for his 1970 Electra. A coffee pot and a kettle were on the kitchen stove, but

Ronnie, who had stayed home the previous day because of stomach pains, didn't make anything for himself. Nor was his appetite stirred by the cast-iron frying pan soaking in the metal sink. He took a blue denim jacket from the hall closet where the family's winter coats were kept and left. There was no one about except for the family's English sheepdog, Shaggy, who was chained inside the back door. The dog hated Ronnie, and the feeling was reciprocal. One night just a few weeks before, the dog had attacked Ronnie while he was sneaking a girl down to the finished basement. He didn't have the cash for a motel that night and the girl disliked scrunching in the car, so they were going to use the cellar. But the dog jumped him and bit him on the arm—the scar was still visible. After that, Ronnie had lain awake nights trying to figure out a way of getting rid of the dog without arousing his father's suspicions. That was another problem: the old man had told Ronnie that whatever happened to the sheepdog would happen to him. "If the dog ends up in the canal," his father said, "you're going to end up in the canal."

At about 4:40 A.M., Ronnie started his car. Not surprisingly, since everyone parked in the driveway, the Electra was blocked. Although the neighbors didn't like it, he jumped his own driveway and used the driveway of the Ireland house on the south to back out onto the street. He drove south to the dock at the end of Ocean Avenue and parked by the entrance to the town dock. Soon afterwards, his blue Buick was heading back north on Ocean, and turning west onto Merrick Road. Ronnie had lived in Amityville since he was thirteen—his family had moved to the waterfront home from Brooklyn—and the route to work was as familiar as his own room. The row of stores at the corner of Ocean and Merrick, where Henry's bar waited to open, and then the discount shoe mart at the corner of Route 110, where one turned right toward the parkway. Just north of Merrick on Route 110, a set-back funeral home reminiscent of the spacious houses that marked the southern tier of the village gave way to the shopping strip and the overhead tracks of the Long Island Rail Road. A private psychiatric hospital flashed by on the left, and then Ronnie was beyond the village limits, driving past a trailer park and a couple of fast-food emporiums onto the westbound entrance of the Southern State Parkway, which quickly moved out of Suffolk County into Nassau County until it crossed the city line into Queens and Brooklyn.

Normally, Ronnie left the parkway at Coney Island Avenue, which ran south into the rusted resort of the same name and north to Brigante-Karl Buick, not far from Prospect Park. But this time, he got off four miles before that at Rockaway Parkway. For the second time since leaving his house, he made a short stop. Soon, he was driving north on Remsen Avenue and then east on Clarendon Road through Flatbush. Shortly after 6 A.M., he arrived at the car agency, where he worked for his father in the service department. He had worked there for more than a year, his longest tenure in any job. As he would explain to a psychiatrist, "Nobody could tell me what to do because my father was the boss. I did what I wanted to do." Ronnie helped with tune-ups, changed oil, got cars washed and ran errands for his father. Although his grandfather Brigante only paid him eighty dollars a week, Ronnie rarely suffered for money. If he lived at home and didn't cause big trouble with his father, the elder DeFeo would give him all the cash he wanted. He got about five hundred dollars a week from his father, and there were nights when he went to Roosevelt Raceway or toured the South Shore bars near his home with as much as two or three thousand dollars in his pocket. And the job was important for another reason. The previous year, Ronnie had pleaded guilty to possession of a stolen outboard motor. He was put on probation for a year, and he needed the pay stubs to show his probation officer as proof of employment. That day, in fact, he was supposed to see the probation officer at the ACE Youth Center in Amityville, anywhere between 2 P.M. and 8 P.M.

The car agency was locked, and Ronnie went to a

25

luncheonette on Coney Island Avenue. Inside, early risers were meeting the fall morning with coffee, but there was no one at the counter whom he knew. He wasn't worrying about his stomach problems anymore; he bought himself an egg cream and a bran muffin for breakfast. By the time Ronnie was finished eating, a Brigante-Karl employee had opened the service department. They were joined by a part-time worker. Ronald DeFeo, Sr., wasn't expected—he had an appointment to take Ronnie's other brother, Mark, to the doctor for treatment of a leg injury the boy had suffered playing midget football. The injury had occurred in September, and Mark was still using crutches and a wheelchair. Ronnie was proud of his eleven-year-old brother's athletic ability, and had attended the game at which Mark got hurt. Afterwards he was furious, telling his girlfriend that he wanted to get the whole opposing team.

Ronnie spent the morning hanging around the car agency. He called home several times. Each time, no one answered. He also called the girl he had been dating for the past five months. That was at 11 A.M., and he phoned her home in Nassau County. He'd be coming home early, he told her, and he'd drop by. Ronnie's hours were 8 A.M. to 5 P.M., but one of the fringe benefits of having your father as the boss was that you didn't have to punch a clock. Around noon, he figured the hell with it, and took off.

Forty-five minutes later, Ronnie's blue Buick came off the eastbound lane of the Southern State Parkway and headed south on County Line Road in Amityville. A black Volvo going in the opposite direction slowed and made a U-turn behind Ronnie, and both cars parked along the curb. The driver of the Volvo was Robert William Kelske, a twenty-four-year-old stone mason who, over the past few years, had become Ronnie's closest friend. A tall, well-built man with light-colored hair and masculine good looks, Bobby Kelske had been everything Ronald DeFeo, Jr., could never be. Butch DeFeo had never excelled at anything. He had been a fat boy who got into fights but paid off bullies and was not much of an athlete. His marks were never more than marginal. He had been dismissed from a couple of parochial schools and had dropped out of Amityville High School in the tenth grade. Bobby Kelske had been a standout athlete at the same high school, a football and wrestling hero who had reason to dream of a college sports scholarship. Instead, he and Ronnie were part of a subculture of drinking and gambling buddies whose lives revolved around cars and bars and point-spreads and sex and sometimes drugs in a suburbia they had never left. It was a good-old-boy milieu in which Kelske's past glory gave him a certain status. In the words of a former teacher, who knew the subculture, "Kelske was a renowned tough guy."

Perhaps it was symbolic of their relationship that Ronnie got out of his car and walked back to the Volvo. Kelske lowered his window and asked what Butch was doing home so early. Nothing was happening at the shop, Ronnie said, and his father wasn't there to check on him because he was taking Mark to the doctor. Kelske had driven past the DeFeo house around 10 A.M. and told Ronnie that the two family cars were still in the driveway.

While Ronnie and Kelske were talking, two men they knew pulled up across the street and joined them. The pair had a stereo they were trying to sell. Nobody asked where it came from, but Kelske suggested that he show it to somebody who might be interested and meet them at Henry's Bar. Ronnie said he'd also be at the bar. Not long afterwards, Kelske returned the unsold stereo to the two men at Henry's, but Ronnie never showed. Kelske went outside and checked the parking area. The blue Buick was nowhere in sight, and Kelske went home. He ate lunch and decided to take a nap.

At about 1:30 P.M., Ronnie appeared at the home of his girlfriend, who will be referred to as Sherry Klein. Sherry was nineteen, a high school graduate whose father was a doctor. She was dark-haired, pretty, not unused to being complimented on her figure by the men to whom she served drinks. She had tended bar at several Long Island establishments. Sherry Klein and Butch DeFeo had eaten dinner with each other's families, and they had been talking about taking a trip together. But their relationship did not always come up roses. In the latter part of the summer, Sherry had not been living at home. She had her own apartment, and Ronnie had come over with four friends and started a commotion. Sherry tried to calm him down and he threw a chair at the ceiling and shoved her across the floor. She had climbed out a bedroom window and fled to her parents' home.

Now, they stayed at Sherry's house for a while, and Ronnie told her that all the cars were in the driveway at his home but that no one was answering the door or the phone. He was locked out because the set of keys he had taken that morning did not include a house key. While he was at Sherry's, Ronnie called home two or three times without getting an answer.

It was early afternoon, and Ronnie and Sherry drove to the Sunrise Mall in Massapequa. They did some shopping in the enclosed climatized mart, and Sherry left a cigarette lighter at a jewelry store for engraving. When they returned to her house, Ronnie phoned home again. There was still no answer, and he made it obvious that he was upset. He left but didn't tell Sherry where he was going.

Around 3 P.M., Bobby Kelske's dogs made a racket that woke him from his nap. He looked out his bedroom window and saw the Buick in the driveway and Ronnie DeFeo walking toward the front door. Kelske's mother told Ronnie that Bobby was resting, and Ronnie went to the bedroom window.

They talked through the window; at first Ronnie asked if Bobby had been able to sell the stereo. Next, he expressed concern about his family. "There's something going on at the house," Ronnie said. "I still can't get in. Something strange is going on over there. The cars are all in the driveway and I still can't get in the house. I called the house twice and nobody answered."

"Someone has to be home," Kelske said. "The cars were in the driveway all morning."

Ronnie asked if Bobby was coming out, and Kelske said that he wouldn't leave till later. "I'm going to lay down for a while," he said. But he told Ronnie that he would be at Henry's Bar around 6 P.M.

After leaving Kelske, Ronnie dropped in at Henry's, sitting at the long, dark bar as the afternoon lengthened towards dusk. He had four or five drinks, all of them vodka-and-7-Up. He stayed for an hour and a half until he decided to visit friends who lived nearby.

While Butch DeFeo and Bobby Kelske were talking outside the bedroom window of the latter's home, a young woman named Junie Reimer left her baby with her mother in Massapequa and walked over to the Sunrise Mall with an older child and a woman friend. She returned around 5:30 P.M., picked up the baby and drove to her own home in Amityville. As she arrived, she saw her husband, Howie, and Ronnie DeFeo talking in Ronnie's car. The two men—who had been locked out because Mrs. Reimer had the door key—helped her carry her bundles into the house.

Junie Reimer had known Ronnie DeFeo for three years and although they had never gone out with each other, they had double-dated. When they were inside, Howard Reimer went out of the living room for a few minutes, and Ronnie and Junie were alone. Ronnie seemed a little nervous. "I'm sick," he said.

Junie Reimer knew what that meant. Ronnie wanted a fix. She said there were a couple of bags of "stuff" on the refrigerator. Ronnie found them and went into the bathroom.

Junie had purchased the heroin in New York City months before; the bags were folded inside a piece of paper and her husband didn't know about them. Ronnie DeFeo did not think he was addicted, but he had been shooting heroin for two years. He had tried LSD a few times, but the trips were always bad. As a teen-ager, he had taken speed regularly and that had kept him on a constant high. Heroin was different. Heroin made him feel mellow.

Ronnie remained in the bathroom while Junie attended to her children. When he came out, he was calm. To Junie Reimer, he seemed fine. The Reimers were in the living room, and Ronnie asked if he could use their telephone. He went into the kitchen and dialed his house, but there was no answer. After he hung up, he handed Junie forty cents for the phone bill and called Sherry Klein. "I'm at Junie and Howard's house," he told Sherry, and he said that he wasn't getting anywhere calling home. "I'm going to go home and break a window to see what's going on," he said. They had a date that evening, and Ronnie said he'd pick her up at ten after eight.

When Ronnie finished the conversation with Sherry, he told the Reimers that he was going to try his home again. He was holding the phone as he spoke. The situation was confusing at home, he explained, because everybody used everybody else's car. Again, there was no answer and Ronnie hung up and left the Reimers. He drove back to Henry's Bar, where he was supposed to meet Bobby Kelske. His home was around the corner, only a half-mile away.

Henry's Bar glowed in the Ocean Avenue Shopping Center, a neighborhood tavern toasting the November night. When Bobby Kelske walked in, he found Butch DeFeo sitting at the bar with four or five other men. Butch was still complaining about his inability to raise anyone at his home. "I'm going to have to go home and break a window to get in," he said.

"Well, do what you have to do," Kelske told him.

Ronnie took his car. Within minutes, he was back—braking to a stop in the parking area. It was almost 6:30 P.M. as Ronnie hurtled out of the car and raced to Henry's, where he stood in the doorway shouting for help. "Bob," he yelled to Kelske, "you got to help me. You got to help me."

Kelske rushed to his friend, who looked as if he might buckle over. What he was shouting seemed impossible. "Someone shot my mother and father."

"Are you sure?" Kelske asked.

"Yeah," Ronnie answered. "I saw them up there."

"Are you sure they're not sleeping?"

"No, I saw them up there."

"Come on," Kelske said then. "Let's go."

For a moment, Ronald DeFeo, Jr., remained in the doorway. He looked at the rest of the men in the bar. "Come on," he yelled. "Everybody come on. Somebody shot my mother and father."

They came running out of the tavern. They were named Al Saxton, Billy Scordamaglia, Joe Yeswit and John Altieri. Most of them were friends of Ronnie DeFeo. They rushed into the blue Buick. It was Ronnie's car, but Bobby Kelske took the wheel. Ronnie huddled in the back.

They got to the house in seconds. On the way there, the others had to tell Bobby Kelske to slow down. As it turned out, there was no rush. The house at 112 Ocean Avenue was quiet except for an alarm clock that had gone off in Dawn's room at 7:15 A.M. It was still ringing.

3 _____

THE ELECTRA PULLED UP behind the two other Brigante-Karl Buicks in the driveway. Bobby Kelske was in the lead, running toward the house. "Be careful going in there," one of the men behind him said. "Somebody might be in there yet."

Kelske pushed open the front door and dashed upstairs to the master bedroom, where Ronnie's parents slept. The bedroom door was open and the light was on. He stood in the doorway, staring at the ornately carved bed and the mirrored wall behind it, and one of his companions had to steady him. "Come on," the other man said. "You better go downstairs."

Ronnie DeFeo had never left the driveway. When Kelske came out, Ronnie was pounding his fists on the car. "I'm not going to go back in that house," he was screaming. Kelske asked whom he should call, and Ronnie named his paternal grandfather, Rocco DeFeo, who lived several miles away in West Islip. Meanwhile, the English sheepdog, which was still inside tied to the back door, was barking incessantly. And one of the men, Joey Yeswit, was calling the police.

"We have a shooting here," Joey Yeswit was saying. "Uh, DeFeo."

Officer Kenneth Greguski of the Amityville Village police Department was in his patrol car three blocks away when he received the call to respond to 112 Ocean Avenue. It was 6:40 P.M. When Greguski arrived, he found Ronnie DeFeo and four other men congregated at the head of the driveway. DeFeo was crying. "My mother and father are dead," he told the officer.

DeFeo and Kelske took the patrolman into the house and sat at the kitchen table while Greguski went up the stairs to the second floor. The master bedroom was in the southwest corner—lush with gold curtains, flowered wallpaper and highly polished mahogany furniture that included a triple dresser and a large television set. There was a sheen to the room—the rich wood, the mirrored wall, the metal and crystal bases of the bedside lamps, the gold-and-marble telephone on one of the night tables. An empty wine glass stood atop a clock radio on the radiator, and two open packs of Lark cigarettes sat on the television cabinet next to a paisley eyeglass case. Religious statuettes and pictures decorated the furniture tops and walls along with photographs of the DeFeo children.

But Greguski's gaze was held by the double bed, which consisted of two mattresses attached to a single headboard. The woman was lying on the left, the man was on the right. Both of them were on their stomachs on the flowered sheets—looking as if it were morning and they were burrowing into the bedclothes for a few more minutes of sleep.

Except that there was no movement. The woman was covered with a gold-colored blanket, but Greguski could see the top of her orange nightgown and what looked like a bullet hole. There were bloodstains on the left side of the bed by the blanket edge and near the place where her brown hair touched the sheet. The man was uncovered, heavy and thickset in blue boxer-style undershorts, sprawled on the mattress with his right leg almost off the bed. Blood streaked his left side and ran into his shorts in a slanting line from a bullet hole in the small of his back. Greguski did not touch either body, but just stared at them. They seemed very white.

Across the hall, the door to the northeast bedroom stood open, and the officer went inside. Even without looking at the beds set against the east and west walls, he would have known it was a boys' room. The print wallpaper carried designs of duck decoys, guns, globes and clipper ships. Sneakers were stuffed next to a radiator, games lay about and pants dangled from a chair. Green-and-tan plaid curtains matched the pulled-down bedspreads, and Napoleonic soldiers rode regal chargers across the figured pillowcases.

Two boys were lying face down in the twin beds—their bodies making grotesqueries of the religious figurines on the brass-handled dressers and the giant, inflated Pepsi bottle leaning on a chair. The covers of the boy on the left were pulled to his feet, and his right arm disappeared beneath his pillow. He was wearing white, ski-style pajamas and the bottom half of his shirt was drenched with blood. Looking closer, Greguski could see the ragged edges of a bullet hole.

Across the room, the second boy hugged his pillow with his head turned to the left. His hair fell over his face, and his left arm almost touched the wheelchair at the side of his bed. Behind the wheelchair, a pair of crutches leaned against the wall. His blankets were also pulled down, but a white sheet covered him to the waist. His T-shirt was hiked up, leaving a broad band of bare skin. A bullet hole pierced the middle of his back, and blood coagulated down his side. The blood formed a pool on the bottom sheet.

Greguski went downstairs to the dining room phone and called village headquarters. There were four bodies in the house, he reported. Detectives from the Suffolk County Police

Department would have to be notified.

As he talked, Greguski could see Ronnie DeFeo, sitting about fifteen feet away in the kitchen. Ronnie was crying softly, but he was listening to the call. Suddenly, he realized that there was something else he should tell Greguski. His sisters, he said. He also had two sisters.

Greguski instantly put down the phone and raced upstairs. By this time, a second Amityville patrol car had arrived and another officer, Patrolman Edwin Tyndall, followed him. There were rooms with closed doors, and Greguski pushed them open. In a bedroom in the southeast corner, he and Tyndall made another discovery.

There were two beds in the room, their curlicued orange headboards as bright as the flowered walls. One bed was neatly made, its embossed white spread barely wrinkled by the sweater, jigsaw puzzle box and teen bra that lay on top of it. A jigsaw puzzle was in progress on a board laid across a dehumidifier, and a completed puzzle interlocked nearby on the carpet. Blue jeans and a flowered top hung over a stuffed panda on a chair. A tape recorder dominated the clutter on the gold-trimmed white desk, and a portable television set perched on the matching dresser. Frilly white curtains and pink shades suited pictures of wide-eyed children and daisies, and a ceramic Madonna stood banked by flowers on an orange radiator.

The girl was lying face down in the other bed, the one closest to the door. A pink blanket covered her slim figure, reaching to the shoulders of her pale pink nightgown, and her dark hair streamed across the pillow. Blood ran down the lower side of her head, down her left arm and down the side of the bed to the floor. Greguski believed she might have been shot in the neck or at the top of the back, but he really couldn't tell. There was too much blood. He was careful not to touch the body, and it was just as well. She had been shot in the face.

The only remaining room on the second floor was a television sitting room, but it was empty and there was another sister unaccounted for. A staircase went upwards. Figuring that the steps led to an attic, Greguski had not climbed them before. This time, he and Tyndall went up the steps and found a finished area. Their search ended in the east bedroom.

It was a vivid but well-kept room. Things were in place—the bottles of nail polish crowding the bright green vanity, the stuffed monkey seated in the slender, red-cushioned white chair, the Tiffany lamp and the wicker box topped by a vase of flowers on the white, gold-trimmed chest, and the electric typewriter protected by its cover on the dark table.

Even the young woman appeared undisturbed as she nestled beneath a pink blanket on a sheet whose orange butterflies seemed ready to light on the big pink-and-orange flowers that bloomed across the wallpaper. She, too, was face down. The blanket almost covered her body completely. Only by standing at the head of the bed could one spot the redness staining the sheet beneath her left shoulder.

The officers returned down the two flights, and Greguski phoned village headquarters again. There were six people dead at the location, not four. He had discovered two more bodies, both female. It was, as the newspaper would point out the next day, the largest number of victims in a single slaying on Long Island in recent memory.

The family's only survivor, Ronald DeFeo, Jr., was at the kitchen table in the home to which his family had moved in search of the better life that waited for them east of the city line. There was a television set on a kitchen counter, and a Papal Blessing on the wall.

Greguski walked over and put his hand on Ronnie's shoulder. He told him to take it easy.

Ronnie's reply was incoherent. He was still crying.

4

THE POLICE came in waves. Detectives from the First Squad of the Suffolk County Police Department hurried up the front steps in the wake of village brass, and county homicide detectives followed within a half-hour. Before the house was cleared of all but homicide personnel at 7:20 P.M., sixteen county and village officers were moving about the building and grounds—checking everything from the marks of animal teeth on the door of the garbage shed to the alarm clock buzzing near Dawn DeFeo's bed. For all practical purposes, the house at 112 Ocean Avenue was no longer a private dwelling; murder had made it a public concern. Through the night, the police snapped photographs, took measurements, searched for expended bullets. They walked through the living room and around the baby grand piano and the alabaster fireplace and looked about the dining room where a gold-and-crystal chandelier glittered above artificial roses on a damask tablecloth.

They searched the basement playroom, where the DeFeo children had amused themselves with a pool table and still another television set and shelves filled with toys and games. The detectives examined the first-floor bar with its built-in sink and shelves on which goblets and glasses stood upside down to dry and bottles of liqueur and whiskey jostled each other like commuters on a rush-hour train. They poked about the laundry room, where there were two washing machines and a dryer, and a small pile of unwashed clothes waited on the floor next to a box of Tide. They stood on the wide patio that was raised five steps above the ground. They walked along the driveway pocked by fallen brown leaves and past the swimming pool to the boathouse that opened onto the canal.

As the news radiated into the night beyond Henry's Bar and bounced back over car radios and television speakers, the outside world pirouetted on the edge of tragedy. Amityville's then police chief strutted among the county detectives, selling chances for his department's annual Thanksgiving raffle. Relatives of the DeFeos moved back and forth, alternating between grief and anger, and reporters pursued police and passers-by with pencils and microphones. "They could not do enough for their children. The whole world was oriented around their children," a neighbor said of Ronald, Sr., and Louise DeFeo. "Oh my God," said another woman, who had just learned of the murders, "that just can't be!"

Early in the evening, a priest arrived and administered the last rites. He was the Reverend James McNamara, an assistant pastor at St. Martin of Tours Church in Amityville. Father McNamara said the DeFeos attended services regularly but did not take an active part in church affairs. The three younger children had been students at the parish grade school, while Dawn had graduated from St. John the Baptist High School in West Islip. "They seemed like an average good family," Father McNamara told a reporter.

Outside the house, the curious gathered—not just neighbors,

but the emotional scavengers who materialize at crime and accident scenes with the mindlessness of slugs in the midst of something rotten. They swayed and surged beyond the police line, alert to rumors, excited by comings and goings and staring ever-avidly at the shrine to the Baby Jesus and the jack-o'-lantern windows and the sign affixed to the lamp post by the front path. The sign, consisting of black letters on a decorative white board, was as much a status symbol as the three Buicks lining the driveway. The sign gave the house a name. "HIGH HOPES," it said.

The first county detective to talk to the family's lone survivor was Gaspar Randazzo of the First Squad. This was at 7 P.M. after Randazzo had come down from the bedrooms, where he heard Dawn's alarm. Randazzo didn't touch the clock, which had been set to ring at 7:15 A.M. He was directed to Ronald DeFeo, Jr., and took him into the kitchen. Ronnie was sobbing but he was able to tell Randazzo where he had been that day and how he had discovered the bodies. When Randazzo asked if he had any idea as to who could have done such a terrible thing, Ronnie hesitated and then blurted a name.

"Falini," he said. A man named Louis Falini [pseudonym] could have done it. Falini was involved with the Mafia. He was supposed to be a hit man. And he had a grudge against the DeFeos.

The conversation was interrupted when the priest took Ronnie aside to comfort him. The homicide detectives arrived, and one of them asked if anybody could get the sheepdog out of the house as it was still making a racket. Ronnie volunteered and put the dog in his car.

By now, police had obtained permission to set up their command post in the home of Mr. and Mrs. Rufus Ireland, next to the DeFeo house on the south. Ronnie walked to the Irelands' sun porch with Randazzo and Homicide Detective Gerard Gozaloff, who would take over the interview. "Call me

Butch," he told Gozaloff, "that's what everyone calls me." He promised his full cooperation. "I'll do whatever I have to do—I'll help you in any way I can." Again, Ronnie mentioned Falini. "It's an idea," he said.

"Okay," Gozaloff said, "we'll get to that."

Gozaloff was taking Ronnie's pedigree when another homicide detective, Joseph Napolitano, brought word that they should interview him at the First Squad, a few miles away. If Ronnie were correct and the murders were tied to organized crime, he could still be a target.

Ronnie concurred. "They could have missed me," he said.

It was shortly after 8 P.M. Ocean Avenue was blocked to traffic, but bystanders watched from the street and the Ireland front lawn. Sherry Klein was in the Ireland house and saw Ronnie leave. She had called Ronnie at 7:30 because of their date and gotten Bobby Kelske. "We'll call back," Kelske said. "There's trouble." Instead, Sherry drove to the scene, where a detective told her about the killings.

They came out single file, with Ronnie between Napolitano and Gozaloff. The detectives unsnapped their holsters and told Ronnie to stay close as they walked to an unmarked police car. Bobby Kelske ran up and asked where they were taking Butch, and the officers motioned him away and told him not to worry. During the short ride, Ronnie was increasingly composed and even showed them a shortcut to the precinct. At 8:20 P.M. in a small interview room at the First Squad, Gozaloff began taking a written statement.

Ronnie went back to the day before, when he stayed home because of a queasy stomach. That night, he watched a late movie, *Castle Keep,* a war film starring Burt Lancaster, and fell asleep at 2 A.M. in the second-floor TV room. At about 4 A.M., he woke with stomach pains and saw Mark's wheelchair in front of the bathroom across the hall. A light shone beneath the door, and he heard the toilet flush.

He'd slept a lot during the day before and wasn't tired, so he decided to go to work. Ronnie told about having breakfast in the luncheonette and leaving work early, and described his visits with Sherry Klein, Bobby Kelske and the Reimers. He told about drinking several vodka-and-7-Ups at Henry's Bar, and about trying to call home and getting no answer. When Ronnie said that one of the reasons he phoned from the auto agency was to have someone leave out his pay stubs for him to show his probation officer, Gozaloff had a question. If he needed the stubs, why hadn't he broken into the house earlier?

He didn't want to get into trouble, Ronnie answered. He'd gotten a beating from his father for breaking in once before. Despite Ronnie's age, his father still hit him.

When he finally entered the house, he forced a kitchen window whose lock was broken from a previous attempt. He said all the lights were out except for one over a picture in the living room. He put on the stair light and went to the second floor, where he saw figures in his parents' bed. He flipped the wall switch and froze at the sight of the bullet hole in his father's back. There was blood by the hole. Seconds later, he raced out the front door, which was double-locked. He had to turn the lock handle and then the doorknob. The only way the door could be locked that way was with a key. When he left in the morning, the door had been single-locked because he didn't have a key. He drove to Henry's Bar and got help. When the police came, he went back inside the house, but he never went upstairs again.

At several points, Ronnie's narrative was jumbled and Gozaloff found it difficult to follow. He asked if Butch would take a blood test to check whether he'd had "a few too many" during the day. Ronnie declined. But he explained that it wasn't because of the drinking. He really did want to cooperate. It was because he'd shot heroin at the Reimers' house that afternoon.

At Napolitano's request, Ronnie rolled up his sleeves, and the detectives spotted a red dot on the inside of his right arm slightly below the elbow.

Butch didn't want them to misunderstand about the heroin. He wasn't an addict, he was a "chippy shooter," a Saturday night user. "I told you I'll be honest with you," he said, "and I am."

He was equally frank in discussing his family's criminal connections. His granduncle Pete DeFeo, who lived in New York City, had gotten his name in the papers as mob-connected. A Mr. Lee, who came to the auto agency, was Carlo Gambino's man. And there was Louis Falini, who could be the person they were looking for. Falini was about seventy; he used to be a good friend of Ronnie's father. Falini had a key to the DeFeo house because he and his wife had stayed there several years before when their own home burned down in Brooklyn. About two years ago—this was after Falini had lived with them—he and Butch had a big argument over the way Butch was doing a paint job at the agency. Butch didn't want the detectives to put this in the statement, but he called the older man a cocksucker. Afterwards, his father told him that Falini was a professional killer. "He's a hit man, that's how he makes a living," his father said. "You don't realize what you've done when you called this man these names."

But that happened a few years ago, Gozaloff said, interrupting Ronnie. Why would Falini go after the DeFeos now?

Ronnie's reply narrowed the gap between the tree-lined avenue of southern Amityville and the tough sidewalks of New York City. Not quite two weeks ago, he and another Brigante-Karl employee were taking several thousand dollars to the bank and they were robbed by two gunmen. Last Friday, he and his father got into an argument about the holdup. His father felt Butch wasn't telling the truth. "Not only do I have to worry about you as far as this phony robbery," his father said, "but I've also had to lose a good friend." The elder DeFeo was talking about Falini—he'd been put in a position where he had to tell Falini that "if anything happens to my son, I'll kill you and your whole family." This meant that Ronald, Sr., had to be on guard for his own family's welfare. "I have to watch Ma and the kids now," he said, and he made it clear that this was all Butch's fault.

At 10:25 P.M., Ronnie signed the statement, which covered eight handwritten pages. The only things he had asked be omitted were the names he called Falini, and the story about his sheepdog biting him when he tried to bring a girl down to the cellar. While Ronnie was checking the statement, Gozaloff, Napolitano and two other detectives were standing in the doorway of the interview room, discussing his safety. They were still worried that an attempt might be made on his life. Ronnie could hear them, and he agreed. He believed the killers had missed him, that he was the prime target. The detectives said they were going to the Fourth Precinct in Hauppauge, and would he come along.

As far as the detectives were concerned, Ronnie was one hundred percent cooperative. "Anything you want to do," he said.

Before leaving, he met another homicide detective, George Harrison, who would become a prime figure in the murder probe. "I hope you find out who did it," Ronnie told the short, square-set officer.

Harrison and Napolitano drove Ronnie to Fourth Precinct headquarters, where they could use a squadroom, while Gozaloff returned to the murder scene. During the half-hour ride, Ronnie and Napolitano discussed their respective stomach problems; Ronnie said he had some kind of ulcer. He was bumming Napolitano's cigarettes and he offered to buy the detective a pack. Napolitano told him it wasn't necessary.

The Fourth Precinct was situated off Veterans Memorial Highway in the same complex as county headquarters and homicide, but the detectives felt it would afford less chance of interruption by reporters than their own office. Each precinct houses a detective squad. In an interview room, Harrison motioned for Ronnie to take a seat while he thumbed through

43

the statement and asked questions as they occurred to him. Both he and Napolitano were impressed by Ronnie's frankness in answering.

For instance, how could he get away with using heroin while he was on probation—didn't his probation officer ask for urine samples? Ronnie told them how he faked the man out. If he'd been shooting up, he would get his sister, Dawn, to give him a urine specimen. At the probation office, he'd go into the bathroom and make believe he was urinating. Then he'd bring back Dawn's specimen as the sample.

The detectives wanted to know if there had been any recent changes in his parents' lives. Ronnie told them that his father had become religious in the last year or two, although he'd never even gone to church in the past. The elder DeFeo corresponded regularly with a priest in Canada. He sent money to the priest, who sent back religious artifacts and medallions. The family had traveled to Canada to visit the priest, and occasionally went on retreat. Ronnie never joined them. He believed in God but he just couldn't get into religion—certainly not as deeply as his father wanted him to.

Around 11:45, Harrison left to take a phone call from Gozaloff, who had left the scene and was at the squadroom in the First Precinct. Ronnie and Napolitano went to the bathroom. At 1:30 A.M., Gozaloff joined the others at the squadroom. During the time he was at Ocean Avenue, Gozaloff had been sent to interview a teen-ager who lived two houses away from the DeFeos and reported being awakened shortly after 3 A.M. by barking coming from number 112. Back at the DeFeo house, another detective showed him scratch marks and animal hairs in the garbage shed outside the rear door. Gozaloff figured that the boy had been awakened by the sheepdog, and asked Butch if it had been tied in the shed overnight.

No, Ronnie said. The dog had been kept there a few weeks ago, but not the night before.

Harrison had not seen any mention of guns in the statement,

and decided to check. It was another avenue. "Maybe a burglar was in there and took one of your guns and shot your family," he explained. He asked Ronnie to tell him about any guns that were in the house.

Well, Ronnie said, if his father had a pistol, he'd never seen it. Ronnie owned three rifles, although his father had taken them away recently as a punishment. "I also had a handgun at one time," he said, "but my father found it and knew I was on probation and got rid of it or told me to get rid of it, or he threw it away or sold it. I don't recall which."

There had been another rifle that he'd gotten rid of, Ronnie added. He couldn't remember what caliber it was. "In fact, I was totally unfamiliar with it," he said. Ronnie did remember that this particular rifle had gone off accidentally at a friend's house a couple of years before. The friend's name was Steve Hicks. No one got hurt when the gun went off; the bullet went into the floor.

The conversation turned to Falini, and Ronnie added another detail about the argument in the auto agency. He'd gotten so angry that he threw his paintbrush at the man. Falini ducked and the brush shattered a window. Also, he'd thought of a way for the police to tell if Falini had committed the murders. When Falini was living with the DeFeos, he'd helped Ronnie and his father chisel out a hiding place in the floor under the sill in a master bedroom closet. "We hid a cash box there," he explained. "It's always full of money and jewelry."

All the police had to do was look under the sill. "If you find a cash box, if it's empty or if it's gone, Falini had to do it. Because the only two other people would be my father and I."

Napolitano left the room and phoned the command post at the Ireland home to have someone look for the box. When he returned, Ronnie was talking about the quarrel he'd had with his father the past Friday over the payroll holdup. At first, Ronnie had told the detectives in Brooklyn that he could identify the robbers. But he had decided that he was wrong,

45

that he really couldn't. The police had phoned his father and said that Ronnie wasn't cooperating, and his father got angry. He said maybe Ronnie had something to do with the robbery. The following Monday, just a few days ago, they'd argued about it again.

Ronnie was becoming more intense in his effort to cooperate. There were two things he hadn't told the detectives. "I want to tell you about these now," he said. "I don't want you to think that I'm hiding anything from you." One admission concerned the vacant house on the north side of the DeFeo home. Ronnie said that he and Bobby Kelske had broken in and stolen antiques, which they were able to sell. The other story was that he had "loused up" the engine of his father's boat, and his father told him to get rid of it. Ronnie set the boat on fire, he said, and his father collected the insurance.

There didn't seem to be anything Ronnie would hold back on, and the detectives asked him a delicate question—did either of his parents have a lover? Ronnie didn't know. Of course, his father was pretty smart. If he had a girlfriend, he kept her in the city and no one knew about her. As for his mother, well, he wasn't sure. In telling about his mother, Ronnie explained why there was a phone in the house without a number printed on it. For a while, his mother was always on the phone and no one knew who she was talking to. Because of this, his father had another phone installed but kept the number to himself. That way, his father could ring the house whenever he wanted to. And if the regular line was busy, he could find out who was using the phone.

By 2:30 A.M., everyone was weary, and the detectives felt that Butch had given them abundant information. Ronnie seemed even more tired than the rest, which was understandable. Not only had he been through hell, but he'd been up since 4 A.M. Where would he like to sleep?

"I don't know," Ronnie told them. "I trust my relatives but I don't want to go there because Falini might get me."

The officers suggested that he accompany them to homicide, where there was a cot he could use. If anything developed—for instance, if they picked up Falini—they could let him know. Also, the morgue was right across the street and they might need him to identify the bodies in the morning. Some member of the family would have to do that.

As he had throughout the night, Ronnie agreed to stick with the detectives. Identifying the bodies was not something he wanted to do, but it was his responsibility. And he wanted to stay on top of the investigation. "I want to know what's going on," he explained.

Homicide was no more than a thousand yards from the Fourth, but the three detectives were wary. They drove in two cars—Harrison and Napolitano taking Ronnie, and Gozaloff following as a backup. Instead of going directly, they took a long route that brought them through the rear of the complex rather than through the lighted area in front of homicide. The building was a converted white frame house, and the door in back was used as the regular entrance. Napolitano went in that way and opened the front door for Ronnie and the two detectives.

There were doughnuts inside, and the squad had a coffee machine. Ronnie explained that he didn't drink coffee because of his stomach problems, and Napolitano offered him a cup of tea instead. Then they took out the cot and put it in a back room used for files. It was a small room, about ten by twelve, with file cabinets standing against the north and south walls, and an evidence locker squatting near the cabinet on the north. There was one window in the room, along with a two-way mirror. There was no lock on the door.

Ronnie went to the bathroom, and when he came out, Gozaloff opened the cot for him. It was about 3 A.M.

Ronnie went to sleep. When he woke up, everything would be different.

5

WHILE POLICE SEARCHED Ronnie DeFeo's memory for leads to the murders, relatives and acquaintances of the DeFeos were being questioned at the scene. Ronnie's paternal grandfather, Rocco DeFeo, and the latter's son-in-law, Vincent Procita, arrived within minutes after receiving the phone call from Bobby Kelske. His maternal grandfather, Michael Brigante, Sr., came in from Brooklyn at 9:15 P.M. with his wife and son. A garrulous, excitable man, Brigante tried to crash the police line.

"You got a gun?" a detective asked.

"What about it?" Brigante answered. "I have a permit for it."

Inside the house, medical and ballistics experts were checking the bodies. Brigante was a police buff, a regular contributor to police benevolent organizations in the city. "If this was New York," he told a detective, "I'd have been inside already. I want to see my daughter before they put her in a bag."

Light from the house glinted off gold badges as the auto

agency owner pulled out his wallet and displayed his collection of police shields. Incensed at being kept out of the home, he tried to overlay anger with authority. "Just two weeks ago, I saw a cop with both arms and both legs off in Chinatown," he shouted. "A month before that, I saw another sergeant dead on a parkway. I've seen many a homicide. I've seen many people dead. I've seen autopsies performed. I want to see my daughter."

Less than an hour later, Brigante found a vent for his frustration. He was standing on the Ireland property, talking to detectives, when they were accosted by a reporter. The detectives weren't giving anything away, but the reporter persisted. "Why don't you get the hell out of here before you get belted in your mouth!" Brigante shouted at the newsman. "Get away from here and leave these people alone."

But if the family had a leader that night, it was not Mike Brigante. The leader was Rocco DeFeo, whose son lay against the mirrored wall next to Brigante's daughter. This was established when Detective Gozaloff returned to the scene after taking Ronnie's statement. He found Brigante, the latter's son, Michael, Jr., Rocco DeFeo and Vincent Procita on the Ireland front lawn, and began asking questions.

Gozaloff started with Brigante, who said that he would have been in the squad room with the detectives if it was New York City. Gozaloff looked at him. "Do you know a man named Louis Falini?" he asked.

"Yes," Brigante answered. "He's one of the most wonderful men I ever met." But he didn't know Falini's address or phone number. And when Gozaloff asked if Falini could have committed the murders, the auto agency owner seemed insulted that anyone could even think that.

He was more insulted by the next question—could Butch have had anything to do with the shootings?

"He's a wonderful grandson," Brigante said. "I'm very proud of him." There was no way Butch could be involved.

Gozaloff asked Vincent Procita the same thing. Ronnie's uncle shook his head. There was a possibility Butch was involved with drugs, and who knew what could happen with drugs. But he was sure Butch couldn't do anything like that. And he never heard of Falini.

Next, Gozaloff tried to question Michael Brigante, Jr., but got nowhere as the latter's father kept answering for him. And moments later, Rocco DeFeo ended the interviews. "Shut up," he hollered. "This is family. Don't say no more."

Rocco turned his back on Gozaloff and ignored the detective's attempt to talk to him. Nor would the others answer any more questions, and Gozaloff drove to the First Precinct and phoned Harrison to keep Butch away from Rocco DeFeo. Rocco was shutting up the whole family—if Butch talked to him, he might stop cooperating.

Meanwhile, another relative, Richard Wyssling, had arrived at the command post. Wyssling, a Babylon attorney whose wife was a cousin to the Brigantes, spoke to the family and then asked a detective where Ronnie was. A year later, the prosecution of the DeFeo murder case would hinge on how Wyssling put the question and what happened after that.

At 12:30 A.M., Mike Brigante got his grim wish. And the emotional scavengers crowded in the street got something to buzz about. The bodies of the victims were placed in zippered canvas bags and taken out of the house on rolling stretchers for removal to the morgue. As attendants lifted one of the stretchers off the front steps onto the driveway, the body dropped partly out of its bag and had to be secured again. Enough of the corpse showed for bystanders to know it was the body of a young boy. To the people grouped nearby, the murders in Amityville were palpably real—it was as if someone had taken a hot brand and forever seared their memories.

Joel Martin, a reporter for radio station WBAB in Babylon, was one of the spectators. "It was a rather horrible, horrible thing to see," he would remember years afterwards. "It was not an easy thing to see and then go home again."

*   *   *

Detective Sergeant Alfred Della Penna, head of the firearms section of the Suffolk County Police Laboratory, arrived at the DeFeo house at 8:10 P.M. Deputy Chief Medical Examiner Dr. Howard Adelman drove up ten minutes later. Both men worked into the next day—Della Penna going from the house to the lab, and Dr. Adelman performing the autopsies at the morgue. If anything, the clinical nature of their findings made the case even more grisly.

The killer had fired eight times. Ronald, Sr., and Louise DeFeo each had been shot twice, and the children once. Ronald, Sr., had been hit twice in the lower back—one bullet exploding through the kidney and exiting near his right nipple onto the bed, and the other entering at the base of the spine and burying itself in his neck. From the nature of the wounds, Dr. Adelman determined that the victim had remained alive anywhere from a few seconds to several minutes after being shot. A waistband imprint on his torso showed that his shorts had pulled down—his body had moved upwards as he died.

Bullets had pierced Louise DeFeo's right flank and chest. One bullet landed on the blood-soaked mattress; the other came out the middle of her chest and reentered her left breast and wrist. The bullets shattered her rib cage, and the splintering bone destroyed most of her right lung, diaphragm and liver. Although she was face down, her chest was slightly raised from the bed, and the axis of her body was turned to the right. The medical examiner postulated that she could have lived for several minutes after being shot, perhaps as many as ten. Her position indicated that she had awakened and lifted her upper body off the bed—possibly looking toward the doorway in the killer's direction.

Both Mark and John were shot in the back at close range—examination of the wounds disclosing that the murderer stood between the beds less than two feet away from each boy. The killer remained in the same spot while turning to fire the second time. The bullets penetrated the liver, diaphragm, lungs and heart of each victim and burrowed through the boys' mattresses into the box springs. In John's case, his spinal cord was severed, which may have caused involuntary twitching in the lower part of his body.

The examination indicated that Allison DeFeo apparently had awakened and turned around in time to stare at the muzzle of the exploding gun less than two feet from her face. The bullet smashed upward from her left cheek through her right ear, lacerating her brain and damaging the skull. The slug tore through the mattress, hit the back wall of the bedroom and bounced to the floor.

Dawn's wound was the most terrible to look at. The killer stood about two and a half feet away and fired at the back of her neck, the bullet entering just below the left ear and slamming through the left temple into her pillow. The left side of her face had collapsed, and brain particles mixed with the blood saturating her pillow. She had been menstruating, and her sheets were sodden with blood beneath the pink blanket.

At the morgue in Hauppauge, where the bodies lay tagged on wheeled tables, Dr. Adelman worked into the following afternoon, performing autopsies. His discoveries included the fact that the stomachs of Ronald, Sr., and Mark DeFeo were about one-third full, which meant they had eaten from two to four hours before death. He removed the second bullet from the father's neck after locating it by X-ray. In each case, Dr. Adelman listed the cause of death as massive hemorrhaging due to bullet wounds.

Elsewhere in the police complex, Sergeant Della Penna worked in the laboratory, going over physical evidence found at the scene. Della Penna had already formed an opinion as to the nature of the murder weapon, but he wanted to make sure before notifying the homicide squad. Now, he put the spent bullets under a microscope and measured them with a micrometer. The key means of identification were the grooves on the sides of the bullets. Such grooves on a bullet come from the channels inside a gun barrel. These channels, which are called rifling, give a bullet the spinning motion that stabilizes it in flight. The grooves are transposed into the bullet as it goes through the barrel. Each type of gun has different channels, which gives experts a basis for making identifications. When he was through counting and measuring, Della Penna called homicide. The bullets all had twelve channels that turned slightly to the right. His determination was that all six victims had been killed with a .35-caliber Marlin rifle.

No such weapon had been turned up at the scene. Della Penna had looked through the house himself and spotted the three weapons in Ronnie DeFeo's room. None was a .35. Nor was Ronnie a suspect. If there was a suspect, it was the mysterious Louis Falini, whom police had not been able to locate.

But at 2:30 A.M., another member of the homicide team, Detective John E. Shirvell, made an important discovery.

A thirteen-year police veteran, Jack Shirvell had been a structural draftsman before he became an officer, and the department took advantage of his expertise. Shirvell was assigned to diagram the rooms at 112 Ocean Avenue, and he went through the house taking measurements and photographs. As other officers left after midnight, he continued to work on the diagrams. It was almost 2:30 A.M. when he went through the rooms for the last time to make sure no police equipment had been left behind. Checking over Ronnie's room, Shirvell spotted two tall cardboard boxes on the northwest wall along the chimney. The boxes were in an alcove and had been overlooked in prior searches. What caught Shirvell's attention were the labels. Both boxes had contained Marlin rifles; a .22 and a .35.

At this point, Shirvell did not know that a .35-caliber Marlin had been used in the mass-slayings. But the boxes could be important, and he decided to bring them back to homicide just in case. When he arrived in Hauppauge at 4 A.M., the others had received Della Penna's report from the lab. The packing cartons were suddenly top priority. One of them had contained a rifle that could have been the murder weapon.

It was a lead, but the detectives needed more information about Butch DeFeo's gun collection. He had never mentioned a .35-caliber weapon, but he had talked about getting rid of a rifle that went off in a friend's house. He couldn't remember the caliber.

Before talking to Ronnie, the detectives decided to try another source. His buddy, Bobby Kelske, was available. Kelske had been interviewed by Harrison at the First Squad during the evening, and had been brought to the homicide building. At 5 A.M., Gozaloff went in to see him.

The interview lasted close to a half-hour. As one question led to another, Kelske made some disclosures about his friend. For one thing, he said, Butch had plotted a hide-in burglary at Brigante-Karl Buick. Kelske knew about it because he had seen the actual burglar hand Butch his seven-hundred-and-fifty-dollar half-share at a gas station in the city. He said Butch had shown the burglar where the money was kept at the agency and where to hide before closing time.

But the most important information involved guns. What about the guns that Ronnie's father had taken away as punishment? That was just for a little while, Kelske explained. Mr. DeFeo had kept the guns in his car and then given them back to Ronnie.

"Do you know the calibers?" Gozaloff asked.

"No," Kelske said. "But Butch does." He said Butch knew the guns inside out and upside down. Butch was a gun buff. Hell, a couple of weeks ago, Butch had been trying to buy a silencer.

While Gozaloff was questioning Kelske, Shirvell and Della Penna checked another lead. They went to the home of Steve Hicks in Amityville, where Ronnie said that the rifle he no longer owned had gone off accidentally. Sure enough, they found a hole beneath the living-room rug. The bullet had gone through the floor into the sand and gravel in the crawl space beneath the house. Someone would have to return later on with more equipment to see if it was still there.

Shirvell returned to homicide. From 5:30 A.M. to 7 A.M., he, Gozaloff, Harrison, Napolitano and other officers working on the case discussed what they had learned. One, the murder weapon was a .35-caliber Marlin rifle. Two, a box for such a gun had been found in Butch DeFeo's room. Three, Butch was a gun buff. It didn't make sense that he wouldn't remember the caliber of one of his guns. Four, he had been looking for a silencer.

Together, the facts added up to a terrible possibility. While he slept on a cot in a police file room, Ronald DeFeo, Jr., became a suspect in the mass-murder of his own family.

Gozaloff and Harrison went home to change clothes and freshen up. They returned to homicide at 8:45 A.M. Fifteen minutes later, Harrison said it was time, and he, Gozaloff and Napolitano went into the file room.

Ronnie was still sleeping, and Harrison shook him by the shoulder.

"Did you find Falini yet?" Ronnie asked as he came awake.

"Butch, we have guys out in the street looking for him," Harrison said. "But to tell you the truth, I think you're the guy we want."

"You're kidding," Ronnie said. "I'm trying to help you guys in any way I can."

Ronnie was on the cot, and Harrison looked down at him. "Ronnie, I'd like you to sit here, and be quiet and listen to me," Harrison said. "I want to advise you of your rights."

Ronnie didn't seem to believe what was happening. "You don't have to do that," he said. "I'm telling you I want to help you guys."

Harrison took his rights card out of the case in which he kept his shield. He turned a straight-backed chair around and straddled it, facing the suspect. They were no more than two feet apart; Harrison leaning forward on the back of the chair, and Ronnie sitting directly in front of him on the cot.

"Ronnie, pay attention," Harrison said. "Listen carefully."

"You don't have to do this," Ronnie repeated. "It's all right. I want to help you guys."

"Ronnie, listen to me." Then Harrison was reading from the card. "You have the right to remain silent."

"I know that," Ronnie said. "Don't worry about it. I want to help you guys. I told you."

"Ronnie, just listen to me. Do you understand this right?"

"Yeah."

"Do you wish to waive this right?"

"Yeah, yeah. I'll waive it. Okay."

"Ronnie, anything you say can and will be used against you in a court of law."

"Get Falini," Ronnie said. "He's the guy you want. Not me."

"You have the right to talk to a lawyer right now and have him present while you are being questioned. . . . Do you wish to waive this right?"

"Yeah, I don't need a lawyer."

"If you cannot afford to hire a lawyer, one will be furnished to represent you before any questioning, if you wish one."

"I'm telling you, if you get Falini you got the guy who did it. You'll have the killer." Ronnie waived the right to counsel.

Harrison was almost through. "Do you understand each of these rights I have explained to you?"

"Yeah, I understand you."

"Do you wish to contact a lawyer?"

"I told you before, I don't need a lawyer. I don't want a lawyer."

"Having these rights in mind, do you wish to talk to us now without a lawyer?"

"Yeah, I'll talk to you. I have been telling you I want to do all I can to help you."

Before they could start questioning him, Ronnie asked about

56

the metal box he had told them to look for. "What about the box? Did you find the box?"

Napolitano said they had found a box in the bedroom that only contained papers. He left the file room and returned with three metal boxes taken from the DeFeo home. "You don't have the box," Ronnie insisted. "None of those boxes are the one."

When they went over the location of the hiding spot, it became obvious that police had looked in the wrong place. The hole was beneath the sill in the floor—in the doorway.

Not a sill, Napolitano said. A saddle. Did Ronnie really mean the saddle? Yeah, Ronnie answered. That was it, the saddle.

Napolitano took off for Ocean Avenue to make another search. Harrison gave Ronnie a piece of pound cake and something to drink. They went to the bathroom at the other end of the building, and Ronnie washed up. On their way back, Harrison picked up the gun boxes. In the file room, he showed Ronnie the labels on the cartons. "Ronnie, do you recognize these? Do you want to tell us about them?"

"Yeah," Ronnie said, examining the boxes. "That twenty-two box—I got a twenty-two rifle. That's probably mine."

"What about the other one?" Harrison asked.

"I don't know. I don't know if that's mine or not."

"Listen," Harrison told him. "We've got other information. We know that you got all your guns back from your father. We know you're a gun buff. You know your guns inside out. You can take them apart blindfolded. And there was never a gun that you had that you didn't know the caliber of. We know the gun that killed your parents and your brothers and sisters was a thirty-five-caliber Marlin."

Ronnie tried to talk about Falini instead, and Gozaloff interrupted him. "Let's go back to the day before and let's start over," the detective said. "Let's start with supper."

Ronnie said he didn't eat with the family that night.

"Why not?" Gozaloff asked.

His answer startled both detectives. It was as if Ronnie

DeFeo had ripped a shroud off his feelings. Suddenly, he was different.

"My mother was a lousy cook," Ronnie said. "She cooked up some brown stuff in a bowl. It looked like shit and it smelled like shit." He noticed the detectives' reaction. "Yeah, if you guys had to eat it, it would taste like shit."

"How about your brothers?" Gozaloff asked.

Again, in the context of what had happened, the coarseness seemed inexplicable. "My brothers is a couple of fucking pigs. I often used the same bathroom that they used on the second floor. And I go in there and sometimes there is toilet paper hanging out of the bowl. Sometimes there is shit in the bowl and there is no toilet paper. The fucking pigs don't even wipe their asses. A couple of times, there was even shit on the back of the seat."

"How about your sisters?"

"That fat fuck, Dawn," Ronnie said. "Dawn is nigger music, fucking nigger music, nigger music. All fucking day and night. And I can't even tell her to turn it down, because if I tell her to turn it down, I get my fucking ass kicked."

"Who'd kick your ass?"

"My father."

He did not mention Allison, but when Gozaloff asked about the hide-in burglary, Ronnie stopped in surprise for a moment and then ranted about his grandfather, Mike Brigante. "That cheap bastard; I'll rip him off every chance I get. I'll go to work late, and I'll come home early." But he refused to say he had anything to do with the burglary.

It was almost 10:30 A.M. Gozaloff left the room, and a minute or two later, another detective entered. His name was Dennis Rafferty. He would spend the next six and a half hours talking to Ronnie DeFeo.

6

DETECTIVE DENNIS RAFFERTY was in bed that Wednesday evening when he got a call from his partner, Tommy Gill. "They got six in Amityville," Gill told him. The village straddles the Nassau-Suffolk border, and Rafferty wasn't sure which county had jurisdiction.

"Are they ours?" he asked.

"Yeah," Gill said.

Rafferty phoned the squadroom but everyone was out. At eleven o'clock, he watched the news and obtained his information along with millions of other people. Six members of an Amityville family had been found murdered in their home. Suffolk County police were investigating.

Suffolk County police, Rafferty thought. The biggest homicide case in more years than anyone could remember, and he didn't have a piece of it. That night, Dennis W. Rafferty, shield number 417, a police officer for nine years and a homicide detective for more than four, barely slept. Although he was off-duty the next day, Rafferty put on his jeans as soon as he got up and drove to the office.

The first people he talked to, Lieutenant Thomas Richmond, the operational officer in charge of homicide, and Lieutenant Robert Dunn of the organized crime bureau, brought him up-to-date on the mass-murders. Listening, Rafferty put mental asterisks on several facts: all six victims had been discovered in their bedclothes, the murder weapon was a .35-caliber Marlin, a packing box for that particular rifle had been found in the room of the family's only survivor. Most important, DeFeo had been advised of his rights, he was being questioned and the clock was running. He would have to be either charged or released by the end of the day.

Nobody was surprised when Richmond asked Rafferty if he would spell the detectives interrogating DeFeo. "I want you to talk to the guy," Richmond said. The homicide lieutenant was facing the pressure of repeated calls from police brass and the press. The clock was getting louder.

It was like asking a wide-receiver in the stands if he wanted to run down-and-out patterns in the Super Bowl. For Rafferty, police work had two highs. One was conviction; the other was confession. A tall, slim man with a direct glance and a low-keyed style, he had built a reputation as an interrogator. His system started with his attitude. If a suspect could prove he was at a party with seventeen people during the time of the crime, he might convince Dennis Rafferty that he was innocent.

"I think when I walk in that the guy's guilty," was Rafferty's self-analysis. "And that it's my job to do the best I can to get him to give us direct evidence." Nor did he become emotionally involved. That only happened early in his homicide career when he questioned the perpetrator of an especially vicious rape-murder. "I remember looking at the guy and thinking, 'You're a piece of shit.' But after that, I talked to a lot of guys that have killed and I never had that feeling at all. My purpose is to get the evidence. I don't have any bad feelings toward them, I really don't. And I think that's part of interrogation—that you have to show enough sincerity to gain their confidence."

When Gozaloff came out of the file room, he gave Rafferty a quick briefing. DeFeo wasn't admitting anything. Rafferty went in with Lieutenant Dunn, a former homicide squad colleague. He asked Harrison if they could talk to the suspect. "Go right ahead," Harrison said. He was tired, and he left the room to take a breather.

The first thing Rafferty did after introducing himself and Dunn was fold up the cot and push it into a corner. He specified that an armless chair be brought for Ronnie—a suspect sitting in an armless chair can't relax; he can't fall asleep on the interrogator. And it had to be a chair without wheels so that Ronnie couldn't move away. Dunn sat to Ronnie's right, and Rafferty took a chair facing him. If a desk were in the room, Rafferty might have perched on the edge to make sure he was looking down on the suspect. But he was much taller than Ronnie, which helped. And when the questioning became intense, he could lean forward and put his knee between Ronnie's legs so that Ronnie couldn't close them.

Rafferty advised Ronnie of his rights, and the suspect gave the same answers he had given Harrison. He didn't need a lawyer; he wanted to help the police.

"Can I call you Ronnie?" Rafferty asked.

"No," Ronnie said, "everybody calls me Butch."

"Butch, I'd like to find out about the day before this happened. Where were you the night prior to this incident?"

"Where do you want me to start?"

"Start the day before in the evening," Rafferty said. Ronnie repeated what he had told the others about staying home Tuesday because he was sick. He took Epsom salts for his stomach around 11 P.M. and then watched the movie, which was an Army movie. His parents and John were watching television in the master bedroom, Allison and Mark were in their rooms and Dawn was upstairs taking a shower.

Ronnie retraced his steps on Wednesday. When he was done, Rafferty made him go through it again. This time, the detective stopped the narrative to ask how Ronnie knew Dawn was taking a shower.

"Did you see her under the shower?"

"No," Ronnie said. "I seen that fucking thing on her fucking head."

Dunn interrupted, "Butch, how can you say that about your sister who has expired in the last twenty-four hours? I find it almost incredible. How can you say 'that thing on her fucking head'?"

"That's the way I speak," Ronnie answered. He said Dawn was wearing a towel around her head, turban-style, to dry her hair. "Later on in the morning, I saw towels lying on the floor in the bathroom upstairs. She was a slob and she left them all laying around."

Rafferty was looking for a weak spot. In most cases, he could reach the suspect by expressing sympathy over the "tragedy." But this was different. An entire family had been slaughtered; there was no way he could minimize that. And when he tried to close in by indicating that something terrible must have happened to make Butch commit the shootings, Ronnie backed off. "What do you think, I'm crazy?" he said. "Hey, that's my own family. Jesus Christ!"

"Somebody did this horrible thing," Rafferty said. "We're here to help you."

It became evident that they had to lock up the time interval during which the murders occurred. Maybe that was the way in. "Butch," Rafferty said, "the whole family was found in bed lying in their bedclothes. That indicates to me that it didn't happen at like one o'clock in the afternoon after you had gone to work."

Ronnie agreed, and Rafferty continued to set limits. Daylight began around 6 A.M., he said. "Do you think this happened between six o'clock and seven o'clock in the morning when it was light out?"

"No," Ronnie said, "because it would be light out."

"Do you think it happened between five and six? Do you think somebody was outside the house, watched you leave and then went into the house between five and six and killed the whole family and not you?"

"No, I don't think that happened."

"Okay. We know it didn't happen between four o'clock and five o'clock because you were awake and were in the house at that time. Right?"

"Yeah, that's right."

"Okay, and we know it didn't happen prior to two A.M. because you were awake at that time earlier in the night."

"That's right."

Rafferty leaned forward. "Butch, that means it happened between two A.M. and four A.M.."

"Yeah," Ronnie said. "I think it happened between two and four."

"Okay. Butch, if it happened between two and four, you were in the house when it happened. You were in the house when this terrible thing happened."

"Yeah," Butch DeFeo answered. "I probably was."

"Okay," Rafferty said. He was speaking quietly and he had his knee between Ronnie's legs. "Butch, you had to hear something. You had to hear something."

Ronnie was sweating, moving his hands. "Did you hear anything?" Rafferty pressed. "Did you hear the dog barking?"

"No," Ronnie said.

It was Dunn's turn. "Butch, I think you're embarrassed. I think you were probably there, you probably heard something. You probably feel you should have done something to protect your family, but you were too frightened. You had a very good reason, so what could you have possibly done?"

"I was scared. I was really scared."

"You had to hear something," Rafferty said.

"I did hear something."

"What did you hear?"

Ronnie was crying. Not sobs, but tears. "I heard two shots," he said.

It was the breakthrough. But they had to go carefully, they couldn't frighten him off. The two detectives sat back. "Take it easy," Rafferty said. "This is what we mean, this is what you have to help us with." Dunn was equally supportive.

They waited, and went forward. "What did you do?" Rafferty asked.

"I didn't do anything," Ronnie answered. "I was scared. I was scared shit. I stayed in the room, in the TV room, for about twenty minutes. I hid in the closet behind the door."

"Did you hear anybody walking around?"

"No, all I heard was two shots." He waited twenty minutes, got dressed and drove into the city. He was too frightened to check anyone. "Put yourself in my position," he said. "I just got out of the house. And that's it, man."

It was 12:15. Miles away, there had been another development. Detective Shirvell had returned to the Hickses' house with two emergency service officers and they had gone into the crawl space with a screen for sifting dirt. They found an expended round eight inches down. At 11:40 A.M., Shirvell brought the round to Sergeant Della Penna at the lab. The bullet was from a .35-caliber Marlin.

In the file room, Ronald DeFeo, Jr., cried for a minute or two. He cried softly, and then Rafferty told him that he had to have heard more than two shots.

"I did hear more than two shots."

"What did you hear?"

"Let's see," Ronnie said, concentrating. "I heard one, two, then there was like a hesitation, and I heard a third shot. Then there was a longer hesitation, and I heard another shot. Then there was another hesitation, and I heard two more shots. And then a longer hesitation, and the last shot. That was the furthest away."

Rafferty made him do it over, and Ronnie went from room to room in his description, again accounting for only seven shots. He said the first shots came from his parents' room, then Allison's, then his brothers'. The last shot was upstairs from Dawn's room.

Now they were getting somewhere, Rafferty and Dunn told him. But it still didn't seem right that he hadn't checked the rooms afterwards.

"I did check my mother and father," Ronnie said. "I saw my father was shot in the back. He had the hole in his back. There was a little blood, but I didn't see any blood around my mother, but I could see she was dead. Then I left the house."

"Why did you do that?" Rafferty asked. "Why didn't you check anybody else? You left your brothers and sisters in their own rooms. Maybe they were wounded, maybe they needed help."

"I was just scared."

Rafferty switched directions. "Neither Lieutenant Dunn nor I were there. Could you draw a diagram of the house, of the layout of all the rooms where everybody was?"

Ronnie nodded. Dunn gave him a black marker and a pad of yellow legal-sized paper from on top of the file cabinet. Ronnie designated his parents with "M" and "F" and used first-name initials for his brothers and Dawn. For Allison, he wrote "ALICE."

The detectives went on. Ronnie must have checked his brothers and sisters. Rafferty and Dunn knew that the experience had been very tragic, but he should tell them what he saw. Once more, Ronnie changed his story. He did check the other rooms.

"What did you see?" Rafferty asked.

"Well, after I checked my mother and father's room, I went down and I checked Allison's room, and she got it in the head."

"What did you do then?"

"Then I checked Mark and John's room. They both got it in the back. And John's foot was shaking and twitching."

Rafferty let it go for the moment, but his thought was that there was just one way Ronnie could have seen the foot twitching. He had to be right there when it happened.

"Then I went upstairs," Ronnie continued, "and I checked Dawn's room, and she got it in the neck. Then I was just so scared, I got dressed and I left."

"Butch, it's incredible," Rafferty said, "it's almost unbelievable. Butch, we know we have a thirty-five-caliber gun box from your room. Every one of the victims has been shot with a thirty-five-caliber. And you've seen the whole thing. There has to be more to it. It's your gun that was used."

"No, it wasn't my gun."

"Butch, it was your gun. It had to be your gun."

Ronnie started to cry again.

"Something happened there," Rafferty said, "and you have to tell us what. Tell us the truth."

"You won't believe it. You won't believe it."

"Take it easy," Rafferty counseled, and in another setting, the litany would have been comic. "We'll believe it. We'll believe it."

"Well, when I was going into Dawn's room, I didn't have any shoes on, I was in my stocking feet, and I stepped on the gun and I looked down and sure enough, it was my gun. My rifle."

"Okay. What did you do then?"

"Well, I knew I'd been framed. I knew I had to get rid of everything. I had to get rid of the evidence."

"What do you mean? What did you have to get rid of?"

"I knew I had to get rid of the gun and the cartridges, the shells."

"Butch, you hadn't seen any shells. Maybe the perpetrator who did this picked up the shells after he did it."

"No," Ronnie said. "When I went in to check Allison, there was a shell, a gold-colored shell like floating in a puddle of blood on the shag carpet. I picked it up, and I got blood on my hands and I wiped it." He showed how he wiped off the blood on his right thigh. "Then when I went upstairs and I stepped on the rifle, I knew I had to get rid of everything."

"Butch, wait a minute," Rafferty said. "Why did you pick up the cartridge if you had nothing to do with it? You didn't know it was your gun that was used."

Ronnie didn't answer, and Rafferty gave him more room. "Let's go on, Butch. After you stepped on the gun and you realized it was yours, what did you do?"

Ronnie recalled taking the rifle and cartridge to his room and putting them into a pillowcase along with the clothes he was wearing. He changed and put the pillowcase inside a second pillowcase. Then he took a 30.06 rifle from his room and shoved that into the pillowcase. Finally, he went from room to room retrieving shells. The shells in his brothers' room were in the middle of the floor.

"They got it like this." Ronnie was talking about his brothers, and suddenly his hands were holding an imaginary rifle, which he cocked and fired. He moved from right to left and cocked and fired again.

After filling the pillowcase, Ronnie said, he found the keys and drove down Ocean Avenue to a village dock, where he threw one of the rifles, he believed it was the 30.06, into the bay. He was going to dump the other articles but he was afraid some of them might float, and he put the pillowcase back in the car. He drove to Brooklyn, dumped all the stuff into a sewer and went to work.

"Where in Brooklyn?" Rafferty asked.

Ronnie described his route—Southern State Parkway to Rockaway Parkway in Seagate. He said the sewer was around the corner from a Shell station.

At the detectives' request, Ronnie drew two diagrams—one of the site, and another showing how to get there. He drew lines for roads and circles for traffic lights. He marked "s.s." for the

Southern State, and sketched a checkerboard square for the sewer grating.

Rafferty left with the diagram and showed it to Gozaloff. Meanwhile, Harrison came in with hamburgers and Cokes and coffee. It was 1:30 P.M., and no one had eaten. Dunn settled for coffee, while Ronnie took a Coke and a hamburger. He was sipping the soda when Rafferty and Gozaloff returned. Gozaloff was having trouble locating the sewer site on a map, and he asked Ronnie to draw a more explicit diagram. The four officers and Ronnie initialed both diagrams, and Gozaloff left for Brooklyn.

Rafferty resumed the interrogation. "Butch, I think you had to see more than what you are saying here. I think that you had to hear something or see something more."

"No. I didn't."

"Butch, it's not logical. It's incredible. Every time we go into another area of questioning, you change your story."

"You won't believe it," Ronnie said. "You won't believe me."

Rafferty and Dunn repeated the litany. They would believe him. "Try me," Rafferty said. "I promise you. We'll believe you. Just tell us the truth."

They waited for Ronnie to break the quiet. "Give me time to think," he said. "You won't believe it." He began to cry.

"Butch, what happened?" Rafferty asked. "Tell us the truth."

"Louis Falini did it," Ronnie said.

"How do you know?"

"He was there." Ronnie continued to cry as he described how Falini and another man had awakened him at about 3:30 A.M. Falini held a large automatic to his head. They went to Ronnie's room, and Falini took a rifle out of the closet and found bullets in a dresser drawer. The other man kept the automatic on Ronnie.

Rafferty asked for a description of the other man, but Ronnie couldn't supply any details. He couldn't approximate the man's height, nor could he give his hair color or eye color.

"What happened then, Butch?"

"Falini took me downstairs with this other guy holding the gun on me. 'You're going to live with this the rest of your life,' Falini told me. 'This is for what you did to me.' They went into my mother and father's room, and Falini shot my father twice. He shot my mother once. Then they went to Allison's room."

"Did they take you with them?"

"Yeah. I had to go with them. I had to see the whole thing." Ronnie said he was forced to watch all the murders. As he described the killings, he kept in the part about John's foot twitching.

"Did anybody wake up?" Rafferty asked.

"Yeah. Dawn did." Dawn opened her door as they were coming up the stairs and asked if anything was wrong. Ronnie said no, and she closed the door. When they got up the stairs, Falini opened it. "Falini opened the door and shot her right in the head, and her head was like blown away. That Falini loved it. He loved it."

"This must have been a terrible thing for you to see," Rafferty said.

"Yeah. That Falini loved it. You should have seen him. He was like a mad dog. The gun was smoking and the barrel was hot."

Ronnie's eyes were lit up as he talked. Rafferty's thought was that Ronnie was really saying, "I loved it." How did Ronnie know the barrel was hot?

"You asked me before about the dog," Ronnie was saying. "The fucking dog was screaming while this was going on. The dog was screaming."

Ronnie added that Falini and the other man took him downstairs after the shootings and left the house. That was when he realized he had been framed and that he had to get rid of the gun and the shells.

There were just a few steps left. Dunn took the next one. "Butch, I think they must have made you shoot some of them," he said. "If they didn't, you can testify against them. They had to make you a piece of it. They must have made you a piece of it. They must have made you shoot at least one of them—or some of them."

Ronnie plunged. "They did. They made me shoot my father and Mark."

"How would that have possibly happened?" Dunn asked. He pointed out that the rifle would have had to go back and forth from Falini to Ronnie as they moved from room to room.

"It didn't happen that way, did it?" Rafferty said.

Ronnie was silent. Rafferty persisted. "Butch, it didn't happen that way. You know it didn't happen that way."

"Give me a minute," Ronnie said. "Give me a minute." He put his head in his hands.

"Butch, they never were there, were they? Falini and the other guy were never there."

"No," Ronnie said.

The horror of what he was hearing pressed in upon Lieutenant Robert Dunn, and he didn't want to hear any more. He got up and left the room. It was close to 4 P.M. Dennis Rafferty's knee was between Ronnie DeFeo's legs, and the suspect's head was on his shoulder.

"If all cops were like you, this would be better," Ronnie said.

Rafferty spoke gently as if he were consoling a child. "Butch, tell me what happened."

"It all started so fast," Ronald DeFeo, Jr., said. "Once I started, I just couldn't stop. It went so fast."

7

"OKAY," DENNIS RAFFERTY SAID, "tell me what happened, Butch. Take it easy."

Butch DeFeo had made the admission of his own guilt in a low voice, and then he gained strength. "It all started so fast. Once I started, I just couldn't stop. It went so fast." After that, it was as if a stuck faucet had been turned on—the interrogation was over in less than an hour. He had awakened near the television set, gone up to his own room and loaded the .35-caliber rifle. He came downstairs and killed his father and mother. He shot Allison in the head, and stood between the beds in his brothers' room and murdered Mark and John. Then he went upstairs.

"Did Dawn wake up?" Rafferty asked.

"Yeah," Ronnie said. "She said, 'Is that you, Butch?' I said, 'Yeah, everything's all right.'"

Dawn returned inside her room, and Ronnie opened the door

and shot her. The dog was screaming. Butch returned to his room and put the rifle in the pillow cases. He went across the hall to Dawn's room and picked up the cartridge. Next, he went downstairs and searched for other cartridges. Finally, he went back to his room and changed. He put the clothes he had been wearing during the murders into the pillowcases. He was at the front door when he realized that he didn't have any car keys, and he looked around and found a set. Then he dumped the 30.06 in the bay and drove to Brooklyn.

Butch was finished, and Rafferty asked if they could put everything he had told them in writing.

"No," Ronnie said. "If I put that in writing, my grandfather will see it."

"No, he won't, Butch. Don't worry about it. We keep things private here. This is the homicide squad."

Butch was adamant. "My grandfather has a lot of connections with cops. If I put that in writing and sign it, he'll have it twenty minutes after I sign it. I'm not putting it in writing."

It was about 5 P.M. when they left the file room. Harrison took Ronnie into another office. Rafferty went into a room by himself and made notes on the interrogation. When he and Lieutenant Dunn left homicide together at 7 P.M., Dennis Rafferty was burned out. He had not eaten or had anything to drink during the questioning, and he thought that he had never been involved in anything as overwhelming. It had been a difficult interrogation, but it had been a good one. He would never forget what was going on inside him when Butch DeFeo leaned on his shoulder and cracked.

"It was nice," Dennis Rafferty would remember. "It was nice, no doubt about it."

During the day, police worked on leads supplied by the suspect. Detective Napolitano returned to the DeFeo home in the morning with Detective Sergeant James Barylski, who had headed the homicide unit assigned to the scene and had stayed with the case overnight. They found the gray metal box beneath the saddle of Ronald DeFeo, Sr.'s closet in the master bedroom. Careful not to touch it with his hands, Napolitano removed the box with paper clips he inserted in the corners. He dusted the box for prints and found it clean; the smooth metal was not even smudged. The box was locked, but the detectives were able to open it with a key Scotch-taped to the top. Inside, they found an empty envelope and another key. There was no money, no valuables.

In the afternoon, Detective Gozaloff drove to Brooklyn, following the map Ronnie had drawn. A block west of Rockaway Parkway on Seaview Avenue, he saw a Shell station. The cross street on the left was East 96th Street. The drain was on the northeast corner of East 96th, built into the curb in front of a white house fronted by a cyclone fence. "LEASH, GUTTER AND CLEAN UP AFTER YOUR DOG," a sign on the fence advised passers-by, and a delicatessen a few yards down the street advertised heros and cold beer. The rear end of a Plymouth sedan partially obscured the sewer, but Gozaloff hunched over the curb and spotted a blue-and-white pillow case crumpled around a Kent box in the damp dead leaves lining the sewer. He could also see a black rifle scabbard and what looked like ammunition boxes.

At Gozaloff's request, New York City police dispatched a tow truck, which was used to pull away the Plymouth and to remove the sewer grating. Along with the scabbard, the pillowcase and a tan pistol holster, the searchers recovered eight expended cartridge casings, two live rounds and two ammunition boxes— one empty and the other unopened. It was all .35-caliber. A second pillowcase fell out of the first one, and Gozaloff found a pair of blue jeans, a blue shirt, a yellow towel, black socks and a pair of green undershorts.

There was no rifle. Nor did any turn up when sewer workers removed the four-inch-thick mat of leaves and pumped the drain dry of four feet of water. By 7:30 P.M., Gozaloff was back in Hauppauge, where Ronnie initialed the recovered articles with a black Magic Marker.

"The least you could do is ask about the burials," Gozaloff told the suspect.

"Oh, is there anything that I was supposed to do?" Butch asked. Gozaloff said a relative was attending to the arrangements, and Butch had another question. He asked if he could collect insurance on his family.

They discussed the murder weapon, and Ronnie switched his story. He hadn't dumped it in the drain. Actually, Ronnie explained, he had thrown it into the canal behind the empty house next to the DeFeo home. At the request of police, he drew a diagram to show the location.

A few minutes later, Gozaloff asked if Butch wanted to call someone. "No," DeFeo said, but he had an afterthought. "They're going to read about it in the papers."

"Maybe you better call somebody," Gozaloff told him, and Ronnie called his uncle's home in West Islip.

They left homicide for the headquarters building, where DeFeo would be fingerprinted and mug shots would be taken. As they were leaving, DeFeo told Harrison and Gozaloff that he was sure the underworld intended to hit him. "If there's any shooting," he said, "just duck. I'll take it all."

It was not, someone on Ocean Avenue said Thursday, as if tragedy had not visited the street before. The first young man from Amityville to die in Vietnam had been a resident of the street. And four years ago, a New York City patrolman who lived on Ocean Avenue had been shot to death on his beat and had been given an inspector's funeral at St. Martin of Tours. But nothing had been as shocking as the mass murders.

Throughout the afternoon, traffic streamed past the police barricades at the DeFeo home. People walked by the house and drove cars and bicycles up and down the street. DeFeo had not been booked yet, but word had gotten out that police were interviewing him. A woman who was pushing two infants in a baby carriage talked to *Newsday* columnist Jack Altshul. "Do they know who did it yet?" she asked. "I've been frightened half out of my mind. I hear they have the son in the police station questioning him. I've got this ambivalent feeling. Some people say he did it. If he did, I guess I could stop worrying. But I really hope he didn't. It's too terrible to comprehend."

That evening, the news became public. Ronald DeFeo, Jr., had been arrested. It was, as the woman pushing the carriage said, terrible. Immediately after the crime, most residents had been stricken by the immensity of the tragedy. But now, another sort of reaction was settling in. Not everybody in the surrounding neighborhood found it difficult to believe that Butch DeFeo was the killer. It depended on how well they knew Butch and his family. Or how much reason they had for not wanting to know the DeFeos. The southern part of the village was a quiet neighborhood, an established neighborhood. Some residents had resented the Brooklyn family that had moved into their midst. The DeFeos were loud, some people said. They were showy; they threw money around. "They all screamed at each other," one man told a detective. And there was a neighborhood story about the time Ronald, Sr., was floating in the pool on a rubber raft, and Butch threw a cherry-bomb into the water. The elder DeFeo came out of the pool, bellowing, and chased his son around the house. Butch jumped into his Buick and took off. Ronald, Sr., drove after him, their cars careening through the village.

There were two places of minimal surprise. These were Amityville police headquarters and Henry's Bar. Village police knew Butch DeFeo as someone who was always on the fringe of trouble but never close enough for them to arrest him. They suspected that he was into dope; they knew about the fights with his father. At headquarters the night of the murders, one officer told another that there had been a homicide at the DeFeo house.

"What'd Ronnie do?" asked the second officer. "Blow his father away?"

"No," came the reply. "He got the whole family."

At Henry's Bar, the tough young men who knew Butch DeFeo were close-lipped in front of the press. "A lot of the guys here know the only surviving member of his family," an auto-body worker had said before the bar regulars heard about Ronnie's arrest. "And we don't want to think he did it."

After the arrest, they were still wary. "They better have a good case," a man in a denim jacket said while a reporter was in the room, "or they're going to blow it."

"Just because he's a wild boy doesn't make him guilty or innocent," said another man.

But that night, and on the nights that followed, no one ever maintained that Ronnie didn't do it. The tough young men drank and played the juke box and pushed and pulled at a red, yellow and blue pinball game and cursed the newspapers for invading their privacy. But no one ever protested that Butch was innocent. No one at Henry's thought of Butch DeFeo as being especially tough, but he got nasty when he drank and he had been known to wave guns around. Once, he had threatened to use his gun on another patron. "Bring your gun," the second man said. "I'm gonna jam it right up your fucking ass." That was one of the times Butch backed down.

If any of the regulars at Henry's showed a marked reaction to the murders and DeFeo's arrest, it was Bobby Kelske. For three or four days, Kelske was in a daze.

Elsewhere in the community, reaction ran from grief for the family to anger at Butch DeFeo. One friend of the DeFeos worried about Shaggy, the sheepdog whose barking had wakened a neighborhood youth the night of the murders. The friend claimed the animal after it had spent ten days at the town dog shelter.

The anger at Butch grew after his arrest. In a bar-restaurant frequented by boating families, the consensus was that Butch was a creep, that he was probably on dope. Several of the patrons were ex-cops, and they shared another opinion—one voiced by a merchant who knew the DeFeos as customers. "He'll never get to trial," the merchant said.

Other residents of Amityville were afraid that he would get to trial but win acquittal on insanity grounds. Or that for one reason or another, the charges would be dropped. Some worried that DeFeo would come back to 112 Ocean Avenue and turn the house into a hangout for hoods. Others had more personal fears. They included a thirteen-year-old girl who had been a close friend of Allison DeFeo. The night of the murders, the girl had been babysitting. When she heard about the killings, she hid in a corner of the house where she was working. She was afraid that Ronnie DeFeo was going to come there and murder her.

The girl had reason for fear. She was a village policeman's daughter, and a year before, Ronnie DeFeo had threatened to kill her and her father. What had happened was that the officer got a tip that a friend of DeFeo's was growing fence-high marijuana plants in his backyard. The officer obtained a search warrant and not only found the plants, but discovered a crop of marijuana leaves drying on a fish line stretched across the attic of the suspect's house. DeFeo's friend was arrested. DeFeo found out and stomped around his own home, yelling that he would kill both the cop who had arrested his friend and the cop's daughter. The girl was in the cellar playing with Allison, and heard Butch yelling. "He was frightening," she would remember, years later.

On Friday, November 15, five scuba divers—from both the Suffolk and Nassau Police Departments—plunged into the canal behind the empty house on the north side of 112 Ocean Avenue. The cold water yielded broken bottles and cans, but no rifles. One of the divers did turn up a weapon, but it had nothing to do with the case—it was a toy machine gun.

After an hour, the divers transferred their search to the canal's mouth alongside a small village dock at the tip of Ocean Avenue. To the south, beyond the steel-blue bay, the barrier beach held the horizon. To the west, gray frame houses guarded the shore. To the east, the canal emptied into the bay. A line was tied to the east bulkhead, and the divers worked off it in a semicircle. Near the end of the last swing, Nassau Patrolman Melvin Berger spotted a weaponlike object lying on the bottom in about ten inches of eel grass. He was less than thirty feet from the dock in ten to fifteen feet of water.

When he broke the surface, Berger was holding a rifle over his head. The rifle was loaded and cocked. It was a .35-caliber Marlin.

Later the same day, in First District Court, Hauppauge, Ronald DeFeo, Jr., was arraigned on one charge of second-degree murder. For the purpose of the arraignment, he was specifically accused of shooting Mark. Dressed in mechanic's overalls, Ronnie seemed relaxed as Judge Donald L. Auperin read the complaint to him:

"Ronald."

"Yes sir."

"The specifications obtained in the information are that you caused the death of another person, you did cause the death of Mark DeFeo, eleven years old, with a rifle, thereby causing his death. Do you understand what I just said to you, that you're accused of murdering Mark DeFeo, who I understand to be your brother?"

"I, well," and he hesitated. "Ahh, huh."

However, he told the judge he had spoken to his lawyer before entering court, and answered in a low voice when asked his occupation: "I work for my grandfather, the Buick dealership."

"What kind of work do you do for him?"

"Mechanic work, everything."

"What is your education?"

"High school."

"Did you complete your high school education?"

"No."

"You dropped out somewhere along the way?"

"Yes."

Ronnie's appearance became part of the proceeding when his lawyer said he wanted the record to show that injuries were visible on the defendant's lips and left eye.

The assistant district attorney handling the arraignment disagreed. "I don't see any injury on the eye. I don't see the injury on the lips."

This prompted Ronnie to speak for himself. "The lips are swollen," he said.

The assistant district attorney had the last word. "It's the people's position we don't know what happened to the lips prior to this incident."

Judge Auperin turned down a defense request for a psychiatric examination to determine whether the defendant was able to stand trial. He ordered Ronald DeFeo, Jr., held without bail, and set a date for a felony hearing.

Butch DeFeo's first day in court as an accused murderer was over. The prosecution was just beginning.

PART TWO

Maneuver and Investigation

8 _____

I HAVE ALWAYS BEEN fascinated by the concept of one person taking the life of another person. This stops being academic when you consider that I practice law. To me, a murder trial is the pinnacle of prosecution. At the time of the mass-slayings in Amityville, I worked for the office of the Suffolk County district attorney. The following year, I would push for the chance to prosecute Ronald DeFeo, Jr.

From here on, you will be seeing the DeFeo case through me. The *cinéma vérité* of people and passions, events and places. The pretrial maneuvering and investigation, and the trial itself. The trial went on for nine weeks and included one hundred and thirty-seven exhibits and fifty-seven witnesses. There were several side paths, and along the way, a subculture was stripped bare. Perhaps a way of life was on trial. From trees to boathouses, Ocean Avenue was a street of American dreams. And what happened at 112 was a suburban tragedy.

I think about that aspect of the case because I have lived most of my life in the same Long Island that spawned Ronnie DeFeo. My name is Gerard B. Sullivan, Jerry to my friends and some of my adversaries. I was born October 22, 1942, in Brooklyn, the first child of Gerard A. Sullivan and the former Mary McGrane. When I was six months old, my parents moved to Queens. When I was eleven, they followed the suburban migration eastward, settling across the Nassau border in Williston Park with me and my two sisters. I attended parochial schools and Seton Hall University in South Orange, New Jersey, where I took prelaw courses but was not at all sure that I wanted to be an attorney. Instead, after graduation, I enlisted in the Navy as a would-be pilot. A week before I was to report to flight training, I was involved in a car accident on Cape Cod, winding up with a broken knee cap and a medical discharge. I spent the next several months on my back, a position from which there is literally and figuratively no way to go but up. My father, a district manager for Rheingold Breweries, impressed me with the need for a direction. He was proud of me—I was the first member of my family with a college degree—but he wanted me to have a goal. I chose law.

For the next four years, I went nights and summers to St. John's Law School in Brooklyn. At the same time, I worked days as an insurance adjustor. I had two years of law school left when I married a coworker, the former Betty Jane Breit. It was one of my more intelligent actions. Betty and I moved from a sixth-floor walkup in Queens to an apartment in Great Neck, and then purchased our own home in Huntington. Our first child, Kim Marie, was born in 1969; our second, Jill Ann, was born two years later.

In May, 1969, I graduated from St. John's, and the following March, I was admitted to the bar. Two weeks later, I obtained a job in the Suffolk County district attorney's office. I had decided in law school that I would never become a law library recluse or bury myself in an oak-paneled inner sanctum. Law libraries were arsenals containing weapons necessary for effective courtroom work, and law offices were where attorneys prepared for trial. I wanted to be a trial lawyer, and the district attorney's office provided an outlet for immediate courtroom experience. I tried all types of cases—working my way up from traffic infractions and misdemeanors in the district court bureau to felonies in the trial bureau. When the DeFeo trial opened, I had appeared in court for more than a thousand different matters, and had tried fifty cases to verdict, winning forty-eight.

To round out the profile, I think of myself as squarely built and Irish-looking. I enjoy my family. I'm a sailing enthusiast, a scuba diver and a football fan. I have always been moved by classical music, and I'm a closet piano player. I'm an extrovert—I have a definite ego need, which trial work satisfies.

It is paramount that I have to believe in what I'm doing. As a prosecutor, I have to be morally convinced of the defendant's guilt. This is a gut necessity; there have been instances when I have helped clear a defendant rather than convict him. A case in point involved a Suffolk police officer accused of committing sodomy with two fourteen-year-old girls. The girls passed a polygraph test, and Internal Affairs wanted the officer convicted. Although he had already been indicted and suspended from duty, I re-presented the facts to another grand jury. In doing so, I put the two girls through a searching cross-examination. The panel returned a "No Bill," effectively exonerating the cop. As a result, the Internal Affairs brass took their complaints over my head to the chief assistant district attorney. They had information that the accused officer went to porno movies, so they decided he had to be guilty of the morals charge. He wasn't. Clearing him was well worth the heat I took as a result.

When the DeFeo murders occurred, I was assigned to the rackets bureau, which handled investigations of organized crime. I arrived at work late that Wednesday and found almost everyone talking about the killings in Amityville. The case had overtones of mob involvement, and Bob Dunn, the lieutenant in charge of our detectives, was at homicide. I read the accounts in the newspapers, and spent much of the day discussing the crime with the rackets-squad detectives who worked for me. By late afternoon, we heard that Ronald DeFeo, Jr., had confessed, and that evidence had been recovered on the basis of what he told police. "They got the son of a bitch," someone said, and that was the general sentiment. We were pleased that Suffolk homicide detectives had brought the case in quickly, and particularly proud that Bob Dunn had a part in obtaining the confession. I was upset that six people had been slaughtered, and that four of them were children, but my ruling emotion was more personal. There was going to be an unprecedented murder prosecution, and it was passing me by. From the beginning, I wanted to prosecute the man who had blasted away six lives. I wanted a piece of that case. And I couldn't see my way clear to getting it.

It would become pertinent that the district attorney's office was in a state of upheaval. Earlier that month, the voters of Suffolk County had made history by electing a Democrat as district attorney for the first time in fifty years. Several of my colleagues were, with good reason, worried about their jobs. I had no such concerns. The man who would take over the office in January was Henry O'Brien, a onetime Republican and former assistant district attorney with a reputation as a confirmed maverick. Although I was a registered Republican and had even gone out ringing doorbells for the party on a few occasions, I thought of myself as politically amorphic. O'Brien and I had opposed each other in court and were in no way close, but I knew he considered me a highly competent trial lawyer. Besides, it was an open secret that he was going to appoint Sam Fierro, head of the rackets bureau, as his chief assistant. Fierro and I worked well together. Although I was committed to the rackets bureau through the remainder of 1974, I had good reason to believe that I would return to the trial bureau the following year as its deputy chief. The trouble was that by then, the DeFeo case would already have been assigned.

*   *   *

The Sunday after the murders, the names of the slain DeFeos were mentioned by the priest during mass at St. Martin of Tours Church. The bodies were on view in a funeral home in Deer Park, where mourners arrived steadily throughout the afternoon. The scene was described by *Newsday* reporter Neill S. Rosenfeld, who wrote that mourners halted in the doorway "as if their knees had hit an unseen barrier." In front of them lay the six murder victims—propped on satiny pillows in dark wood coffins at the head of a room in which flowers lined three walls. After paying their respects to the dead or resting in chairs arranged in semicircles in the room, many of the mourners went outside and stood in the drizzle that sprinkled the crowded parking lot.

Most of the people who came to the funeral parlor were reluctant to comment, but a few discussed the incredibility of what had happened. The sight of the six bodies in the flower-banked coffins seemed to make the murders more unbelievable. "'They were such beautiful children,'" Rosenfeld quoted one woman as saying. The woman, who described herself as a distant cousin of Louise DeFeo, twisted a yellow tissue in her hands and stared at a wall mural. "'Look at them. . . . I can't look any more,'" she said.

At 11 A.M. Monday, a mass was said for the victims at St. Martin's. Burial followed at a Catholic cemetery a few miles away. There were six hearses; the long procession was supervised by the Suffolk Police Department. The route was marked out, and officers were stationed around the church.

At St. Martin's, police had to control Michael Brigante, Sr., the slain children's maternal grandfather. Brigante had been composed throughout the ride from the funeral home to the church. But as the mourners were entering St. Martin's, a newspaper photographer jumped in front of them. Brigante reacted instantly, swinging at the photographer and missing.

The church was across the street from St. Martin's Catholic School, where Allison DeFeo and her younger brothers had attended classes. Nuns at the school had discouraged conversation about the tragedy and frowned at the idea of pupils attending the funeral. The children in Allison's class could see the cortege arriving outside their classroom window. They could see people coming out of the church in tears. But they could not discuss it.

Seven years later, I would meet one of the girls who had watched the mourners through the window. She described Allison as a shy, sensitive girl who would close the door of her room when Ronnie came home because she did not want to hear him fighting with their father. The young woman said she and Allison spent time at the DeFeo pool during the summer, but that otherwise, Allison liked to stay over at her house. "I still dream about Allison," the young woman said. "I have dreams and I see her face. She was very sensitive. Like at school, she had money and everybody knew it. But she didn't go around buying snacks for people and things like that. She didn't want to buy friendship. Why did she have to be killed? She was so nice, so sweet." Allison's former classmate had a fond memory of John DeFeo, the youngest child. "He was adorable," she would tell me.

I read about the mass funeral for the DeFeos, and I was affected by one of the pictures I saw—a photograph of the six dark coffins being carried out of St. Martin of Tours. A few days later, the photograph flashed back into my mind. This occurred after our bureau received a report from street informants that an attempt might be made to kill Ronnie DeFeo. The speculation was that organized crime was behind the threatened hit. Although the report was uncorroborated, the district attorney's office could not take any chances with DeFeo's safety. He was scheduled to appear in county court that day, and would have to be brought there from the Suffolk County jail. Despite the fact that the buildings are a few hundred yards apart in the county seat in Riverhead, the transfer involved some risk. Because of the assassination report, the judge agreed to move the hearing to the chapel on the third floor of the prison. When I heard the switch being discussed, I couldn't help thinking that it seemed a sacrilege. Only a few days before, the coffins had been carried out of the House of God after the dead were given the Church's last rites. Now, the man accused of murdering the people in those coffins was being led into a chapel for the protection of his legal rights and his person.

In January, 1975, my job expectations were realized. Sam Fierro was named chief assistant district attorney. I was appointed deputy chief of the trial bureau under its incumbent boss, John Buonora, and given my own case load, which included several murders. As I expected, the DeFeo case had already been assigned. The accused mass-killer would be prosecuted by Assistant District Attorney Edward Connors. At fifty-six, Eddie Connors was senior man on the staff and had more trial experience than anyone else in the office. His seniority gave him a built-in advantage over the other assistants. The minute Eddie walked into a Suffolk courtroom, he engendered respect. In court, his self-assurance bordered on arrogance. I was a tyro out of law school when I came to the district attorney's office, and I had learned a great deal by watching Eddie Connors. Where we differed was that Eddie felt it was up to the police to do all the investigating; he would work with what he had in front of him. I felt that prosecutors should be innovative. I believed in thorough investigation and I thought the prosecutor's job started with it.

From what I heard, it seemed to me that more investigation was required on DeFeo. I knew as much about the case as most of the other assistant district attorneys on the trial staff. There was a confession. There was a good deal of physical evidence. Forensic experts would testify to the physical facts of the crime. Terrific. But nobody was talking about motive—the why of the murders. Not unless you counted speculation in the newspapers about DeFeo expecting to get insurance money, but that wouldn't hold.

There was a lot of talk about whether DeFeo would use legal insanity as a defense. I had tried several cases involving psychiatric defenses, and they were tough—the distinction between legal and medical insanity can be difficult for a jury of laymen. "If DeFeo killed six people without a reason, he had to be crazy." That would be any layman's reaction; hell, that would be my reaction. The prosecution needed a motive. If there was proof of a motive out there, it wasn't being sought. I knew that investigative activity on the case had gone stagnant in January. Nothing is more perishable than testimony, and I was disturbed that DeFeo's chance of acquittal might be improving with time.

On several occasions, I was in the county courthouse on my own cases when Ronald DeFeo, Jr., was brought there for calendar appearances. There was no official reason for me to watch him, but I didn't need one. The first time I saw DeFeo, I was struck by the fact that no member of his family was in the courtroom. And I was caught by his eyes, which were squinty but expressive. He wore a perpetual smirk, but it was all in his eyes.

Everytime I watched DeFeo, I wanted the case. I was haunted by the memory of those six black coffins being carried from the church. The mass-murder trial stalked the back of my mind, a daydream on the edge of reality. One night in early spring, I did something about it. The DeFeo case was kept filed with hundreds of others, including mine, in the trial bureau's secretarial pool. I took the case from its place among Eddie Connors's files and locked myself in my office with the bulging folder. For the next few hours, I examined photographs, read police reports, studied DeFeo's account of the murders, went over witnesses' statements. By the time I finished, I wanted that trial even more intensely than when I first heard about the killings. Okay, it was already assigned. But I could still try to get it.

The fact that I was deputy bureau chief didn't help. John Buonora was fair, but he ran the bureau like an autocrat, and my title, I soon came to learn, was more nominal than real. There were a dozen assistant district attorneys in the trial bureau, and case assignments were a matter of jealousy. I couldn't even look like I was pulling rank to usurp somebody else's case. I might have to stoop to guile, but I also had to rise to diplomacy.

My first idea was to bring up the DeFeo case in discussions with Connors. I was looking for an opening, and I wanted to find out how he felt about the trial. Eddie was little more than a half-year away from retirement. His health was giving him trouble, and his general outlook seemed dour, if not pessimistic. As it developed, his attitude toward prosecuting DeFeo was no exception. Instead of discussing positives, he stressed problems. There were very real problems. I didn't add to Eddie's pessimism, but I have to admit I did nothing to dispel it.

The glaring problem was the one I had sensed—the lack of a definable motive. Ronald DeFeo had admitted murdering his family, but he never said why. Insanity was DeFeo's most obvious defense, and he could go two ways with it. He could plead not guilty by reason of insanity, and he could also defend on grounds of extreme emotional disturbance, which would lessen his responsibility from murder to first-degree manslaughter. A manslaughter conviction carried a penalty of only eight-and-a-third to twenty-five years. Murder carried twenty-five years to life. Connors figured that anyone who could wipe out his family without a definable motive had to be extremely emotionally disturbed at the very least, and probably was insane. He felt he couldn't do any better than manslaughter.

My feeling was that Connors's approach did not suit the case. Eddie was going with what he had, and it wasn't enough. The case cried out for the investigation that would prove DeFeo was legally sane. Whoever prosecuted DeFeo needed a concrete motive to show the jury. In effect, he had to be able to say, "Look, there it is—that's the reason Ronald DeFeo, Jr., murdered his family." When I had studied the case file, I had spotted something that hinted at the motive. Something that might provide a very solid reason for the killings. But it was only a shadow. A lot of work would be required to develop it into hard evidence.

As my discussions with Eddie continued through the spring, I began to feel that he really didn't want the DeFeo case but had too much professional pride to give it up. Under the right circumstances, I thought, he might be willing to trade. In mid-June, our vacation plans provided a catalyst. Betty and I planned to go sailing with another couple during a week in July; Eddie was scheduled to take his vacation later in the year. His long-range plan was to retire to a horse farm he owned in Virginia, and he needed time off to fix up the property. The DeFeo case was sure to cut into his plans. I mentioned to Eddie that one of my cases was interfering with my vacation. It was a murder case that would probably go down to manslaughter—the defendant had caused the death of another motorist while fleeing from police in a high-speed chase.

"I'll try it for you," Eddie said.

"I'll try one of yours," I said, and I took my shot. "How about DeFeo?"

For an instant, I felt like a place-kicker watching his field goal attempt arching forward in a sudden-death overtime. Then I was exultant. Eddie went for the idea immediately. In minutes, we were in John Buonora's office. The bureau chief ascertained that Eddie had no qualms about the trade, and when we walked out, I was prosecuting Ronald DeFeo, Jr.

I wasted no time making my first move. I took the DeFeo file out of Eddie Connors's cabinet and put it in mine. I stamped my name all over the file, changed all the necessary records to reflect my assignment, and notified the detectives who had worked on the case that they would be dealing with me. I told them to gather every piece of paper in their possession that pertained to the case. We would meet within two weeks to reevaluate everything we had.

At home that evening, I discussed the trade with Betty. In April, we had moved from Huntington to a new and larger house about thirty miles farther east, and much closer to Riverhead. The house was considerably more expensive to carry, and I was trying to save money by doing my own landscaping. I told Betty that a lot of jobs around the place would have to be postponed because of the new case. A great deal of investigation was required, and the trial would not be a short one. There would be night work and preoccupation— moments when I would sit at the dinner table with the DeFeo case filling my mind. "I'll be a pain in the ass for a long time," I said. "Do you want me to give the case to someone else?" I knew I wasn't being very fair.

"No," Betty said. "If you want the case, I want you to take it." We talked about the tragedy itself, the destruction of a family and the importance of prosecuting the guilty person. "You can do as good a job as anyone else in the office," Betty said. "You should try the case. We'll live through the side effects." I think she was as moved by the enormous sense of tragedy in the DeFeo case as I was.

I was more than pleased by her response. Lack of confidence is not one of my problems—that's a luxury a good trial lawyer can't afford—but it matters that Betty believes in me. It matters very much.

And if she had gone the other way, if she had asked me to drop the case, I'm not sure what my answer would have been. I was grateful to her for making that answer unnecessary.

9

"SIGNORELLI?"

The name followed by the question mark topped my list of things to deal with in the DeFeo case. Ernest L. Signorelli was the judge to whom the trial had been assigned. At the time, he may have been the best judge on the county court bench. But not for the DeFeo case. And not for me.

First the case. Ronald DeFeo, Jr., had not signed a written confession, which meant that police credibility might well be an issue at the trial. Judge Signorelli was something less than a police buff; he had a reputation for being critical of officers who appeared before him as witnesses. Since so much of my case would depend on police testimony, that could be a problem.

So could my presence. In 1971, Judge Signorelli and I made local judicial history together. He cited me for contempt of court—something that, to my knowledge, had never happened before to an assistant district attorney in Suffolk County, and has not happened since. It was pertinent to my worries about the DeFeo trial that the incident involved a police officer, my top witness in an assault case. Not only did Judge Signorelli take over the officer's cross-examination, but he swiveled around in his chair and sat with his back to the witness. This forced the witness to answer questions looking at the back of the judge's chair, while the judge looked out the window. I objected, pointing the situation out for the record, and the judge ordered me to sit and be silent. I wasn't about to sit down until I had finished objecting, and whammo—the judge cited me for not following his orders and for impugning his impartiality. He ordered me to appear in court to defend myself against the charge, but an agreement was worked out before this became necessary. Over the next four years, nothing had occurred to change the aura between us. His Honor did not like me; I did not like him. I had prosecuted a few cases before Judge Signorelli, and each time I felt the friction. I did not look forward to prosecuting the most important case of my career before him. If there were any way the case could be reassigned, the prosecution would have to benefit. If not, I would make sure this was the best-prepared and most aggressively prosecuted case over which Judge Signorelli had ever presided.

On June 30th my vacation began, and Betty and I sailed to Martha's Vineyard with our friends. I brought part of the DeFeo file and studied in the fog that accompanied us all the way to Massachusetts. The mist cloaking the gray sea matched the haze still hanging over the mass-murders, and areas of investigation formed in my mind. The investigation would entail problems, but I could deal with them. I wasn't sure that I could do anything about Judge Signorelli.

I also wondered who my trial adversary would be. Since his arraignment, DeFeo had gone through three attorneys. Money was a problem, so was his attitude. If he were acquitted, DeFeo could obtain his family's assets and be more than able to pay a lawyer. Otherwise, unless his family or the estate provided the money, there was no surety of recompense. On May 27th,

DeFeo's third lawyer, Jacob Siegfried, a highly respected Suffolk trial attorney, had withdrawn from the case. In a phone conversation with Eddie Connors that day, Siegfried referred to DeFeo as "nuts," and said that his client had tried to assault him. Although DeFeo apologized later in court, saying that "I was wrong about something that somebody said to me," Siegfried remained adamant. He told Judge Signorelli that the lawyer-client relationship prevented him from going into details but "this defendant expressed specific desire, in no uncertain terms, in the presence of others and threatened physical harm to me. And I don't feel in all good conscience—my own conscience and justice to this defendant—that I should represent him."

The matter of counsel remained unsettled for several weeks. DeFeo wanted to pick his own attorney, but approval was required from the administrator of the estate, who was out of the country. On July 7th, Judge Signorelli phoned William Weber, a well-known Suffolk defense lawyer, and asked him to take the case under the county's assigned counsel plan. As an assigned counsel, Weber would be paid by the county, with the amount to be decided by the judge who presided over the trial. I knew Bill Weber as a bright, shrewd lawyer with a talent for dominating a courtroom. Equally important, I suspected Weber would be as drawn to the case as I was.

In addition, he and Judge Signorelli had a relationship that was sure to be mentioned at some point in the case. An important trial is like a play with subplots that crisscross the main theme. The difference is that the players write their own lines. The DeFeo murder case was no exception. Judges, lawyers, witnesses—each carried their own drama. Personal ambitions, frustrations, emotions flared and subsided and flared again on the great dark frame of the case itself.

My own desire, my campaign to get the trial, was one example. Judge Signorelli's ambition to higher office and pride in himself as a jurist, Bill Weber's drive; they were others. Suddenly, it mattered to the prosecution of a mass-murder trial

The floor of Butch's room was covered with a gray, white and blue shag rug, and the walls were brightly papered in red-and-blue polka dots on a white background. At the head of his bed, the polka-dot motif changed into mock road signs and posterlike drawings, the latter including a nude blonde whose lower torso was blanketed by the legend: "NOT NOW, DARLING."

All six victims were killed with a .35-caliber Marlin rifle. At 2:30 A.M., a police officer went through the rooms for the last time to make sure no police equipment had been left behind. Checking over Ronnie's room, Shirvell spotted two tall cardboard boxes on the northwest wall along the chimney. The boxes were in an alcove and had been overlooked in prior searches. What caught Shirvell's attention were the labels. Both boxes had contained Marlin rifles: a .22 and a .35.

The two DeFeo girls: Dawn at right, Allison at left. When Dawn was found by the police, she nestled beneath a pink blanket on a sheet whose orange butterflies seemed ready to light on the big pink-and-orange flowers that bloomed across the wallpaper. She was face down. Only by standing at the head of the bed could one spot the redness staining the sheet beneath her left shoulder. When Allison was found, she, too, was lying face down. Blood ran down the lower side of her head, down her left arm and down the side of the bed to the floor. She had been shot in the face.

Dawn's room was vivid, but her things were in place—the bottles of nail polish crowding the bright green vanity, the stuffed monkey seated in the slender, red-cushioned white chair, the Tiffany lamp and the wicker box topped by a vase of flowers on the white, gold-trimmed chest, and the electric typewriter protected by its cover on the dark table.

There were two beds in Allison's room, their curlicued orange headboards as bright as the flowered walls. One bed was neatly made, its embossed white spread barely wrinkled by the sweater, jigsaw puzzle box and teen bra that lay on top of it. A jigsaw puzzle was in progress on a board laid across a dehumidifier, and a completed puzzle interlocked nearby on a carpet.

Butch returned to his room and put the rifle in the pillowcases. He went across the hall to Dawn's room and picked up the cartridge. Next, he went downstairs and searched for other cartridges. Finally, he went back to his room and changed. He put the clothes he had been wearing during the murders into the pillowcases. He drove to Brooklyn, where he dumped all the stuff into a sewer and went to work.

Along with the scabbard, the pillowcase and a tan pistol holster, the searchers recovered eight expended cartridge casings, two live rounds and two ammunition boxes—one empty and the other unopened. It was all .35-caliber.

Shirvell and Della Penna went to the home of Steve Hicks in Amityville, where Ronnie said that the rifle he "no longer owned" had gone off accidentally. Sure enough, they found a hole beneath the living-room rug. Della Penna later used a microscope with a dual eyepiece to compare test-fired bullets with those found in the DeFeo house, as well as with the bullet unearthed in the crawl space at Steve Hicks' home. In all cases, the striations on the bullets matched up.

DeFeo had never mentioned a metal box, but he did refer to the secret place where the money and jewels had been kept. "In the bottom. In the floor, like."

Nassau Patrolman Melvin Berger spotted a weaponlike object lying on the bottom of the canal in about ten inches of eel grass. He was less than thirty feet from the dock in ten to fifteen feet of water. When he broke the surface, Berger was holding a rifle over his head. The rifle was loaded and cocked. It was a .35-caliber Marlin. (Arrow in aerial photograph at right shows recovery site.)

The shed where Shaggy, the family sheepdog, was normally kept at night. "You asked me about the dog," Ronnie said. "The fucking dog was screaming while this was going on. The dog was screaming."

that County Judge Ernest L. Signorelli was running for surrogate. The relevancy centered on the fact that William Weber was actively supporting Signorelli's candidacy. Describing the judge's race as a "lawyers' campaign," Weber was calling on other attorneys for contributions. There was nothing wrong with any of this, but it could be a basis for reassignment of the DeFeo case. However, that was not an action I could or would initiate. It would be up to Judge Signorelli to decide whether there was a conflict of interest.

On July 14, 1975, I made my first court appearance as prosecutor in *The People of the State of New York* V. *Ronald Joseph DeFeo, Jr.* The hearing on the third floor of the county court building was held to confirm Weber's selection as defense counsel, but that was merely the surface. The undercurrents were more interesting. Both defendant and judge were learning for the first time that there had been a switch in prosecutors. I avoided looking over at DeFeo, whom I had started thinking of by his last name. He was a dealer in stares and I didn't want him to think he worried me, rather that my attitude was one of indifference. But I knew he was watching me constantly. Judge Signorelli was equally aware of me. His Honor was a cornucopia of body language. When we faced each other, he furrowed his brow and glanced downward. His jaw muscles flexed, and a vein on the side of his head bulged out. He rubbed a pencil back and forth along the desk—rolling it lengthwise with the palm of his hand as if it were a barrel. All that, and I could detect the rhythmic movement of his foot beating a tattoo behind the bench. He had just discovered that Sullivan had replaced Connors for the prosecution.

The question of Judge Signorelli's impartiality did not come up that day, but the following week he called Weber and me into his chambers and confronted the issue. Judge Signorelli said he wanted the prosecution to be aware of Weber's activity in his campaign. Further, he wanted both defense and prosecution to have ample opportunity to object or consent to his presiding over the trial. As warily as a blindfolded man putting his hand in a lobster tank, I said that His Honor was on the verge of a time-consuming campaign for surrogate, knowing that this was going to be a time-consuming case, was he going to be able to . . . and he came down on me like a trap door, emphatically letting me know that his judicial obligations came first. I said I would have to talk to others in the district attorney's office, and would respond at our next court date.

That came a week later. Directing himself to DeFeo, Judge Signorelli referred to Weber's support of his bid for surrogate. He added: "I want everybody to be perfectly clear in this matter that I will only try this case if everybody is satisfied that they want me to try this case."

I could think of greater satisfactions, but my office was in a bind. We could not say anything that would hint of prejudice on the part of Judge Signorelli. The record speaks for itself.

Mr. Sullivan: "All right, I'll be as complete as I can, Judge, with respect to the People's position. Since Your Honor made that known in the conference in chambers I think Wednesday of last week I took it under advisement to discuss it with others within the office. And the position is stated thusly: first, we do not object to Your Honor presiding over any portion of these proceedings because of Your Honor having assigned Mr. Weber as defense counsel and Mr. Weber being active in Your Honor's campaign; secondly, the district attorney does not want to try the case—"

The Court: (Interposing.) "I just want to stop you and the reason I did assign Mr. Weber is not because he was active in my campaign. I know you didn't mean it that way. I assigned him because I have the greatest confidence in him, in his ability to give this defendant the best possible defense he knows of. All right."

Mr. Sullivan: "Yes, Judge. We considered the fact that Mr. Weber was apparently chosen off the 'A' list."

The Court: "Right."

Mr. Sullivan: "I had originally thought the 'A' list was administered by the rotating system or that the clerk chose the lawyers assigned off the 'A' list. And that I was—that misapprehension was cleared up recently by Your Honor.

"Secondly, to go on, we do not want your Honor to try this case, nor do we not want Your Honor to try this case. We have no preference as to any of the county judges or in fact any Supreme Court justices sitting at criminal term to preside over this case. . . ."

For the record, we were saying we had no feelings one way or the other whether Judge Signorelli did or did not preside over the trial. I doubt that anyone in the courtroom had any illusions about how we really felt. But our office had no choice—you cannot infer partiality to a judge without strong support. I added, however, that my office was "chiefly concerned with any objection that the defendant personally might see fit to make concerning the arrangement whereby Your Honor preside and Mr. Weber represent him as defense counsel." I was falling short of unqualified approval, and I could tell from the judge's body language that my choice of words was troubling him.

Weber came on next, explaining that he had met five to seven times with DeFeo, sometimes for as long as three hours. He said he had explained his relationship with the judge, and his client had no objections.

DeFeo agreed. "No, I'm satisfied," he told Judge Signorelli. "I'd like you to be the judge and Mr. Weber my lawyer."

His Honor turned to me. "Then I take it from what you have said the People are satisfied to having me remain in this case?"

I didn't hesitate. "Yes, sir," I said. His Honor had gotten the response he was waiting for.

I had other problems. In a few weeks, Weber had done more than DeFeo's previous lawyers had done in eight months. Not only was he the first to hire a private investigator and retain psychiatrists to examine the defendant, but in a cogent twenty-four-page motion before the court, he was demanding that the prosecution turn over the names and addresses of all prospective witnesses.

I argued that a previous judge had rejected a similar motion by Siegfried. I offered Weber copies of the laboratory reports and police photographs, and even the names of police officers who might testify. But not the civilian list. I didn't want my witnesses harried by the defense, and I didn't want to booby-trap myself. I was reopening the investigation; there were sure to be new witnesses. I might not be allowed to call them if Signorelli granted Weber's motion for a list of all my witnesses.

By the end of the week, Judge Signorelli handed down his decision. As I expected, he found for the defense. Within ten days, we were to supply the names and addresses of all "potential prosecution witnesses to be called at the trial."

There was a small saving grace. The DeFeo case was placed on the calendar for September 15th, but Judge Signorelli was going on vacation until September 3rd. We would hold off on the witness list while he was away. Although it probably would do little good, I could argue truthfully that we were continuing to develop witnesses. Further, I was committed full time to another trial. His Honor would be angry, but I had survived his wrath before.

The prosecution occupying my attention at the beginning of August was the second-degree murder trial of Vito Coscia, a twenty-one-year-old man accused of killing an eleven-year-old girl the previous November. Coscia had visited the victim's home in Lake Ronkonkoma and stayed there while the child's mother and a woman friend went to a nearby 7–11 store for food and cigarettes. During the half-hour they were gone, he sexually attacked the girl and stabbed her several times about the torso with a large kitchen knife. Then he used the knife on her seven-year-old brother. When the women returned, they went into the kitchen and began making the food. Coscia kept them company as if nothing had happened. After a while, he went into the boy's bedroom. Quickly, he came out holding the bleeding child. He acted surprised. The mother's friend ran into the girl's bedroom and found her dead. Police were called, and Coscia was arrested. At first, he claimed that a burglar had attacked the children. Within an hour, he changed his story. He had been despondent and had picked up the knife with the idea of killing himself. Instead, he had gone into the bedroom with the knife in his hand and attacked the children.

I was emotionally committed to the Coscia case because of what had been done to those children. I figured I would work on it days and spend nights and weekends on DeFeo. Before the trial began, a hearing was held to determine if Coscia had made his confession voluntarily—he claimed that police had beaten it out of him. The judge ruled in our favor, and on August 14th, the jury selection was completed. No sooner had I made my opening statement, than Coscia's lawyer asked permission to approach the bench. His client would plead guilty as charged. The following year, after a lengthy hearing in which he attempted to withdraw the plea, Coscia was sentenced to fifteen years to life. Until then, he had been imprisoned in the Suffolk County jail, where he met another accused child-killer in sickbay. The other man's name was Ronald DeFeo, Jr. Near the end of the DeFeo trial, Vito Coscia would be called as a defense witness.

The morning after Coscia pleaded guilty, I was putting all my time and energy into the DeFeo case. It gripped me as no other prosecution ever had. It became a preoccupation, perhaps an obsession. I had seen guilty persons go free because of a lack of admissible evidence. I wouldn't let it happen in this case. The expenditure of time I was putting into the prosecution was enormous; I worried about my family suffering as a result. At home, I was often uncommunicative at the dinner table; afterwards I would hole up in the fourth bedroom, which I used as a den. I knew Betty understood but the children were another matter. "Is Daddy mad at us?" one of them asked her.

I read the files until I could almost recite them. I made notes, formulated theories, outlined areas that demanded further probing. The investigation had been dormant for eight months; now we had little more than a month in which to prepare for the pretrial hearing.

Weber had inadvertently apprised me of an issue that could dominate the hearing. We had walked out of the judge's chambers together on July 29th and were in the well of the courtroom, chatting, when he told me he was sure he could beat the case. I asked how, and he said his witnesses would include a lawyer who had been denied access to DeFeo while the latter was being questioned by homicide detectives. He even told me the lawyer's name, Richard Wyssling.

I said nothing, but I was steaming. Why the hell hadn't anyone told me about this? If the defense could prove that an attorney had been kept away from DeFeo, we were beaten before we started. Fundamental criminal law holds that evidence obtained from a suspect after he has been denied counsel has to be suppressed. In this case, that evidence would include DeFeo's confession.

Meanwhile, I didn't want to hold off totally on the disclosure order. Along with supplying the witness list, I was required to give Weber all statements, written and oral, that DeFeo had made to police. Eddie Connors had already turned over material, but it was sketchy. I sat down with Rafferty, Harrison, Gozaloff and other officers who had talked to Ronald DeFeo. I wanted exact sequences, specific wording. The result was twelve additional pages of statements made by the defendant.

And I was looking ahead to evidence we needed for the trial itself. I wanted to send detectives into Brooklyn, where Butch DeFeo worked for his grandfather's auto agency and where the possibly phony robbery had taken place. I wanted to dig more deeply into the Long Island subculture in which he drank and played. I wanted to peer beyond the religious statues scattered around the DeFeo home into the heart of the turbulence that led to mass-murder. Hate, greed, it was all there from the way DeFeo disparaged his brothers' bathroom habits to his concern with the empty metal box hidden beneath the saddle of his father's closet. I wanted DeFeo examined by a psychiatrist—but not before we had developed some picture of sanity. I had seen psychiatrists fooled by defendants. We had to show outside evidence to the psychologists.

My list of things to do became longer. But the first item remained constant. The name followed by the question mark. "Signorelli?"

On August 25th, William Weber came to my office in Riverhead and spent four hours going through the physical evidence, which we kept in a locked vault. When he left, I gave him the new DeFeo statements and a closed envelope containing copies of more than one hundred photographs taken at the crime scene and the morgue. From my fourth-floor window, I spotted Weber as he walked to his Cadillac, carrying the photographs in a briefcase.

I continued to watch as he drove out of the parking lot onto the exit road. His motor kept running as he pulled over and stopped. He seemed to be taking something from his briefcase, and I surmised that he was examining the photographs. I could empathize with his curiosity. The photographs of the victims made the crime as real as anything could make it in retrospect—there was nothing theoretical about the visual impact a hurtling bullet makes on a human face. They were pictures of torn flesh and bloody wounds and death close up. They repelled and fascinated at the same time. When I first stared at them, I thought how important it was to prosecute Ronnie DeFeo. Watching Weber, I wondered if he felt how important it was to defend him.

During his visit, Weber had mentioned Wyssling again, and asked if I had read a detective magazine article on the DeFeo case. The author was George Carpozzi, a reporter for the *New York Post*. I tried to show mild surprise, but a strong wince would have been more natural. Months before, Eddie Connors had shown me the article and pointed out several factual errors, a few of which worried him. For instance, the most flagrant mistakes were that the victims were found with their hands clasped behind their heads, and that DeFeo had been a prime suspect from the minute homicide detectives arrived at the scene.

If the defense had the article, the prosecution had a problem. Eddie would hate to do it, but he might have to put a police officer on the stand and discredit him in order to expose the mistakes.

Weber not only knew about the article; he sounded as if he was going to use it. As soon as he drove off, I phoned Lieutenant Tom Richmond of homicide, who was mentioned in the magazine piece and had a good relationship with Carpozzi. I told him to set up a meeting with the reporter as soon as possible.

Our sit-down was held in Richmond's office at 9:45 the next morning. No problem; we could deal with the article if the defense introduced it. As I suspected, Carpozzi had made conclusions based on inaccurate information. It was clear that he didn't want to reveal specific sources, but he was willing to concede the mistakes.

When we finished, Carpozzi asked why I was so concerned about the story, and I indicated that it might come up in the trial. I said DeFeo was being represented by William Weber, whom I knew as a good, thorough attorney.

"You think there's a conflict of interest in this case so far as the defense is concerned?" Carpozzi asked.

There are times when impassivity can be a virtue. This was one of them. "Well, why?" I asked back. "There could be, but I'm wondering what you've got in your mind."

Carpozzi asked me to repeat the lawyer's name.

"William Weber," I said. I spelled the last name. "W-E-B-E-R."

"And the trial judge?"

"Signorelli."

"What's Signorelli's present political ambition?"

"Well, he's running for surrogate," I said. "First week in

September, there's a Conservative primary that he hopes to be successful in."

By now, Carpozzi reminded me of a prosecutor working a friendly witness. "What is the attorney's position in relation to his campaign?"

"I believe he's pretty active in his campaign."

Carpozzi came to the point. His wife had two cousins in the same county in New Jersey. One was a judge and the other was an assistant district attorney. There was an absolute agreement between them that none of the prosecutor's cases could ever go before the judge.

This was different, I said. Judge Signorelli had put everything on the record. If there was an objection, we would be implying that the judge was going to be less than impartial.

"So you mean you really couldn't do it," Carpozzi said.

"The point is that I wouldn't do it. I have no basis."

"Oh, I think it reaches to a higher source than that," said Carpozzi. "I think it's the judge himself who should extricate himself from the case. I don't say there's anything wrong, but I say it isn't right."

"Well, he was certainly right in what he did in making both sides aware of it."

"Certainly the other side isn't going to object to it," Carpozzi said. "And the D.A.'s office, I don't think would do it, either. So I mean it's somebody else's job."

"Well, I'll tell you, George," I said, "he's probably the most competent judge on the county bench. He's the most experienced judge, and for that reason alone, if for no other, I would probably look for him to preside over a case like this."

Carpozzi asked when the case was scheduled. "So that I don't put you on the spot or anything," he told me, "just before September 15th, I'll get in touch with you. Things may change between now and then. But what I'll do is run an advance in the *Post* on the fact that the hearing's coming up. Now the relationship between the lawyer and the judge, is it an embarrassing thing if the paper wrote a story about this? You think I'd be barking up the wrong tree, so to speak?"

I picked my words with care. "Well, you know, I'm a big advocate of minimizing pretrial publicity," I said, "and I'd be somewhat dismayed to see a prominent article read by potential jurors in this county on any aspect of the case. I don't know how to answer your question, but it would be an embarrassment. I will tell you that there is no overt conflict of interest in Judge Signorelli presiding."

"That's what I want you to tell me," Carpozzi said.

It seemed to me that Christmas had come in August. There really was a Santa Claus, and his name was George Carpozzi. I was positive that George had provided the basis for Ernest L. Signorelli's departure from the DeFeo murder case. The next day I took what now seemed a very small risk—I sent Weber the witness list. No other judge assigned to the case was likely to prevent me from developing additional witnesses in an ongoing investigation.

During the following weeks, I concentrated on the reopened investigation. Signorelli returned from vacation, and on September 15th, Weber and I conferred with him in his chambers. All I had to do was mention my conversation with Carpozzi and say there was a strong likelihood that he would write an article about a possible conflict of interests. His Honor never hesitated. He would remove himself from the case.

In court, a few minutes later, Judge Signorelli made it official. Addressing himself to counsel, he said: "Upon reflection, although I appreciate your expression of confidence in me, both of you, I deem it advisable to disqualify myself from the case. And I am going to ask the administrative judge to reassign the case. . . ."

"Signorelli?" The name followed by the question mark was crossed off my list. But I hadn't finished maneuvering. I was about to engage in a time-honored strategy that defense lawyers and prosecutors have honed into an art form. Some called it "judge shopping." By any name, it is something most lawyers practice but don't preach. When judges do it, they call it "case shopping." In this case, it was good advocacy. Bill Weber was an aggressive lawyer, able to exert the force of his personality in a courtroom. Weber could do that well; he was a bulldog. I could do the same thing. But if it came down to a shouting match between the two of us, we'd have bedlam in the court. We needed a judge who absolutely could not be pushed around. The only judge in Suffolk County who possessed that kind of total control was Thomas M. Stark, a hawk-nosed, hazel-eyed, Harvard Law graduate who had been a Suffolk Supreme Court judge since 1969, and a county court judge for six years before that. Stark, who already had presided over twenty-seven homicide trials, came to court armed with a resonant baritone voice, an encyclopedic knowledge of the law and the rare ability to immobilize an obstreperous attorney with a single stare over the silver-framed half-glasses he wore halfway down his nose.

The hitch was that Judge Stark sat in Suffolk's Supreme Court. Almost all criminal indictments were tried in county court. A criminal case could not be heard in Supreme Court unless it was specifically assigned by Arthur Cromarty, then the administrative judge for all the courts. I met with John Buonora, and we decided on the argument to use in approaching Cromarty. In 1975, the county court bench had switched to a new system of giving each judge his own calendar. Judge Signorelli not only had had the DeFeo case on his calendar, but he had more than fifty other criminal indictments. The DeFeo trial could extend over a couple of months, and any county court judge who heard it would have to let his other cases languish. Assigning the trial to a Supreme Court judge would be more efficient.

Buonora and I decided to enlist the new district attorney, Henry O'Brien, in our crusade. My feeling was that since I barely knew Cromarty, I needed all the horsepower I could get. O'Brien was ready; the reform district attorney had his own reasons for wanting our office to win the DeFeo case. His independent posture had upset the Suffolk establishment, and he was embroiled in a public feud with the county police commissioner. O'Brien could stand some good publicity. He had tried cases in front of Judge Stark as a private attorney, and agreed that Stark would be an ideal choice for the DeFeo trial.

The day after Signorelli disqualified himself, O'Brien, Buonora and I went to Judge Cromarty's chambers in Amityville. We made our pitch about the fragility of the new assignment system in county court. Cromarty agreed. "How about the Supreme Court?" he asked.

"Fine," I said. So far, so good, I thought.

It got better when Judge Cromarty made his next suggestion. "How about Judge Stark?" he said.

Two days later, we appeared before Frank Gates, the assigning judge for county court. Judge Gates said he had contacted Judge Cromarty and recommended that the case be transferred to the criminal term of Supreme Court. "I understand Judge Stark is sitting in that term," said Gates. "I called him yesterday and he wants it for Monday, September 22nd, at 9:30 A.M."

The cast for the DeFeo trial was complete. I could have used an extended delay for the investigation, but I didn't want to take a chance on losing Stark as the judge. If Cromarty knew there was going to be a long break in the case, he was likely to return Judge Stark to civil trials. In time, he might have considered another judge for the DeFeo trial.

Like most attorneys worth their briefcases—and that goes for defense lawyers as well as prosecutors—I have always been a big believer in pretrial preparation. I can't stress this enough. Cases are won or lost on preparation. I had been pressing the DeFeo investigation; I would press harder.

10

AUGUST 27TH was a Friday, and I was actually home for dinner. I had talked to George Carpozzi the day before and felt confident that my problem with Judge Signorelli was under control. For the first time in weeks, I was beginning to relax. I could tell the girls were delighted. It was the start of a weekend; as I remember, Betty and I were planning to take them on an excursion. Then the phone rang, and I never finished dinner.

The caller was Tom Spota, a longtime friend and fellow assistant district attorney. That year, Tom had been switched from the trial bureau to the anticorruption bureau, a new boat-rocking outfit whose formation had been one of Henry O'Brien's campaign planks. The bureau was investigating several members of the sheriff's office, which administered the county jail, and Tom had been interviewing corrections officers.

He said that a jailer named James DeVito had just laid a bombshell on him. At the prison, DeVito had become friendly with Ronnie DeFeo. He had been reluctant to come forward because a duty lieutenant had put out an order saying that corrections officers shouldn't consider themselves investigators and go running to the district attorney with things they heard from prisoners. But DeFeo had told him a great deal. Not only had DeFeo discussed the murders with him; he had named other people as accomplices.

Spota was calling from Riverhead, where he had been questioning DeVito in the chief assistant's office. "Will you come out?" he asked.

It was a needless question. "I have to go," I told Betty. "There's a guy in Riverhead who might be able to give us the kind of thing we've been trying to get for two months."

Betty looked at the kids. I could see they were unhappy, but all I could do about it was feel guilty. I was on my way out the door as I finished giving excuses. We had an aging, orange VW station wagon that we'd named Clementine, and I made believe she was a Porsche. I broke the speed limit most of the way to the office.

Spota was waiting with DeVito and two detectives from the anticorruption bureau. Ordinarily, I would have been uncomfortable with the idea of detectives from another bureau listening to details of the DeFeo case. But these two guys not only were friends, they were probably the best men on the anticorruption staff. Besides, DeVito was their witness. What was upsetting was that only one homicide detective was available to help with the questioning. The officer, Eddie Halvorsen, was a pro at his job, but since he hadn't worked on the DeFeo case, he knew very little about it. The lack of manpower was something I would have to deal with pretty damn quickly, I thought. In the meantime, I took over the interrogation.

110

I felt sorry for the man in front of me. James DeVito was a portly man, a little under five-eight, with a stutter and an unsure manner. He was almost too willing to please—I didn't think he was lying, but I got the impression that Jimmy DeVito felt he had to please almost everyone he talked to.

For the past three and a half years, said DeVito, he had been assigned to sickbay, which consisted of four cells in a separate room on the first floor of the prison. The place was known as the suicide squad; most of the inmates were put there for their own protection. Ronald DeFeo, Jr., had been sent there after his arrest the past November.

The insanity issue was an immediate concern. "Was he thought to be suicidal or mentally unstable?" I asked.

"No," DeVito answered, "they thought someone had a contract out on him." He said DeFeo himself seemed convinced that he was targeted for assassination. DeFeo's meals were brought in separately by kitchen personnel, and he was under constant supervision. Near the end of December, he and DeVito started talking. Their relations were "strictly friendly" until DeFeo was transferred to a regular jail tier. That happened two months ago, and DeVito hadn't spoken to him since.

Their first conversation about the crime occurred in the exercise yard. "We're sitting there," DeVito recalled. "I said, 'Ronnie, come on, your case, did you do it? You know, it makes no difference to me.'"

"'Mr. DeVito, you ought to know I did it,'" the jailer quoted DeFeo as answering. "'But I didn't do the actual shooting.'"

DeVito said DeFeo never admitted that he pulled the trigger. Although he changed details in different conversations, his basic story was that he was in the house with Bobby Kelske, Sherry Klein and another man and woman, searching for seventy-five thousand dollars that his father had hidden in the premises. One of his parents, apparently his father, came out of the master bedroom and caught them. One of DeFeo's companions—DeVito did not recall him saying which one—shot the parent with Ronnie's rifle.

DeVito's impression was that this first killing might have taken place on a stairs. DeFeo said something about a stairs, and mentioned that a picture of one of his grandfathers on the stairway wall was spattered with blood. Remembering this, DeVito chuckled. "He said he could have sworn that the grandfather was watching—was looking at him."

The searchers put the body back in the bedroom, and murdered the other parent. After that, they herded DeFeo's brothers and sisters together and took them out one at a time to be shot in their beds.

"I asked him, 'Didn't you feel bad?'" DeVito recalled. "He said he felt very bad for his brothers. I said, 'But how could you let these kids see what was happening?' He said they were going to die anyway."

DeVito remembered Ronnie telling him about Allison's death. "I don't know whether they blew her head off when she was laying on the side of the bed or they hit her with the shot and the head rolled off on the side of the bed, and they had a white rug there and he said that the rug got full of blood."

"Did he say it was her head or pieces of her head?" I asked.

"Pieces of her head," DeVito said. "He said he would never forget the smell. A horrible smell."

DeFeo did not express his feelings toward Allison, but he was vehement about his older sister, Dawn. As DeVito put it, "The older one, he really couldn't stand."

"What'd he tell you about the older one?"

"He was always fighting with her. He was very jealous of her. . . . She was a pothead. She was a slob. He said she was a fat slob. He got into a fight with her boyfriend downstairs in the playroom there; they had a big playroom or something."

DeVito said the fight was over Dawn's music, which she played very loud. "He said she used to drive him crazy."

I was very interested in what DeFeo had told DeVito about searching the house for cash. "Did he say they ever found any money?"

"No. He says he knows where it is, but they never found it."

"Did he tell you where?"

"No."

"Did he say it was someplace in the house, though?"

"He said people think his father had it buried under one of those floorboards or something. He said it's not in the house. What the heck else did he tell me about that? About the piano. He said he had an old antique piano there; it's worth a lot of money. He says, 'If you go over the house, and if you could get it out, you could have it. You could have the piano. But it's going to smell in there.'"

"That's how it started about the money," DeVito went on. "We were kidding around. 'Hey, where's the money? We get the money and I'll get you out.' And he says, 'No, no, no. I know where the money is. It's not in the house. People think it's in the house, but it's not in the house.' And he wouldn't tell me."

DeVito recalled DeFeo saying that the second man kept searching for the money when he, Kelske and the women left the house. The accused killer told DeVito about throwing the rifle in the bay and disposing of the bullet casings in Brooklyn. "That's what he said," DeVito remembered. "In a pillow—not far from where his grandfather's Buick place was."

According to the jailer, he and DeFeo talked about guns. DeFeo claimed that he dealt in guns and silencers, which he bought in Harlem and sold on the Island. They argued about whether a silencer could be fitted to a rifle. DeFeo said it could, but did not explain how. Nor did he say whether a silencer was used the night of the killings.

DeVito said that DeFeo mentioned underworld contacts. They included a "known hit man," with whom DeFeo claimed a close acquaintanceship.

"Lee?" I asked.

"That name sounds familiar. I don't . . ."

"I've got another one for you. Falini."

"That's him," DeVito said. "That's right. He said you never would think he was a hit man; he was very well-dressed and a few things. . . . That's the name."

"Did he ever tell you that he tried to pin the killings on Falini?"

"No. No, but he told me that he was a hit man . . ."

A minute or so later DeVito had a thought that made him laugh:

"He said one of his grandfathers sent him a letter."

"In jail?"

"Yeah, said he bought him a cemetery plot."

"You remember which grandfather it was?"

"No, but I thought it was funny."

There was no need to hold back a laugh; I did not share Jimmy DeVito's sense of humor. "Yeah. When did he tell you he got the letter?"

"Couple of weeks ago. Before he went upstairs."

"Was he scared of the grandfather?"

"Yeah. He was."

"Was he convinced they were going to try and hit him?"

"Oh, yeah. . . ."

I questioned DeVito for a couple of hours, and then asked Halvorsen to follow up my interrogation. In talking to the homicide detective, DeVito added several details to what he had told me. He quoted DeFeo as saying that he couldn't stand his family, that his mother had a boyfriend and his father was no good. He said DeFeo talked about the family's sheepdog—the dog was always attacking Butch and he used to lie awake nights, thinking of ways to kill the animal and make it look like an accident. The night of the murders, the dog barked at DeFeo.

DeVito recalled DeFeo boasting about how he fired a gun out

the window of his room. DeFeo said that he used a silencer, and nobody knew where the shots were coming from.

"Do you think the guy's an outright bullshitter?" Halvorsen asked, midway through the questioning.

"I really don't know," DeVito said. In the next breath, he told about DeFeo describing Allison's shooting. "He showed no remorse at all."

The jailer said DeFeo told him that he had committed a murder prior to the mass-slayings. DeFeo claimed that he had drowned a man with whom he got into an argument in a bar. "You know what bothers me the most?" DeVito said. "That he's telling the truth about this guy that he killed. Here's a poor guy, people might think he drowned, and he was killed."

The most important information DeVito gave Halvorsen was that DeFeo deliberately played crazy. The corrections officer recalled DeFeo saying that he would never go to prison. If he couldn't win acquittal, he would feign insanity.

"What did he tell you he was going to do?" Halvorsen asked.

"You know, do the crazy act. He was going to forget things, he was going to sit in the corner, he was going to sit up on top of his shelf like he did, a little shelf they have in the cell, and stare down at you. A couple of times, I had to call in and say DeFeo's up on the bars."

"Did anybody in the jail think that he was sincere? Did they all know it was an act?"

"They knew. Everybody knew."

"Did he tell you why he was putting on the act?"

"Oh, yeah. He said, 'I can beat this case, but I want a psychiatrist.' He got out of the Army on a psychiatric discharge or something.'. . . He said, 'I been going to psychiatrists all my life.' He said, 'I can really beat this.'"

DeVito would be questioned again. He had given us plenty to look into. Although the accomplice theory would turn out to be bull, we would investigate it thoroughly. Much of DeVito's story supported basic elements of the case—the barking dog, the description of Allison's murder, the disposal of evidence. I was intrigued by the idea of hidden cash in the house; it fit into the theory I was forming about motive. And DeVito's account of DeFeo's insanity act could be blockbuster testimony at the trial. Jimmy DeVito's manner flawed him as a witness, but what he had to say could be substantial.

In addition to information, DeVito provided us with contacts. He supplied the name of a fellow corrections officer to whom DeFeo had talked, and told us about a prisoner named John Kramer, who had occupied a cell adjoining DeFeo's in sickbay. Kramer would become a key prosecution witness.

The questioning of DeVito lasted well past midnight. Instead of dinner, I had coffee and sandwiches. They tasted fine, but I suspect I would have been happy eating gruel. Sitting in the chief assistant's office, questioning a man I had never seen before, I was working in the present to set up the future. I could see the case in front of me, almost as if it were an entity that had been crouching in shadows and now was coming into daylight.

There were two immediate results concerning personnel—I got an assistant and a staff. Once Tom Spota gave me DeVito, he had a vested interest in the case. I couldn't blame him for staking his claim; I would have felt the same way. There is a striving that goes beyond ambition, a burning to do what you're good at. If anybody understood that, I did; it was part of what had driven me to the DeFeo case months before. Tom asked if he could work with me on the prosecution, and I said I'd love to have him. He was an excellent book lawyer as well as a first-rate courtroom tactician. The DeFeo case could use two lawyers. I asked Henry O'Brien to reassign Tom. The anticorruption bureau didn't want to lose him, but O'Brien went along with me.

The other development stemmed from my disgust over not having detectives available when I needed them. My stumbling block was Captain Daniel Mueller, the commanding officer of homicide. Mueller did not like giving detectives to the district attorney's office, and he was super-concerned about overtime. Under the circumstances, I felt he was dead wrong. Nor did I have any sympathy for arguments that the case was nine months old and the work had been done, or that the men would have to be yanked off other assignments. Tough. This was one of the most important prosecutions in the history of Suffolk County. We were dealing with a mass-murderer. It was ridiculous for me to have to go begging for personnel, to have the police department nickel-and-diming me to death.

The issue was resolved that Monday at an 8 A.M. sit-down in the office of Sam Fierro, the chief assistant district attorney. Sam attended, along with Tom Spoda and John Buonora. The police department was represented by Chief of Detectives David Buckley, and his deputy chief, Bub D'Armitt. In effect, I was going over Mueller's head, but that wasn't one of my concerns. I wasn't dealing in personalities. I was arguing that the DeFeo case was too important and required too much work to be handled on a routine basis. Within minutes, I was making a full presentation—explaining the need for additional investigation and outlining my theories on what we had to look for.

Mueller hadn't bought my ideas. His contention had been that we had a confession, and that was all we needed. This was a traditional police position, which had about as much relevance to modern jurisprudence as spats have to Bermuda shorts. Bill Weber had already filed written notice that he would rely on proof to support a defense of mental disease or defect. At the time of DeFeo's arrest, insanity was not an issue. Now it was. Therefore, the confession was no longer enough. Sure, it was vital to the case. Although it was oral, I considered it as good as a written confession because it had been corroborated by the recovery of evidence from the Brooklyn sewer. But the confession did not supply a motive. And we needed one. We needed a substantial motive to prove that Butch DeFeo was legally sane when he slaughtered his family. Establishing that motive was the single most important reason for reopening the investigation.

Buckley was receptive. The chief of detectives, for whom I had great respect, seemed sensitive to the case's importance. Besides, if we lost it because of inadequate investigation caused by police stinginess, the department would pay the tab in public censure. When the meeting ended, I had been assured of complete cooperation from the Suffolk County Police. I had gotten the two men I most wanted on a full-time basis. George Harrison had handled the original squeal; Dennis Rafferty had obtained DeFeo's confession. I had worked with both Harrison and Rafferty before, and respected their abilities. (Nor did it hurt that Rafferty was a personal friend. Dennis and I shared an abhorrence for losing; we understood each other.) I was also given another first-rate detective, Alan Rosenthal, full time. And if that wasn't enough, I could ask for additional officers whenever I needed them.

I don't know how Captain Mueller took the news. I did learn that he was summoned to Chief Buckley's office later that morning. When he returned to homicide, he was livid.

What mattered was that we had the manpower to do a job. We organized immediately. As I saw the investigation, there were three major areas:

• Rafferty would develop DeVito and any contacts the jailer could provide. For instance, he would talk to John Kramer, the inmate who lived next to DeFeo. And I wanted to examine prison logs, to know who visited DeFeo, and to check his correspondence. We would get our subpoenas out immediately.

• Rafferty and Rosenthal would go into Brooklyn. They would talk to people who worked with DeFeo, and who could elaborate on his relationship with his father. They would find out whatever they could about the operations of Brigante-Karl Buick. They would talk to police about the payroll holdup in which DeFeo was a victim. Perhaps his father's suspicion was correct—Butch had staged the holdup himself. Their argument over the robbery could have been a catalyst for the killings. Rosenthal would be extra-helpful; his brother was a New York City homicide detective who could give us contacts.

• Harrison would work on Long Island. He would talk to anyone who had been involved with DeFeo over the past several years. People in his neighborhood, drinking buddies, girlfriends. Outside of 112 Ocean Avenue, DeFeo was not a family person. I suspected that the people with whom he shot guns and dope knew more about him than his surviving relatives. It would be necessary to have him examined by a psychiatrist, but that would be only part of the profile. I wanted to scrutinize school data, job records, arrest records, even his birth certificate. I wanted to be able to dissect Ronald DeFeo, Jr., in front of a jury.

My hope was for the three separate areas of investigation to produce pieces of information that would interlock like the jigsaw puzzles in Allison DeFeo's room. For that reason, I was interested in anything that touched on the metal box hidden beneath the saddle of the closet in the master bedroom. Back in June when I stayed late in the office and took the DeFeo folder from Eddie Connors's files, I was struck by mentions of the box. I stared at photographs of the dark-gray case both in and out of its roughly chiseled hiding place. The latter photos showed the key Scotch-taped to the top of the case; the former showed how the foot-long box fit sideways into its niche. Reading the detectives' notes on their conversations with DeFeo, I felt that the box had something to do with the crime. Before confessing, DeFeo had used it to point suspicion at Louis Falini. If the box was empty, he said, Louis had to be the killer. Well, the box was empty, but DeFeo was the killer. Detectives had found Falini several days after the crime, and he had produced motel receipts showing that he was in Massachusetts when the murders occurred—he underwent an annual medical check at the Leahy Clinic.

My suspicions grew when I questioned the detectives who

had worked on the case and learned that there were no fingerprints on the box. The hiding place was too narrow for anyone to have removed the box without touching its sides. And someone had taped on the key. The police had been careful to extricate the box with paper clips; they could not have smudged any prints. It was obvious that somebody had wiped the box clean of fingerprints. Why? The logical answer was that whoever emptied the box wanted to remove evidence that he had been at it. Certainly, Ronald DeFeo, Sr., the owner of the box, would have had no reason to do that.

This was where some of what DeFeo had told Jimmy DeVito began to fit. Actually, money had been found in the house. The day after DeFeo's arrest, Detective Joseph Napolitano had returned to 112 Ocean Avenue with a representative of the public administrator's office, which was responsible for the property. Michael Brigante, DeFeo's maternal grandfather, was present. Brigante kept glancing up the stairs toward the master bedroom and asking questions about jewelry. Napolitano decided that a hiding place might have been overlooked and conducted a grid search of the bedroom. He spotted a corner of carpet that seemed slightly raised. When he pulled the carpet back, he found a yellow-green envelope containing about six hundred and fifty dollars. Either someone had searched the house and missed the envelope, or there had not been a search as much as a direct raid on one place in which thousands of dollars were known to be hidden. Suppose that part of DeFeo's story was correct—a large sum of cash had been secreted in the house. Why couldn't that money have been hidden in the metal box for which a hole had been chiseled out of the floor? Why couldn't Butch DeFeo have been the one who removed the contents of that box and wiped it clean? Why couldn't he have killed over those contents? He could have committed murder to keep the theft from being discovered. Or, more likely, the truth lies in the story he told DeVito. He had been caught in the act of taking the money. Or his father had discovered the theft and confronted him.

I wanted answers. For that matter, I was open to new questions. Clearly, there was a great deal to do, and only weeks in which to do it. Along with the investigation, I was preparing for the pretrial hearing. Our pace was tremendous. And so, I admit, was the police overtime. If I ever get reincarnated, I want to come back as a Suffolk County cop. I figure that the detectives on the case made anywhere from three to five thousand dollars in overtime. When the trial was over, Dennis Rafferty bought a new MG, which he called his "MGD", the "D" standing for DeFeo. I didn't begrudge any of it—those guys worked their butts off, and the results can't be measured in overtime pay. The pretrial hearing was held the last week in September, and Rafferty and Harrison, both of whom were witnesses, had to spend their days in court and their nights working on the investigation. Besides, I would be remiss if I didn't confess that I made money, too. I was getting the enormous sum of five dollars and fifty cents in lieu of meals for every night I worked past 8 P.M. From start to finish, I made about one hundred and eighty dollars extra on the DeFeo case.

When we went to trial, I would have interviewed almost all our witnesses. The district attorney has two offices—one in Riverhead, and another near the county police complex in Hauppauge. The latter office is closer to the Amityville area, and most of my interviews were conducted there at night. On other occasions, they were held in the field. Four days after the sit-down with police brass, I talked to DeFeo's uncle, Vincent Procita, at his pharmacy on the North Shore. Soon after that, I interviewed him and his wife, Phyllis, at Hauppauge. I was impressed by Phyllis Procita. A strong, warm-hearted woman in her forties who visited her nephew once a month in jail, she seemed to be carrying the brunt of the tragedy for her family.

The Procitas confirmed much of what we already knew about the case, and supplied information that was helpful in my preparation for the pretrial hearing. They said they had talked to DeFeo after his arrest, and that he never complained about being mistreated or deprived of his rights. Mrs. Procita recalled an incident in late May when DeFeo came into the visiting booth, shouting that Jacob Siegfried, then his attorney, was not doing enough for him. He told her that Siegfried had better come in with guards the next time he visited the jail.

Mrs. Procita tried to calm her nephew down. She told him that Siegfried had been on vacation and had informed Butch that he would be away.

DeFeo turned on his aunt. "Butch said that all you people are interested in is the money from the estate and that we have probably hired Siegfried to take a dive and then we could have the money," Mrs. Procita would say in a signed statement. "He also asked what right we had to sell his car. I said it wasn't his car since it was under his father's name. Butch then demanded the twelve hundred dollars that we got for the car." This occurred around the time that Siegfried said DeFeo had tried to attack him and resigned from the case—sticking to his decision after Butch apologized in court.

Whenever possible, I tried to get a firsthand feeling for the case by visiting scenes. I made two visits with George Harrison to Henry's Bar, the neighborhood ginmill where DeFeo had stood at the front door and yelled for help. The first time, we tried to pass as ordinary citizens, leaving our ties in the car and sitting at the bar and having a couple of beers and listening to its patrons, young men in workclothes, killing the afternoon with small talk. They made us right away. The second time, we identified ourselves and asked about some of DeFeo's friends. On both occasions, we learned next to nothing. But I picked up the flavor of the place; I could visualize Butch DeFeo buying rounds, playing the big shot in his chosen world.

On several occasions, I visited the house with the jack-o'-lantern windows on Ocean Avenue, where death struck in multiples. Two visits stand out. One was with police, including a department serologist, to check something DeFeo had told Jimmy DeVito—that his father had been shot outside the master bedroom, near the stairs. We were searching for blood traces on the wall or the hallway rug. Phyllis Procita came with us to open the house. She knew we were looking for her brother's blood, and she was understandably emotional. We noticed some reddish spots on a wall, and the serologist applied a chemical. Whatever the spots were, they were not blood. The serologist, who happened to be Italian, didn't stop to think. "You know these goombahs," he said. "It's probably tomato sauce. They were probably throwing spaghetti or lasagna at one another and some of it bounced off the wall."

The serologist laughed, and one of the cops echoed him. I wasn't thinking either. I smiled until I realized that Phyllis Procita had overheard the remark. Tears and horror mixed in her eyes. I felt about a half-inch tall. The wisecrack was inexcusable, and I apologized afterward for it.

The incident was incongruous for other reasons. The house was vacant, but most of the furnishings had not been disturbed. The beds were an exception; the bedding had been removed and the frames dominated the rooms with their bareness. The blood-drenched rug had been taken from Allison's room, but an irregular white spot showed where bleach had been used to remove the traces that soaked through onto the floor. And it had been difficult to explain, but as I walked through the house, I had known a sense of reverence similar to what I feel in church on Good Friday. The aura of death was oppressive, but it was also solemn.

The other visit that remains sharp in my memory was one I made with my daughters. It was a weekend, and I was having a conscience attack about not spending time with them. Only I couldn't let the case go. "How about going to Amityville?" I said, making it sound like an excursion. We would drive to a nice place by the water and we would go to McDonald's for lunch. Big fun.

When we stopped at the vacant house on Ocean Avenue, the girls weren't quite sure what we were doing. Neither was an Amityville Village police officer who pulled up.

"What the hell do you think you're doing?" the cop asked.

"When are we going to McDonald's?" one of the kids asked.

I shushed the girls and identified myself to the cop. He didn't believe me until I mentioned Amityville Patrolman Kenneth Greguski, who had been the first officer to respond to the murder scene and was one of my witnesses. Even then, I couldn't accomplish much. We didn't have a key and we couldn't go inside the house. I strolled around the property, looking at the boathouse and the pool and the patio and the wide canal. I examined the garbage shed where the sheepdog had been tied, and stared at the windows of DeFeo's room.

I looked at 112 Ocean Avenue from the street and thought about the people who had lived inside in a welter of television sets and religious symbols. It was just an empty house. Anything else depended on your imagination.

I thought about the portrait of Allison and Dawn DeFeo that had hung above the stairs. It was a nice day, and I took my daughters to McDonald's.

11

THE ONLY IMPAIRMENT for which John Arthur Kramer ever offered an explanation was the three fingers missing on one of his hands. Kramer never told us what had caused him to become cross-eyed or why so many of his teeth were missing. He said he lost the fingers while working on a garbage truck. He was in a situation where it looked like he was going to get crushed between the truck's hopper and an oncoming car. So he jumped in the hopper.

At twenty-eight, John Kramer was Runyonesque material from his "deeze-and-doze" style of elocution to his cluttered police record. He had been in and out of jail since 1967, and his first offense established the tone—he got six months for setting fire to an outhouse. In 1970, while facing charges for the attempted heist of one 7–11 store, he acted in the best "if-at-first-you-don't-succeed" tradition by trying to rob another 7–11 store. In 1974, he was convicted of car theft. Kramer described the victim as a friend, but said this came as a surprise. "At the time," he explained, "I did not know it was his car."

He was doing three-and-a-half to seven years upstate for stealing the car when he was transferred back to the Suffolk County prison to await the disposition of a more serious charge. He had been accused of rape and burglary by a thirty-five-year-old woman he met in a bar. Kramer's story was that the woman paid him to go home with her, and made the rape accusation when her husband discovered them. But Kramer compounded his problems by taking off with her purse, which contained twenty dollars. When the case was finally disposed of, the only charge to which he pleaded guilty was third-degree burglary.

Not long after his return to the Suffolk jail, Kramer was beaten by six other inmates. His story was that he had been unjustly accused of ratting to the guards about a sneaker full of marijuana someone had smuggled into the slammer. What was important to the DeFeo case was that when he got out of the hospital near the end of March, John Kramer was put in sickbay for his own protection. The man in the next cell was Ronald DeFeo, Jr.

Although a steel wall divided their cells, Kramer and DeFeo could talk through the bars and even play cards—dealing them onto a chair placed in front of their quarters. On one occasion, they switched meals. According to Kramer, this was an act of altruism on his part. He was interested in showing DeFeo that his food was safe to eat.

The jail investigation produced quick results. Rafferty obtained usable information from guards and other inmates, but John Kramer was easily his most valuable contact. By the end of their first conversation, the gap-toothed convict was telling his police buddy, "Den," most of what Ronnie DeFeo had confided to him. Although Tom Spota and I took part in later sessions, there was no question that Rafferty deserved the credit for developing Kramer as a witness.

The story DeFeo told Kramer differed from the one he told

DeVito in two important respects. There were no accomplices; he committed the murders by himself. And there was no search; he knew where to find the hidden money. Despite his big-spender image, or perhaps because of it, Ronald DeFeo, Jr., always needed money. In the fall of 1974, he told Kramer, he needed it for his girlfriend. She was expensive, and he was planning to take off with her. He wanted a bundle. The night before the murders, he got one. He told Kramer that he stole two hundred thousand dollars in cash and at least as much in jewelry from a hiding place in his home. After taking the cache, he buried it somewhere. But his father discovered the theft, and the following night, DeFeo had to kill him. After shooting his father, he went "beserk" and slaughtered the rest of the family.

Kramer's recollection of the word "beserk" bothered me, but it was a small minus compared to the plus he gave us regarding motive. DeFeo had never mentioned a metal box to Kramer, but he did refer to the secret place where the money and jewels had been kept. "In the bottom," Kramer recalled. "In the floor, like. In the bottom."

I could understand Kramer's difficulty. Even the police who interrogated DeFeo after the murders had trouble understanding his description of the hiding place. The bottom of the master-bedroom closet, I thought. The floor beneath the saddle. The chiseled-out crypt. The empty box. As far as I was concerned, we had a motive. We could use John Kramer to show that Ronald DeFeo, Jr., killed his family for money.

In addition, Kramer could testify about the purported holdup in Brooklyn. DeFeo told him that he helped stage the robbery and that his father did not merely suspect him. His father believed that Butch had planned the whole job.

"He hated his father," Kramer told us. "He always had fights with him."

As he did with everyone who talked to him for any length of time, DeFeo went on with Kramer about how he hated the rest of his family. When he got to his mother, he said that not only was she unfaithful, but he made money on her indiscretion. He had been taking cash from her to keep quiet.

It was a sordid picture—a man shaking down his mother for cheating on his father. I could easily believe Butch DeFeo's role as a blackmailer, but I had difficulty believing that his mother was the way he painted her. Louise DeFeo's alleged infidelity was out of keeping with all else that I had learned about her. Yet, if it were true, it was as much the real Long Island as split-levels and lawn fertilizer. The DeFeos lived in the suburbia that doesn't make the humor columns. John Kramer described Butch DeFeo, suburbia's child, as a heavy gambler who plunged on cards, dice and horses. He was a pot-smoker who used methedrine, acid, cocaine and heroin. He was a would-be big shot who bought new acquaintances drinks in bars. He was a gun buff who took a shot at a friend on a hunting trip, and wondered what was wrong with that.

Ronald DeFeo, Jr., was all that, Kramer said, plus a killer who played crazy to beat the charges against him. Kramer reinforced what DeVito had told us about DeFeo's insanity act. He said Butch told him he would beat the case by pleading insanity and then live happily ever after. There was the loot he had taken from the house and buried, and all the money due from the estate, including one hundred thousand dollars' worth of insurance policies. DeFeo's scenario was that his relatives would pay for him to go to a private institution, and he would be out in a couple of years. Or as Kramer quoted him: "'I'll be free, like a bird.'"

DeFeo outlined his crazy routine for Kramer, and then put it on the boards. Butch hid under his bunk. He sat on the shelf in his cell and stared downward and whistled like a bird. He threw his mail through the bars. He ripped up his mail and flushed it down the toilet. In his most dramatic performance, he started a fire in his cell.

Information we obtained from Kramer and DeVito was

supported by others in the jail. Two corrections officers, Emil Ross and Vincent D'Augusta, filled out the picture of DeFeo's antics. Ross recalled a conversation in which DeFeo asked about an inmate who had been sent to a facility for the criminally insane. DeFeo said he could accomplish the same thing. D'Augusta remembered DeFeo hiding beneath his covers and trying to climb his cell bars, and then asking that his behavior be noted in the sickbay log. On another occasion, said D'Augusta, Butch had asked him questions about suicide. D'Augusta told him this could be accomplished in two ways— he could either "hang up" or "cut up." The crudest way to "cut up" was with a comb.

No, that would hurt, DeFeo said. He wouldn't do it that way.

Some of what we learned from jail sources was substantiated by prison records, which we obtained through subpoena. This was true of the sickbay log, which was studded with references to inmate DeFeo's words and actions and heralded his arrival in the following manner on November 19, 1974: "Receiving inmate DeFaio. He will not be let out of cell or go anywhere unescorted. Escorted by Duty Lt. *only,* as per Control. Inmate will be fed personally by kitchen personnel (cook only)."

A notation on the following day showed that inmate DeFeo (his name was now being spelled correctly) was talking about trying to hire F. Lee Bailey—then handling a case in Nassau County—as his defense counsel. By December 15th, he was not worrying about his future as much as his present. He complained of pains in his stomach and said he thought something had been slipped into his food.

On January 2, DeFeo's problems seemed to be accelerating. At 2 A.M., according to the log, he was the only resident of the section who was still awake. "Inmate DeFeo told me he can't sleep," reported a corrections officer. "All he can think about is that he wiped out his whole family." A few hours later, DeFeo ate breakfast. But at 10:30 A.M., he announced that he would refuse lunch and supper "and that the show is just beginning and the first person to mess with him is going to have trouble." Subsequent weeks showed similar complaints; on one occasion, DeFeo said there was broken glass in his food. A March entry confirmed Kramer's story about switching dinners.

DeFeo's crazy act engendered several notations. At 11:15 A.M., March 31, he was reported threatening to "blow this place up." An hour later, the log read: "DeFeo starting to burn his personal prop. Control notified." On April 2nd, there was a more cryptic entry. "Inm. DeFeo is shaving. Changed his mind and said he might cut his throat." Or on April 15th: "Inmate DeFeo is threatening suicide in a joking sort of way. We are not sure how serious he is about it. Notified Control. (We must assume he is serious!)" If he was, he didn't try it. Three days later, the log showed inmate DeFeo being discharged from sickbay.

The corrections officers assigned to DeFeo sent memos to their superiors that demonstrated the accused killer's concern with violence. "Re: DeFeo Sickbay #3 cell," began a memo written three days after the prisoner's arrival in the section. "Above inmate said if he gets out of jail he will get even w/all his neighbors and friends of his sister for saying things about him.

On November 21, 1974, a memo from a corrections department lieutenant reflected DeFeo's attitude toward police. "DeFeo told inmate Cella that if he goes to jail for something he didn't do he would kill everyone of those motherfuckers." Three weeks later, two corrections officers reported separately to the warden that DeFeo and Vito Coscia (the child-killer I would also prosecute) had been discussing their cases. "Both said they were innocent," wrote one of the officers. "DeFeo said he would not be tried in Suffolk County and would request a change of venue on the basis of the Angela Davis trial. Said if he didn't get the change, he would take someone with him, if not the entire court. . . ." The second officer noted DeFeo's declaration that he was wrongfully accused and added: "Stated that if he didn't get his way in ct. 'today,' he would take the judge or a deputy

MANEUVER AND INVESTIGATION

out. He stated he was fed up w/all this bullshit. He further
stated he would definitely 'hang up' if everything else failed."

And there was DeFeo's mail. Jail regulations required that all
inmates' outgoing mail be examined and read. We obtained
DeFeo's letters by subpoena. My belief was that if I wanted to
see inside DeFeo, his letters might help. Inconsistencies,
emotions, even protestations of innocence. I read the lines and I
tried to read between them, and I could see Butch DeFeo.
Following are two letters DeFeo sent to his maternal grandparents. The first was written December 1, 1974; the second
was written nine days later.

Dear Grandma & Grandpa
  I hope you and grandpa are Okay, and Michael
to. I know you hate me and don't care what
happens to me but, I figured I better write to you,
and let you know a few things. Ive don't a lot
wrong in my times, pleanty to a lot of people but I
never killed nobody. Nobody loved my parents
more than me or the kids. There all gone know
and I have nobody, and it doesen't fell to good. My
father was the best freind, it probably didn't look
that way to you, but my father gave me
everything I wanted, and bailed me out of pleanty
of jams. I was wrong making my worry about me
all the time, but I loved her more than my father.
There's a lot of things that were going on that
none of you's knew about, and the ship was
sinking quick. My Father is the one responesable
for getting them all killed, but my mother some of
the blame to. The only reason I'm alive is because
I wasen't there. But I wish I was there, so I be
dead to. My father hated you and you hated him,

131

and the only one you didn't hate was my Mother.
Ive been reading the newspapers and I know you
don't care about me at all. All you care about is
your share of the money. For once in my life I try
to help the police becuase of what happend, and
they turn around and blame me for it. I want you
to know I didn't do it and I didn't confess to doing
it. I am hard real hard but no one knows what
they put me threw, and they would of had to
killed to make me say what they wanted me to
say. I've all ready been found guilty by the stuff
they write in the papers about me, and by all you
people. By the way I'am not a user of herion. So
for something I didn't do Ill go to jail for the rest
of my life. I figured I just let you know what was
going on. You'll never see or hear from me again.
Take care of your self Micheal, and take care of
Grandma, and Grandpa.

Love, Butch

Dear Grandpa

I'am very fedup with you's people, because you
all think I did it. All of you's are either sick or
money hungry. I don't understand how you think
that I am capable of doing what has been done. I
may have been a theif and alot of other things but
am not a murder. There is no way I will get a fair
trial out here. This lawyer dossn't care one way or
another, to what ever happen's to me. As long as
he gets is money. There is no way I will be found
innocent out here, Because what garbage and
lair's they said. If you use your head you should
know that there was more than one person
involed in this, and am not one of them. So I am
going to notervey the paper's. My Mother your
daughter made things bad for every body in that

house. My father the bigest theif and con man
had you's all fooled. My father is fulley
responsseble for the death's of the family. Its a
shame that the kids had to die for them.

Butch

12

IF THE JAIL INVESTIGATION was direct, the inquiry in Brooklyn was serpentine—extending in time past the pretrial hearing to the trial itself and leading Dennis Rafferty and Alan Rosenthal beyond the suspect robbery and the Brigante-Karl Buick Agency into the shrouded territory of a secret probe being conducted by the Brooklyn rackets bureau.

The starting points were the car agency and the holdup in which Ronald DeFeo, Jr., and a coworker were supposedly robbed on their way to the bank to make a cash drop. About eighteen hundred dollars in cash and twenty thousand dollars in checks were taken in the robbery, which occurred a little less than two weeks before the murders. Butch had told detectives that he and his father argued over his failure to cooperate with police investigating the robbery, and that the elder DeFeo suspected the holdup was phony. He went even further with John Kramer, telling his sickbay neighbor that his father had accused him of planning the whole thing. I wanted to know more about the argument, as well as the robbery. It had taken place too close to the murders not to have influenced them.

The story we pieced together from Brigante-Karl employees was that on the day of the holdup, Butch DeFeo and another employee had driven to the bank at 12:30 P.M. But two hours elapsed before they came back and reported that they had been robbed. Soon after that, Ronald DeFeo, Sr., returned from lunch and learned what had happened.

The elder DeFeo exploded. He took his anger out on a subordinate, pushing the man to the ground and shouting at him for sending Butch on the bank errand. Twenty minutes later, police arrived, and it was Butch's turn to blow up. When a detective who was questioning him commented on the time lapse, the younger DeFeo began screaming curses and banging on one of the nearby cars, denting the hood before he was restrained.

The argument between the two DeFeos took place on Friday of the following week, just four days before the killings. On the subsequent Tuesday, Butch did not show up for work. That day, Ronald DeFeo, Sr., left the agency at 2 P.M. It was the day before the murders. According to Lucy Burkin, a bookkeeper who had been with the firm for many years, Ronald, Sr., said he "was going to go home and have a confrontation with Butch over the robbery."

This locked into another piece of information—one that homicide detectives had uncovered during the original investigation. Two days after the murders had shocked the community, John Donahue, a nine-year-old student at St. Martin's Catholic School, told his teacher that he had witnessed a fight between Butch DeFeo and his father that same Tuesday afternoon. The boy was a friend of Butch's youngest brother, John. His mother had driven him to the latter's home after school. The two youngsters played games in John DeFeo's room for a half-hour, and then they went down to the finished basement, where they played pool and constructed models. They were working on the models when Mr. DeFeo and Butch came downstairs. Mr. DeFeo told the boys to leave, but instead they sat on the steps leading to the first floor and watched what was happening. The two DeFeos started punching each other near the pool table. Mr. DeFeo hit Butch in the face, and blood ran from Butch's mouth. John Donahue repeated the story to police in the presence of school authorities. According to his teacher, something he had learned recently in class had caused him to tell about the fight. He had compared it to the story of "The Prodigal Son."

Along with checking the car agency, Rafferty and Rosenthal introduced themselves at the precinct that conducted the robbery investigation. City cops labor under the misapprehension that they are somehow superior to their suburban counterparts, and the introduction provided by Rosenthal's brother helped. But nothing very startling developed. My own feeling was that the Brooklyn detectives stopped sweating over the holdup once they figured it was a phony. One of the things they did have was a tape on which a former Brigante-Karl employee admitted participating in the robbery. The precinct detectives gave Rafferty and Rosenthal access to the man, who was never arrested. He admitted his voice was on the tape, but denied having anything to do with the stickup. Nor did he tell the Suffolk officers anything that would make him worth calling as a witness.

Our break came from another source—our own office. In a sense, we could thank Henry O'Brien's election as district attorney. One of O'Brien's first moves had been to raid the Brooklyn rackets bureau for talent—namely, Dave Freundlich, an assistant D.A., whose knowledge of the underworld was such that his former colleagues still called him for help. One of his old friends phoned Dave and told him that Brooklyn had tapes bearing on the murders in Amityville. The tapes had been obtained during a secret investigation the rackets bureau was conducting. The investigation was big; his friend couldn't say anything about it. But he wanted Dave to know about the tapes.

Rosenthal and Rafferty quickly cultivated the police detectives assigned to the Brooklyn rackets squad. Meanwhile, I phoned the office of Brooklyn District Attorney Eugene Gold, and spoke to an assistant district attorney, who seemed to be an intermediary between Gold and the rackets bureau. I tried to impress him with the significance of our case, and explained that if lack of cooperation by his office impaired our case, we would have to make that public. I was polite, but I think he got the message.

I told him that we had learned of the tapes and wanted to hear them. We had to go gently. It was Brooklyn's stadium, and we were coming from the end zone. We didn't know what the tapes contained or what the Brooklyn investigation was about. Gold was keeping it as secret as the identity of the Lone Ranger, and he wasn't handing out any silver bullets, either. All we knew was that it was sensitive, which meant that it probably centered on a name politician. And, as the assistant district attorney emphasized, that an indictment was expected around the time our case was slated for trial.

Gold's people were suspicious of us. Like most district attorneys, Eugene Gold had a reputation as a publicity-conscious prosecutor. I couldn't knock him—his kind of gangbusters P.R. inspires respect among hoods. In addition, Gold was considering a run for the United States Senate. But I had to contend with all this. The Brooklyn rackets-busters were not about to let interlopers from Suffolk County blow their case or, almost as bad, steal their headlines.

We had two things going for us in Brooklyn. One was an assistant district attorney named Stu Klein, with whom Al Rosenthal established a rapport. I never met Klein, but I grew to admire him. According to Rosenthal, Stu Klein was a mod dresser whose blond hair flowed past his shoulders; not exactly the prototype of an assistant D.A. But he was the kind of prosecutor who went on raids with the cops who broke the doors down. I got the picture of a bright, energetic law-enforcement official totally outside political considerations. Secondly, there were the New York detectives attached to the rackets squad. They were cops before anything else; they wouldn't glorify a rackets investigation over a mass-murder case. The most helpful was Teddy Phillips, a detective who lived in Suffolk and with whom Rafferty and Rosenthal met several times.

Brooklyn agreed to give us the tapes. Because of a continued need for confidentiality, the source of the tapes and the means of obtaining them will have to remain secret. Gold's office gave us copies with the understanding that they were being supplied as information only, and could not be introduced as evidence at the trial without specific permission. As it turned out, I didn't need them. It was just as well—introducing the tapes would have opened a Pandora's box on the issue of admissibility.

The tapes had been made the past spring and consisted of conversations dominated by the hoarse voice of Mike Brigante, Butch DeFeo's maternal grandfather. Brigante was not a target of the Brooklyn investigation, and nothing on the tapes hinted at who was. But there was plenty that related to our case. The tapes corroborated our suspicions about motive, and they offered a family's-eye view of Ronald DeFeo, Jr. "He's a nut job," Brigante said of his grandson during one conversation. "This guy is crazy." A minute later, he said, "If somebody killed this kid, he's better off. . . ."

The possibility that Butch might be hit in jail came up when Brigante described a conversation between him and a family connection listed by police intelligence as a Mafia capo. On the tape, Brigante reported telling the man: "'You I'll talk to . . . because you understand my language, and I understand your language. They want to kill if he killed, go ahead. . . . But you better find out what's going on. And if they kill that kid in prison . . . you better get it squared away, boy.'"

When I heard the tapes, I was most impressed by a conversation relating to my belief that Butch DeFeo killed over a hidden fortune. In this section of the tape, Brigante was talking about jewelry. "From Dawny, and Allison and my daughter, and anybody else, where's the rest of all that other jewelry?" he could be heard telling an acquaintance. "That's what I want to know. I want to know where the hell it's at. Naw, the detectives didn't take all that stuff, that's bullshit. And Butch told them where the box was, you know."

The box again. Brigante wondered aloud how Butch could have known about the box, and the man to whom he was talking theorized that Ronald, Sr., had put something in the hiding place without knowing that Butch was watching. "And, ah, who knows," the other man told Brigante, "this fucking kid may have walked in, you know, he used to come in at all crazy hours. He may have saw his father with the thing out."

Later in the conversation, the second man worried about the possibility that Butch might be acquitted. "This kid can hang everybody," he said.

"That's right," Brigante answered. "He knows what was in that house."

Another conversation that held my attention did not bear directly on the murders, but said a great deal about Ronald DeFeo, Jr. Brigante was talking about his daughter's life with her oldest child. "That boy had my . . . had my daughter crazy."

"Well, that's why she had all them aches and pains," said the second man.

"Jesus Christ," Brigante answered. "She was living with a torture."

The tapes were followed by a bigger breakthrough. In the course of their nosing about, Rafferty and Rosenthal were tipped off to the existence of a secret witness, who was connected to Gold's hush-hush investigation but happened to be involved with the DeFeo-Brigante family. But the rackets people were playing him as close as their inquiry. Forget his name—they wouldn't even give his occupation.

I called Brooklyn and got an assistant district attorney working on the rackets probe. He said they were holding back on the witness because of the timing—their indictment was too close. He told me that, and held out a carrot. "When you find out who he is," said the rackets A.D.A., "when you talk to him, you'll want to call him as a witness. He was right there with the family; he was tight with them."

I put in another Brooklyn call. This time, I phoned Inspector Herbert Nevins, commanding officer of the police assigned to the rackets bureau. Although he had specialized in rackets work for much of his career, Nevins had a reputation as a cop's cop. From what I'd heard, I figured he would have a visceral feeling for what it meant to put Ronnie DeFeo away. My intention in calling was to discuss the case in general and see if Nevins would be amenable to a meeting. Instead, we talked for a half-hour and he gave me the name of the mystery witness. He made it appear accidental, but I have always thought he knew what he was doing. Nevins was too experienced a cop to make that kind of slip.

What happened was that I was telling him about the trial, which was about to start. The defense had retained a well-known forensic psychiatrist, Dr. Daniel Schwartz, who worked out of Kings County Hospital in Brooklyn. Nevins agreed that Dr. Schwartz would be a formidable witness and I would need a lot of ammunition to offset him. I discussed what I had just heard about the rackets bureau's secret informant. I never said I didn't know his identity but referred to him as "the guy."

"You know the guy," I said.

"Oh, you mean Burt," Nevins said. "You mean Borkan."

"Who?"

"Well, you know who I'm talking about?" Nevins said.

"Sure," I answered. I had a lined white pad on the desk in front of me. Beneath the name and number of the assistant district attorney I had just called, I printed the name "BERT BALKAN" in capital letters and underlined it. My spelling of both the first and last names was wrong, but my phonetics were fine.

I squelched my elation until we finished the conversation. This was in the office in Riverhead, and Rafferty and Rosenthal were with me. "Son of a bitch," I said as soon as I put down the phone, "I don't believe it but I got the name."

Rafferty and Rosenthal said Nevins had to know what he was doing. It was important that we didn't jam him up—we couldn't admit he was our source. We decided that when we contacted the Brooklyn district attorney's office again, we would imply that someone at the Brigante-Karl Agency knew about Borkan and had informed us.

I waited a few days to avoid compromising Nevins, and then I called the assistant district attorney who had told me that when I talked to the mystery informant, I'd want to call him as a witness.

I enjoyed myself. "It's getting close to where we can't put off sitting down and talking to Burt Borkan any longer," I said.

"Who! How did you get the name?" And then, "Did you find out from somebody in our office?"

"Well, I really don't know that I can tell you exactly how I got the name." I was being as coy with him as he had been with me. I implied that the information had come from outside his office. Actually, I said, we'd known about the witness' existence for several weeks, and we'd been breaking our backs to find out his identity.

"I can't blame you for that," said the Brooklyn A.D.A. "We each have our own jobs to do. I'll have to discuss it with somebody higher-up in the office and get back to you about whether or not we'll give you access."

"I don't want to impair your investigation in any way," I told him. "I don't want to compromise your confidentiality. If you make him available so we can meet with him, I'll do it with you guys there. I won't insist on interrogating him alone."

"We'll never let you do that, anyway," he said.

"You really don't trust us at all, do you?"

"It's not that we don't trust you," he answered. "If the tables were turned and you had a confidential investigation as significant as ours, especially to the D.A., you'd do the same thing."

He was right. "No problem," I said. "We'll agree to do it under any conditions that you set. Let's just do it soon."

The A.D.A. called back that day. District Attorney Gold was incensed by our discovery, but since we had the name, we could have the witness.

By now, I had discovered what the secret investigation was about, and I could understand Gold's concern. The probe's targets were Brooklyn's "Mr. Democrat," Stanley Steingut, the speaker of the New York State Assembly, and his son, Robert, a city councilman. In November, the Steinguts would be indicted and charged with violations of the election law—specifically with offering someone a nonpaying job as adviser to the Civilian Complaint Review Board in return for his running a fundraising dinner for Robert Steingut. The appellate division of the State Supreme Court would dismiss the indictments on the grounds that the alleged offer was made in Manhattan, and the Brooklyn district attorney's office lacked jurisdiction. In 1978, Manhattan District Attorney Robert Morgenthau, to whom the case had been transferred, would announce that there would be no prosecution. Morgenthau said an exhaustive investigation showed that the evidence did not support criminal charges.

To this day, I do not know how Burt Borkan, the mystery witness, was connected to the Steingut investigation. Borkan was a New York City patrolman who ran a used-car business on the side. A twenty-two-year police veteran, he was assigned to the department's community affairs division. For several years until 1974, when he was defeated for reelection, he had served as financial secretary for Brooklyn South's Police Benevolent Association. Brigante-Karl Buick serviced cars for P.B.A. members, and Borkan had bought several autos from the agency. He was a close friend of the DeFeo family. He had known Ronald DeFeo, Sr., for more than sixteen years, and he was Allison's godfather. And the Friday before the murders, he had heard Butch DeFeo threaten to kill his father.

In October, Borkan was made available to us. The DeFeo trial was underway, which meant we had to meet in the evening. The Brooklyn people said they would come to Suffolk, and I insisted that we take them all to dinner.

They arrived five strong—Borkan, an assistant district attorney, Teddy Phillips, Inspector Nevins and another police officer. Burt Borkan was in his forties, overweight, wearing a suit and tie. He struck me as a glad-hander, a P.B.A. politician type. It was clear that he was a cop in trouble—the only time we were stopped from asking questions was when we touched on how much trouble. He acknowledged that his finances were in the balance. He was going to retire and he was worried about losing his pension.

We interviewed Borkan at the district attorney's offices in Hauppauge. Cops are intrinsically suspicious of assistant district attorneys, and Borkan had to be doubly suspicious. I thought he would be more relaxed if Rafferty and Rosenthal talked to him first. They interrogated him for an hour and a half with the Brooklyn assistant present, and then I questioned him for about an hour. At no time did the assistant district attorney create any obstructions.

Borkan and I sat on opposite sides of a long table. There was a desk in the room, but I stayed away from it because I didn't want to come on as a big authority figure. For one thing, he belonged to Brooklyn. For another, I wanted to reach him through his feelings for the DeFeos. In questioning him, I stuck to the case. I did not want to gather extraneous information that could be helpful to the defense in discrediting Borkan. There was no rule that required me to seek such information, which I would be ethically obliged to turn over to

Bill Weber. As I talked to Borkan, however, I realized that Brooklyn had a big nut on him—they would save his pension if he cooperated with their investigation. I said that the nut might come out under cross-examination if he testified at the DeFeo trial. Borkan shrugged his shoulders. He was completely willing to testify, which I ascribed to his close relationship with the DeFeo family.

Borkan had tears in his eyes when he described his friendship with Ronald DeFeo, Sr. But he made no secret of his disdain for Ronald, Jr. He said he had acted as an intermediary to persuade Butch to cooperate with police in the robbery investigation. Since he knew the family, detectives on the case had asked him to get Butch down to headquarters to make a statement and pick out mug shots. Apparently, that attempt failed and police had to call Ronald, Sr., and tell him that his son was not cooperating. On the Friday before the murders, Borkan went to the Brigante-Karl Agency to pick up his own car, in which an oil pump was being replaced. This was between 5 P.M. and 5:30 P.M. The DeFeos were about twenty-five feet away from him, near the polish line—the father and son facing each other. Ronald, Sr., was saying that he had the devil on his back and he had to get rid of the devil.

Butch DeFeo glared at his father. "'You fat prick,'" Borkan recalled him answering. "'I'll kill you.'" Then he ran into his car and drove away. Ronald, Sr., remained standing in the same spot.

Borkan returned to the auto agency the following Wednesday. It was between 11 A.M. and noon, only hours after the killings had taken place. He was in the rotunda looking for Ronald, Sr., when he saw Butch. Borkan asked the young man to have his father phone him. Butch just looked at him and took off. Borkan noticed that the younger DeFeo had a bruise on the right side of his lip.

It was important testimony. Borkan had heard Butch DeFeo threaten his father's life several days before the killing—long enough to show premeditation. This struck right at a defense of extreme emotional disturbance. We had evidence that Ronald DeFeo, Jr., had thought about killing his father over a period of days; he had not acted in a fit of sudden passion. As for the bruised lip, that fit with what Lucy Burkin had heard and John Donahue had seen. Additionally, it shredded a case Weber was trying to make for police brutality. He was contending that DeFeo's face was bruised because police had roughed him up during his interrogation.

I was convinced that Borkan was telling me the truth and would make an effective witness. He wouldn't have to be led; he would be able to express himself without prompting. Nobody would like him, nobody likes a tainted cop. If I were a juror, I thought, I would despise the guy. But I would believe what he had to say. I would believe that he cared too much about the slain family to lie. If he could convey as much emotion to a jury as he had shown me, Burt Borkan would be believed.

After questioning Borkan, I made good my rash promise and took the company to dinner. I felt I owed them that, and the sociability wouldn't hurt. But it was a sizable group. There were five of them and four of us—myself, Tom Spota, Rafferty and Rosenthal.

We went to a nearby Red Coach, where we had several rounds of drinks—I didn't want the boys from the big city to think we were country bumpkins. Then everybody ordered the most expensive steaks on the menu.

When the bill came, I couldn't pay it. I couldn't even come close. Once again, Tom Spota filled the breach. Having him transferred to the case had been a master stroke in more ways than one. We used his credit card.

Naturally, I saw that he was recompensed. The bill was nearly two hundred dollars. It was worth every penny.

I would never find all the pieces of the jigsaw puzzle that was the Amityville murders, but with Borkan, I felt I had enough to nail Butch DeFeo. I was sure of one thing. I knew DeFeo in all his aspects; I could show all his sides to a jury.

The Long Island investigation would take care of that.

13

SOON AFTER THE NEW YEAR in 1974, Lucianne Canella [a pseudonym] got a job at Henry's Bar in Amityville. She worked there into late March, when she was badly injured in an auto accident. She wracked up her car after an argument with Ronald DeFeo, Jr.

Lucianne was twenty-three, nine months older than Butch DeFeo. They met soon after she started at Henry's. They saw each other in the bar, and sometimes he followed her home at night after her shift. In their world, that passed for courting. One night in March, they were seized by a romantic notion. Or as Lucianne would explain to Detective Harrison, "Ronnie and I got it into our heads that we wanted to get married."

They were at Henry's when the idea took hold, and they got into Butch's car and drove around the corner to the house that was built sideways to the street at 112 Ocean Avenue. When they told Butch's parents, there was trouble. Butch and his father got into an argument, and Lucianne fled outside and waited in the car.

Shortly afterwards, Butch came out and he and Lucianne returned to Henry's. Their notion had turned sour and they began quarreling; their voices counterpointing the hoarse rumble of the juke box and the scraping of glasses on old wood. The argument worsened. Lucianne flurried from the bar and gunned her car onto Merrick Road. Butch roared after her in his Buick.

The chase was short-lived. A few miles west of Henry's, Lucianne lost control of her car, and the auto smashed into a tree. Butch pulled up and helped her out of the wreck. Lucianne sustained two broken legs and a broken arm and was hospitalized for a week. After that, she spent almost four months confined to her apartment.

Butch visited Lucianne frequently the first month. On his very first visit, he brought a present—a black pistol, which he carried in a brown paper bag. He told Lucianne to keep it in a dresser drawer in case she needed it. Two weeks later, he took the gun back. He never said why.

The bedside visits were not always tender. There was an argument that ended with Butch grabbing Lucianne around the neck. He was choking her when her twelve-year-old sister walked into the room and started screaming. Only then did he stop.

During another visit, Butch stashed junk in Lucianne's nighttable. When he left, she looked in the drawer and counted fifteen tinfoil packets. Lucianne wasn't shocked. When she first met Ronnie, she thought of him as "pretty heavy on heroin." And he had shown up at her apartment once claiming that he had bought a suitcase full of dope in New Jersey and was bringing it to Amityville. He had promised to return that night but hadn't appeared until the following morning.

This time, Butch returned in a few hours and took the stuff he had left in the nighttable. Lucianne was fed up. She phoned a friend in the Nassau County Police Department, and told him about Ronnie DeFeo, who was driving around with fifteen packets of dope.

It was still night when Butch returned to Lucianne's apartment for the second time. She'd never guess what happened. He'd been stopped by police. But they missed the junk. That was the funny part; he'd been carrying it in his undershorts.

After three weeks, Butch lost interest in his convalescent girlfriend, and the visits stopped. Lucianne only saw him once or twice after that. The last time she ran into him was in August or September. Time changes feelings, and she wasn't sure about the month. What was certain was that, in November, she read about him in the newspapers.

Lucianne Canella told her story to George Harrison when he investigated Ronnie DeFeo's life and good times on Long Island. Her account fit the picture of a heavy-drinking braggart, swaggering through the South Shore bars. "Ronnie was always trying to impress people and was quite often throwing a lot of money on the bar," Lucianne told Harrison. "Ronnie was always bragging about his family being in organized crime. In fact, he used to comment that he could have someone taken care of if he wanted."

His relationships with women were in character. Ronald DeFeo, Jr., had money, cars, a macho style that went with his dark stare and denim clothes. Girlfriends did not appear to be a problem. His taste ran to the women who were most visible, most sexually desirable in his world—the formfit barmaids with professional smiles who were the stewardesses of the saloon circuit.

Sherry Klein, for instance. At the time of the murders, Butch and Sherry had been seeing each other for five months; they were talking about going off together. Several weeks before the killings, Sherry lost a barmaid's job in Massapequa, and Butch retaliated by shooting a gun off outside the place and threatening to knock out the windows of the owner's car unless she was rehired. When I heard about the incident, I knew I had another part of the DeFeo composite to show a jury. Violence wasn't his last resort; it was his first and, sometimes, only remedy.

In January, 1975, with DeFeo in jail awaiting trial, Sherry was working in another saloon in Nassau County. Teddy Phillips, the New York City cop who, months later, would help in the Brooklyn investigation, visited the place and got into a conversation with her. Sherry was attractive, at home behind the bar, easy for an off-duty cop to talk to. She told him that Ronnie DeFeo was her boyfriend—a fact that brought her status in the South Shore bars. Phillips listened carefully. He recalled the meeting in a signed statement: "During the course of the conversation, Sherry Klein told me that she had received letters from Ronnie DeFeo which he had written in jail since his arrest for the murders. I remember that Sherry Klein told me that Ronnie DeFeo had stated in the letters to her that he killed his family. She also told me that DeFeo wrote in the letters that if he goes down, he is not going alone and he is going to take somebody with him."

Or there was Mary Kosky [pseudonym], who was able to describe his quickness to violence. Ms. Kosky met Butch DeFeo in the latter part of 1973, when she was not quite eighteen. They had a single date, and she did not see him again until she got a job at Henry's as a barmaid. This was a year later, one week before the murders.

Butch started talking to Ms. Kosky as soon as he spotted her. He was drinking and he did not seem to be thinking about Sherry Klein. "I want you to be my girl," he told Mary Kosky. "Only my girl."

When the barmaid said she didn't want to go out with him, Butch kept pressing the issue. Meanwhile, he was backing her into a corner. He grabbed her left arm, squeezing hard enough to leave a bruise. "Mary," he said. "I love you. Why are you doing this to me?"

As the night wore on, DeFeo's belligerence increased. "Later that evening," Ms. Kosky would tell police, "Ronnie started threatening me and said he was going to smack me around and run me over with his car."

A man standing at the bar heard the threats. "Leave her alone," he told DeFeo.

It was a challenge. In the next instant, a crash silenced the room as DeFeo knocked over a couple of bar stools. But the man wasn't intimidated. "Knock it off," he ordered, and he used one of Butch's favorite threats. All he had to do was make one phone call, and he could have Butch taken care of.

"Go get your people," DeFeo answered. "I'll get my gun."

Five minutes later, the man turned to leave. Before he reached the door, he and Ronnie were pummeling each other near the cigarette machine. Other patrons pulled them apart, and the man went out. Soon afterwards, Mary Kosky closed the bar and DeFeo left peacefully.

Violence, threats, braggadocio. All of it fueled by drugs and drink. I never believed that Ronald DeFeo, Jr., was a psychopath; I did think he might be a sociopath. This is an antisocial personality—of which jails are full—who does not conform with the dictates of society and will do whatever he thinks necessary to get what he wants. Such a person is easily aroused and likely to be explosive. Such a person tries to impress others with his virility. Such a person is hellbent on self-gratification.

This was the picture left by Ronald DeFeo, Jr., as he strutted through his South Shore subculture. It came from the women who dated and served him, and from his male buddies—the good old boys of suburbia, who hung out on Merrick Road instead of the levee. Especially his best friend, Bobby Kelske.

Throughout the case, Kelske struck me as a sad figure. Of all the acquaintances of DeFeo who were to take the stand, Kelske alone gave off a sense of tragedy. In high school, Bobby Kelske had seemed a good bet for a career in professional sports. Instead, he ran into drugs and the bar scene. He had an early marriage that turned sour. He became close with Ronnie

DeFeo. My feeling was that DeFeo might have contributed to Kelske's involvement with drugs, but that Kelske, who was a year older than Ronnie, played the dominant role in their friendship. One story we heard was that Butch paid Bobby as much as fifty dollars a week just to hang out with him. DeFeo was drawn to super-masculine figures, and Kelske fit the bill more than any other member of their group.

When we reopened the investigation, Kelske and another man were under indictment for promoting gambling. It was a penny-ante sports-betting operation, but it was enough so that at one point, we considered offering Kelske a deal. However, we never had to. Kelske would testify for the defense at the trial, but he would help me more than he would Weber. I never thought this was a conscious effort on Kelske's part, but that it derived from a need to have the truth known. For example, there was an incident in which DeFeo passed out at the Buick agency about two months before the shootings. DeFeo had claimed that someone was trying to poison him, which Weber and a defense psychiatrist would use in an attempt to show that Butch was paranoid. But Kelske knew the real reason for the collapse, and told George Harrison. Butch had confided that he'd gotten sick as a result of mixing pills and liquor.

When he had been questioned after the murders, Kelske had supplied clues to DeFeo's character. He told how Butch masterminded a hide-in burglary at the Brigante-Karl Agency and he described his buddy as a gun buff who on several occasions had fired a snub-nosed .38 in the parking area at Henry's. In talking with Harrison, Kelske filled in the profile by describing incidents involving DeFeo's relationship with his father. We were very interested—we knew far more about DeFeo's life outside 112 Ocean Avenue than inside it.

Kelske described an argument he witnessed between the DeFeos after Butch's arrest in 1973 for possession of a stolen outboard motor. Butch had threatened to "blow the head off" Sergeant Pasquale Cammaroto, an Amityville cop he mistakenly believed was responsible for the collar. Ronald, Sr., became furious. He told his son to shut up, that the house might be bugged. The elder DeFeo hurled a silver pitcher at Butch, who made no effort to retaliate.

Not long before the murders, said Kelske, the DeFeos argued about money. Ronald, Sr., was threatening to cut back on his handouts. "Ronnie told me that he was pissed off at his father because he spent five hundred dollars on knee braces for Mark but couldn't give him any money." Kelske added that the elder DeFeo was incensed over "the phony holdup" in Brooklyn and the fact that Butch had forged about three hundred dollars' worth of checks. "Ronnie told his father that he needed the money to pay for an abortion," Kelske explained.

Two other cronies of DeFeo to whom Harrison talked were Chuck Tewksbury and Barry Springer. Tewksbury, unemployed and separated from his wife, lived with his parents, two blocks away from DeFeo on Ocean Avenue. Springer was a clam-digger who had worked the bay with Butch. Both men had known DeFeo at Amityville High School and had hung out with him afterwards at Henry's and the Chatterbox, another local bar. They were DeFeo's buddies, and did not tell Harrison everything they knew. But he found out enough to get the picture.

Springer was the more cooperative. "Ronnie never had a problem getting money," explained the clammer. "His father would usually give him what he needed." Springer said he had seen Butch in several fights, but they were usually the result of an argument or drinking. Once at the Chatterbox, DeFeo smashed a glass against the wall. "This was also after he was drinking and I provoked him," Springer said. Another flare-up occurred when Ronnie and Springer were playing pool. Butch wrecked Springer's shot, and the latter aimed the cue ball in Butch's direction. DeFeo reacted with instant violence, swinging his pool stick at Springer. Fortunately, Springer said, he was able to block it and neither man was hurt.

Although his buddies agreed that DeFeo became belligerent when he drank, none of them described him as crazy. We knew that insanity was going to be a defense, and foreshadowed this issue in our interviews. In a signed statement, Bobby Kelske summed up the consensus. He described DeFeo as "a rational person and the type of guy that liked to impress people."

DeFeo's school and police records added to the composite of what he was. Even photographs helped. One of the items in the DeFeo file was an old snapshot of Butch, his sisters and his brother, Mark, standing on the front stoop of their Amityville home, dressed for a special occasion, probably Easter. All wore flowers in their lapels. The girls had on spring suits and white hats and carried pocketbooks. Mark wore an Eton cap and a bow tie and a gray suit with shorts. The girls and Mark were animated; the little boy's mouth was open in a big grin. Behind them—somber, staring—stood Ronald DeFeo, Jr., a fat kid in a red blazer and matching tie. We would find out that Butch had lost a great deal of weight during a methedrine episode in his late teens. When the photograph was taken, he was only fifteen. He was massive.

I could sense him, the first and least-appealing child of Ronald and Louise DeFeo. Ronald Joseph DeFeo, Jr., was born at 2:10 P.M., September 26, 1951, in Adelphi Hospital, Brooklyn. His father, who listed his occupation as textile worker, was twenty; his mother was nineteen. I could imagine Ronald, Jr., growing up in Brooklyn, and moving to Long Island at thirteen when his mother was pregnant with her fifth child. Five children, but the most pressure had to be on young Ronnie. He was the firstborn, the eldest son in an Italian family. His father was a powerful man with a hot temper. Butch got his lumps, along with most of the things he wanted. Overweight, spoiled, having problems living up to what was expected of him, he threw tantrums at the world. After a troubled history in parochial schools, he attended Amityville Memorial High School, east of Ocean Avenue on Merrick Road, a building that was aging like the village, with red bricks showing through the white paint. In the tenth grade, he turned sixteen and quit school. His marks for the first semester of that year showed only one passing grade—seventy-five in physical education. The other marks were fifty in world history, fifty-nine in English, "U" in biology, and "U" in typing.

He was a school dropout, inept at sports, unskilled. Jobs were sporadic. DeFeo would claim he was fired from most of his jobs because of fighting and playing the tough guy, but our investigation showed otherwise. Usually, he quit or was fired for absenteeism. One of his first jobs was as a delivery boy for a pharmacy operated by his uncle. He quit several weeks before customers started complaining about overbilling. They said they had already paid the delivery boy.

In 1969, he lasted three months doing small assemblies at a pool-table factory near his home. Near the end of his tenure, he began losing time. He quit shortly after he was told that he would have to put in a forty-hour week. The following year, he managed forty-four days as an assembler at a Fairchild Camera and Instrument plant in Copiague, a community just east of Amityville. He was released because of absenteeism.

That same year, 1970, Butch helped a building contractor put in a raised patio and a finished basement at the DeFeo home. The contractor took Ronnie on other jobs, employing him as a helper for about five weeks. The contractor was pleased with DeFeo's work, but had to lay him off when jobs became scarce. After that, DeFeo went to work at the family car agency, living on the eighty-dollar-a-week salary and his father's largess.

In March, 1973, DeFeo's name cropped up on a Suffolk police blotter. The county P.D. responded to a report that an unknown person had brought the stock and breach assembly of a 12-gauge shotgun into Henry's Bar. According to the field report filed on the incident, the stock and assembly were "part of a gun owned by one Ronald J. DeFeo of 112 Ocean Avenue, Amityville." Butch was in the bar and told police that the gun had been in his car, broken down in two parts since hunting season. He said he didn't know who had taken the stock and assembly into Henry's. The barrel was still in the back seat.

That summer, Butch received a warning from Sergeant Cammaroto, whose daughter was a friend of Allison DeFeo. One evening, while driving home from work, Cammaroto stopped in front of the DeFeo home to talk to Butch.

"You know, Butch, we're having an awful lot of larcenies of outboard motors," the sergeant told the young man whom he had known since the DeFeos first came to Amityville. "We have reason to believe you may be involved. If you are involved, you better stop because we're going to get you."

"I don't steal outboards," DeFeo answered.

Near the end of September, Cammaroto spotted Suffolk County Police arresting Butch DeFeo outside the latter's home. The officers were standing next to the open trunk of DeFeo's car, which contained an outboard motor.

Cammaroto stopped to get the details. The seventeen-hundred-dollar motor had been stolen from a marina in Copiague. Although Cammaroto had nothing to do with the collar, he couldn't resist saying something. "See, Ronnie," he told DeFeo, "we did get you."

A few weeks later, the sergeant's daughter told him that Butch DeFeo had threatened his life. The sergeant phoned Ronald DeFeo, Sr., who blew up at his son.

At that, Butch's threat may have been more than mere posturing. Several homicide detectives thought there was a possibility that he had already taken a human life. We had been looking into the story DeFeo told Jimmy DeVito—that he had drowned a man after a barroom argument. In 1972, homicide detectives had investigated the death of a man whose body was found in the canal at the foot of Ocean Avenue. Death was due to drowning; there were no marks of violence on the body. The victim had been drinking the night before, and his brain showed an alcohol content of point-one-five. Detectives theorized that he could have stumbled into the water in a drunken stupor, but unresolved odds and ends bothered them. The day before his body was discovered, the victim borrowed two hundred and eleven dollars, most of it in tens and twenties, from a finance company. When he was found, his wallet contained only two cents. He visited several bars that night and bought rounds, but as the investigating officers pointed out in their report, "Two hundred and eleven dollars is a lot of generosity and consumption." And although he reportedly took a cab home, he lived almost a mile from where the body was found. The report concluded that the victim apparently died when he drowned in the Amityville River "under circumstances still not conclusively established." The file has never been closed.

By the time the DeFeo trial opened, many people in Amityville were afraid that Ronnie would win his freedom and return to the village. I knew that even before the murders, there was reason to worry about his capability for violence. I knew that he had assaulted friends and even shot at them. I knew that the year before he destroyed his family, DeFeo had come within a hair's breadth of killing his father. My source material for this information consisted of hours of conversation between Ronnie DeFeo and a forensic psychiatrist named Harold Zolan.

Dr. Zolan was retained by the prosecution.

14

DR. HAROLD ZOLAN'S REPUTATION was as impressive as the diplomas decorating his Massapequa Park office—not to mention the Wyeth prints, objets d'art, gleaming furniture and long leather couches. At fifty-seven, Dr. Zolan, an impeccably groomed man who looked as if someone polished him and whose silver eyebrows matched his hair and mustache, had been a psychiatrist for thirty-one years. He was a diplomate of the American Board of Psychiatry, a consulting psychiatrist at the Nassau County Medical Center and attending physician at Long Island Jewish-Hillside Medical Center, where he lectured to the staff on forensic psychiatry.

Dr. Zolan defined his specialty as "any point of interface between psychiatry and the law where the two disciplines have some impact on each other, and where psychiatry is hopefully expected to assist in legal matters of a civil or criminal nature." At the time of the DeFeo trial, he had been retained by defense attorneys or prosecutors to provide such assistance in approximately one hundred and seventy criminal cases. In about ten, he had been asked to consider the limited issue of whether the defendant was competent to stand trial. In the remainder, he had been asked to determine whether the accused were responsible for their acts when they committed them.

It was pertinent that in half of the dozen or so cases he had handled for our office, Dr. Zolan had supported defenses of mental disease or defect. One of the cases was mine; it involved a man accused of trying to murder his girlfriend. I figured that Dr. Zolan would help me disprove insanity. Instead, he was called by the other side. He testified that the defendant suffered from a psychosis at the time of the crime.

I knew that you didn't bring in Harold Zolan to examine a defendant unless you were willing to accept his objectivity. If he decided that DeFeo was mentally diseased at the time of the crime, the case would be wrecked. In all likelihood, DeFeo would be acquitted by reason of insanity, sent to a state hospital and released in a few years. But if Dr. Zolan found the reverse to be true, if he determined that DeFeo was legally sane when he committed the murders, and if we prepared properly for his testimony, we could wind up with an overpowering witness. Harold Zolan's rapport with jurors bordered on magic.

There was another factor. Dr. Zolan had testifed before Judge Stark several years before in *The People of the State of New York* versus *Sugden*, a murder case that was appealed to the New York State Court of Appeals. The state's highest court set a precedent for trials involving insanity defenses by ruling that a testifying psychiatrist could use information that normally would be excluded from evidence as hearsay. In effect, the appellate court said that such material was usable if it was the sort of information the psychiatrist would rely upon in clinical practice. This meant we had solid authority for arguing that Dr. Zolan be allowed to use most of the information we had developed. We could give him our composite picture of DeFeo, and, through him, we could show it to the jury.

Dr. Zolan examined Ronald DeFeo, Jr., at the Suffolk County Jail on two separate occasions. Under state law, the prosecution could not have a psychiatrist examine the defendant until the defense announced that it would rely on expert medical proof of legal insanity at the trial. As a result, our first opportunity to have Dr. Zolan examine DeFeo did not come until midway through the pretrial hearing. The hearing was recessed for a day to permit the session.

The first examination took place on September 29th. Weber was present, and I sat in with a stenographer from our office. The stenographer was an extremely attractive young woman, and DeFeo reacted to her by opening the top two buttons of his gray prison shirt and showing off his hairy chest. I watched Butch DeFeo from the opposite end of a long metal table, and I listened carefully as he answered Dr. Zolan's questions. There were moments when DeFeo lied, times when he worked hard at sounding crazy. But his substance as well as his style came through. His relationships with his friends, his experiences with drugs. The love-hate festering between him and his father. The violence that characterized life inside 112 Ocean Avenue, Amityville.

Dr. Zolan started by questioning DeFeo about childhood and school. Butch seemed frank as he said that he managed to get promoted each year, but that he disliked school and fought with teachers, as well as students. Usually, the arguments were triggered by the need to get his way. "Just the way I wrote my name," he told Dr. Zolan. "Stupid things, the date, where I put it, on what corner of the paper."

"They wanted you to put your name and date on one part of the paper?" asked Dr. Zolan.

"And I put it on another part of the paper."

"Was there any reason why you didn't do it the way they asked you to do it?"

"No, Sir. I just wanted to do it my way. . . . I just didn't want to give in to them. I wouldn't let them tell me what to do."

Most of DeFeo's education took place in parochial schools, where he had one taboo. "I never hit a sister," he said. "I think I might have thrown a book at one of them. . . I didn't get angry. I just had to have my way. If I didn't have my way, there would be no way at all."

After quitting school ("They were going to throw me out, gave me a choice between throwing me out or quitting"), DeFeo hung around for a year before going to work for his uncle. It was during this period that he started using drugs.

"What kind of drugs?" Dr. Zolan asked.

"Pills, marijuana, acid. That was about it then."

"How about the hard stuff?"

"That came later."

DeFeo said that although his parents were disturbed by his indolence, "they always gave me all the money I wanted. Whatever I wanted, it was there."

Suppose he wanted a boat, suggested Dr. Zolan. "Nobody would say to you, well, you know that's a lot of money and you've got to save for it or anything like that?"

"No, Sir. When I was fourteen, I believe my father went out and bought me a four-thousand-dollar speed boat." When he was seventeen, his father gave him a car. And when it came to cash, he never even had to say what he wanted it for.

During this period or just before it, his parents sent him to a psychiatrist in Brooklyn. The psychiatrist wanted to know what he was doing with his life.

"What did you tell him?"

"I don't think I could answer that. I don't think I ever gave him an answer for that." DeFeo saw the psychiatrist several times and then stopped. He was vague as to why. "I enjoyed our talks and all, but I didn't particularly not like seeing him. I wanted to see him but I didn't."

He talked about going to work at Brigante-Karl when he was

eighteen. He said he was able to stick there because his father was the boss and nobody could tell him what to do.

"What did you do then?" Dr. Zolan asked.

"Nothing really. Some days I had to do work, you know, tune up the car or grease and change the oil, or take one down and have it washed, a new car, that was about it, mainly. I just hung around."

"While you were hanging around, what were you doing?"

"Well, I believe at that time I really got into speed," DeFeo said. "I used to run like a maniac all the time."

"All right, then you got into the strong stuff too, besides speed, like horse?"

"Just recently. Through the course of the years, speed was the main thing. I think I was strung out for a year and a half or two years. . . . I had a lot of trouble. I used to weigh two hundred and fifty, sixty pounds. Within a year I went down to about a hundred and fifty-five or a hundred and sixty."

"Did you ever crash or did you stay on a high?" Dr. Zolan asked.

"No, Sir. The longest was seven and a half days, but I was on it every day, day after day. I don't know what it did to me but later on when I tried to quit, I had a hard time doing it, and I had to go upstate to see a doctor . . . about a condition I had." He described the condition as consisting of destructive episodes which occurred when he came off the drug. "I would break up a place. I would get very destructive, like a crazy man. I was like an animal."

The doctor had been his parents' physician in Brooklyn. They chose the physician because at the time, DeFeo had refused to see a psychiatrist. Instead, he saw the doctor every two weeks—about twenty to thirty visits in all—and was put on thorazine, an antipsychotic medication.

"Do you remember how much thorazine?" asked Dr. Zolan.

"He gave me a bottle," DeFeo answered. "He told me to take them if I felt this thing coming on, to keep me quiet, and I kept going up there and it kept happening and he wanted to put me in a sanitarium and I never went back to see him after that."

DeFeo said the episodes continued after he stopped seeing the doctor. He gave several examples, some of which were corroborated by his friends. Once he was driving on the Southern State Parkway, and the man who was riding with him had to reach over with his foot and hit the brakes. "I held the car," DeFeo said, "stepped on the gas and held it to the floor, and there were cars in front of us. The traffic was at a dead stop and I was going to hit the cars that were stopped. We did get into a very bad accident."

"How come? You said your friend stopped you."

"He shut the engine but the car kept going and we hit a pole or a couple of trees and wiped the whole back of the car out."

Zolan asked about other drugs. "All right, when did you finally start on horse?"

"I believe it was twenty-one, twenty-two, around there."

"Did you get hooked?"

"No, I wouldn't call it hooked. I did a lot of heroin though."

"Now, I heard you say you dropped acid too?"

"On occasion, not an everyday thing, once a week."

"Have any bad trips?"

"Maybe one or two."

"What happened during them, do you remember?"

"Not really. One trip, I had a rough time. I had to stay in my house. One of my friends stayed with me because I don't know, I was starting to go a little crazy."

"What do you mean?"

"I don't know. I thought I could fly or something. I was going to jump down—we had a, not a spiral staircase, three flights of stairs in my house and I believe I jumped off the top and jumped down and there was a fountain there and the fountain fell down and I almost killed myself and he stayed with me for a while until, you know, it wore off the next day, whatever it was. He spent the night there. I was really bad."

162

DeFeo described going after Barry Springer with the pool cue, but said he broke the stick over Springer's head. He told of a second attack on Springer, which occurred when they were clamming in the Great South Bay with another friend, Steve Hicks. "I was standing on the deck," DeFeo said, "and I don't know what happened but I picked up a chowder clam and I smashed it over my partner's head, started taking all the clams and throwing them in the water, all the clams that I worked for that day, like a crazy man, and he fell in the water and he was out. Good thing I snapped out of it. He might have drowned. . . . I remember hitting him with the clam in the head and I remember jumping in the water and saving him."

Another scene occurred when DeFeo spent a night drinking and wound up at his girlfriend's home. "I got to her house," he told Dr. Zolan, "and started smashing the place up, took a chair and I put the thing through the ceiling—the legs went through the ceiling. The landlady came down. I don't remember what I did to her, started arguing with her, dragged my girlfriend out of the house in her pajamas and I took her in my car to the bar and I don't remember, my father came down there. . . . He had to come down there and drag me out of the bar, started a big scene in the neighborhood and all. I don't know. All my friends had to jump on me."

DeFeo said he was off speed at this time, but he was taking other drugs. "I was using heroin and acid, not acid too much, heroin."

"How much heroin were you using? I mean, how often?"

"I don't know. When I get high, at a time I usually buy a quarter of dope, fifty, fifty-five dollars. I would do the whole thing at that one time, you know—two or three shots and that would be it. When I want to get high again I would do it that way again."

"How often would you be doing that?"

"Well, I had to watch because I was on probation and they did take my urine so I couldn't do it that often."

Dr. Zolan asked DeFeo if he knew what crime he was charged with.

"Murder," DeFeo answered.

"Can you tell me what that means?"

"It means you took somebody's life."

"Did you kill them?" Dr. Zolan asked a few minutes later.

"I don't know," said the accused murderer who had given police a confession so detailed that it resulted in the recovery of evidence. "I can't remember certain periods of time in that night . . . I don't know what I did. I can't remember taking a gun and shooting my family. I can't remember none of that . . . I don't see how I could have did it, but it looks like I did do it."

"So to this moment, you don't have any recollection of shooting anybody with the gun?"

"No, Sir. I try hard—it's hard to believe; I have my family's pictures upstairs. I still, to this day, don't remember taking that gun and shooting anybody in my house with it. Like I said, I must have did it, but I can't place myself doing it."

Dr. Zolan asked if DeFeo thought something was wrong with him.

"Well, if I did what they said, there must be something wrong with me."

"Why is that?"

"There's no reason for people to do things for no reason. There's got to be something wrong."

"Is there something wrong with what they charged you with doing?"

From a legal point of view, it was a key question. There are two criteria for determining legal insanity. Did a mental disease or defect deprive the defendant of the capacity to understand the nature of his act, and did he know that what he did was wrong? But DeFeo's answer was not responsive. "I honestly don't know," he said. "I believed in the beginning that somebody else did it, but I don't think so."

"I don't think you understood my question, Mr. DeFeo,"

persisted Dr. Zolan. "I'm asking you, regardless of whether you or anyone else did it, is the crime itself that was committed, is there something wrong with that?"

"Sure there's something wrong with it. My family's dead."

"Why is that wrong? What makes something wrong with that?"

"It's my family. They had no reason to die."

"Suppose it wasn't your family?"

"I don't see why any person has a right to take another person's life. I don't believe that's right."

"In other words," asked Dr. Zolan, "are you telling me that it's wrong to kill somebody, to take someone's life?"

"Yes, Sir," said Butch DeFeo.

"And that if you did that, that you did something wrong?"

"Yes, Sir."

"But you are still not sure of whether you did it?"

"No, Sir."

"I see, but if you did do it, then there was something wrong with it?"

"Yes, Sir. If I did it, there's plenty wrong with what I did."

"Because it's wrong to take somebody else's life?"

"Yes, Sir."

The examination had been going on for more than two hours. Just before it ended, Dr. Zolan asked if DeFeo cared that his family was dead. "Yes, Sir," Butch said. "I loved my family. I'm never going to get another family."

During the examination, I kept my reactions to myself. But I was surprised when DeFeo said he didn't know if he had committed the murders and that he couldn't remember much of what had happened that night. It didn't seem like a very smart way to prove insanity. About the only pathology anyone could draw from "I don't know" was amnesia, and DeFeo was no amnesiac. He had described the killings to police, and to

John Kramer and James DeVito, without complaining about any loss of memory.

But it wasn't that simple for Dr. Zolan. In order to make a determination, the psychiatrist told me, he needed more time with DeFeo. He felt DeFeo had lied, but he needed details of the killings from the defendant's own lips. He wanted another session, and he didn't want any phony lapses of memory.

Bill Weber and I argued the issue in court. Weber contended that the prosecution should be limited to a single examination. In return, I argued that Judge Stark should bar the defense from offering psychiatric testimony because DeFeo had failed to cooperate with our expert. Actually, I was gambling. As far as I knew, there was no precedent regarding the credibility of a defendant's claim of amnesia. Even if Judge Stark granted my motion, the decision might be reversed by a higher court.

Instead, the judge arranged a compromise. During the argument, Weber had said that DeFeo objected to my presence at the examination, as well as that of the stenographer from my office. Under the the compromise, the defense would agree to a second examination in which DeFeo would be fully responsive. In turn, I would waive my right to attend, and the court reporter would take the place of a district attorney's stenographer. Both Weber and I would receive copies of the transcript.

The trial was recessed for the second examination, which took place on October 15. Quickly, DeFeo admitted that he held back at the previous session because of me and the stenographer. He said he hated me, and that he had heard us talking about him during the break, and the stenographer had wondered out loud whether he was flipped out on LSD at the time of the killings.

"But apparently you were turned off by her presence before she even said this?" Dr. Zolan said.

"Yes, Sir," DeFeo replied. "In the street before this happened—like Doc, I'll be honest with you about everything. I was not like a sex maniac or nothing, I went out with a lot of girls and I had a lot of sex. Women just started to turn me off right before this happened. I couldn't have sex. I just couldn't do anything. Like you know, I thought it was me. Then I thought it may have been the girl I was going out with. But I kept going out with all these girls. I mean a lot of girls. It wasn't the girls; it was me."

"At what age did this start?" asked Dr. Zolan.

DeFeo counted backwards. "I'm twenty-four. Twenty-three—two years—twenty-one, I'd say."

"Isn't that when you were starting on heroin?"

"Yes, Sir. I fooled around with heroin," DeFeo answered. "I knew what heroin did to you. But even when I was on heroin, I could still have sex, do whatever I wanted. It wasn't that. When I wasn't on heroin, in fact, I was having a lot of trouble. . . . When I was on it, I could do it."

"Was that before heroin, after it, or in between?"

"No, in between times. It's just when I was on heroin, I had sex with women. I had no problem. It's just that I don't know. They just completely turned me off."

Dr. Zolan tried to clarify the extent of DeFeo's drug usage. Actually, Butch said, he had tried LSD only a few times—most of his experiences had been with speed, or mescaline. "The mescaline is what I did use. But actually what it did to me was an upper. It made me feel good. You know, never stupid things. Never a bad time with any of that."

"Why did you take the heroin?" asked the psychiatrist.

"I started to change. I was violent. This and that. The heroin kept me calm. It kept me mellow. When I was on heroin, I was a nice person. It didn't put me in another world or anything. Just like downers would, it kept me mellow. I tell you, when I was on medication, like heroin, anything like that, I never did nothing to nobody. I was fine. I was calm."

When "things did happen," said DeFeo, he wasn't taking any drugs. Zolan asked what things, and DeFeo claimed that people were trying to kill him. Someone had tried to poison him in a

Wantagh bar, and he went back to the place several times with two hand grenades he had purchased in New York City. Only he couldn't do anything because police were watching the bar. (We knew from Bobby Kelske that DeFeo had not been poisoned, but had gotten sick from mixing pills and liquor.)

Another incident involved a ginmill from which Sherry Klein had been fired because of DeFeo's carryings-on. Butch's story to Zolan was that the bar owner had threatened him. "I went down there with a gun. I mean, I have a twenty-five caliber automatic, and I went down there. Boy, and I was going to kill the owner. That's the guy I wanted. I was going to blow him away. And I took that gun, got out of the car and two of my friends, or three of them, jumped on me and took the gun away from me."

DeFeo said he began having trouble with everybody. He was arguing with his friends, he couldn't get along with his family. People were always talking about him, or starting in with him. Even people he didn't know.

"You were saying that you were having trouble with your family, too," Dr. Zolan said. "What was that about?"

"There were a lot of incidents, Doc," answered DeFeo. "Two years ago, I told you, was when all this happened to start. Now, my mother and father had—this is the truth now—since I've been a young kid, very, very bad fights. I'm talking about with the hands. I have seen my father beat my mother so bad—I mean she's bleeding and black eyes. This is all the truth. And when I was younger was one thing. As I started getting older, you know, it was getting kind of, you know, bad. . . . Like I said, about two years ago when this started—I don't remember the night—but they were having these bad fights again. And I happened to be in the house that night, and the kids were all in there, and everybody. And they are all screaming and they are all yelling and fighting. The kids were yelling, 'Butch, come down and break it up. Come down here. Daddy is killing Mommy,' or something like that. And my sister, Dawn, is down there trying to break it up. Now, I got sick of this. I got sick of my mother and father fighting. . . . I had a twelve-gauge shotgun on the wall, Doc. I put a shell in the gun. It was a single-shot gun. I took the gun and came down the stairs and I said, 'Listen, that's it.' And I pointed the gun at my father. I told him I was going to kill him. 'Leave that woman alone. I'm going to kill you, you fat fuck. This is it.' I took that gun and pointed it at him and I pulled the trigger, and the gun didn't go off. I snapped the handle again, and the gun still didn't go off."

"All this time you were pointing it directly at him?" Dr. Zolan asked.

"Yes, Sir. He looked like he seen a ghost. He shit. I dropped the gun. I didn't do nothing. I just walked away. It's very lucky for him, my mother and everybody else in that house that I didn't have any other guns at that time in my presence because I would have killed them all. That's the way I felt about it."

"If you were concerned about the fights between your mother and father—this is going back two years—particularly the fact that your father was beating up your mother, why would you have killed everybody?"

"See, you don't understand. I didn't want to be bothered. I was upstairs. My family and brothers and sisters—supposed to be my brothers and sisters—come up there, and they were bothering me."

"Excuse me. You say supposed to be."

"I got doubts about that being my family . . . I didn't believe that they were my family, my real mother and father. I honestly don't believe this to this day."

"Excuse me. You say you didn't fit in with them. In what way didn't you fit in with them?"

"I couldn't get along with them neither. I didn't hate them. I have to admit the people that were supposed to be my family—"

"Would you like some water?"

"No. Now, Doc, the people that are supposed to be my family, mother, I loved them all. I'm not going to lie about that."

"Yes?"

"But you know, they have done things to make me believe that, you know, they weren't my family, you know."

"Can you give me an example of some of the things that they made you think that they are not your family?"

"It seemed to be, Doc, everyone in that house—I don't know. They were trying to kill each other, always do harm to each other. It was like a bunch of animals. You know, these people wanted to do harm to me, Doc. They wanted to kill me. . . . This is why all this led up to this in the end."

"All right now, how was this demonstrated to you that they wanted to kill you?"

DeFeo answered in disconnected half-sentences that hung separately like pieces of freezing wash on a winter line. "Well, a number of times, Doc, like my sister as she got older. Now, my father was a very violent person. Yes, I wanted to say one other thing, Doc, about this bit with the shotgun with my father."

"Right."

"What happened right after that was that my father, I went to work with him one morning—my mother came—and he told me he wanted me to drive them to New York to take my mother to the doctor, and he wanted me to sit in the car. Now, I went to New York with them and we got to this place. I told Mr. Weber—he's trying to find the address. I didn't remember the name of the doctor. He's got an address book. And when we get there, he says, 'Come on in. Come on upstairs.' I didn't want to go in. When I got up there, it turned out it was a psychiatrist. . . . The guy called me in the room. He's asking me all these questions about these different things leading up to this incident."

"The shotgun?"

"Yes, Sir . . . he came right out and said, 'Mr. DeFeo, you got no business being in the street. You belong in a mental institution.' I said, 'What do you mean?' He said, 'You are a sick man.' I had an argument with him and I left. Now, I was told this a number of times before this by other psychiatrists that I didn't care for. And apparently my mother and father went in, and the man told my father that he was a psychotic or a psychopath, and your son is going to wind up killing all of you. This is what the man told me. He's going to wind up killing all of you."

"He told you or he told your father?"

"He told me and he told them, too. They were warned . . . these people were warned. When the doctor told my father that he was sick, my old man laughed at him, paid him his money and he left."

"When he had told him that you were sick?"

"Beside telling me I was sick, you know, after he was through talking with me."

"Then he told your father he was sick?"

"Told my father he was sick. My mother is crying and my father is laughing. He said, 'You are not sick; this doctor is sick.' You know, passing the buck over on everybody. And it sort of became like a buddy-buddy. You know, we became friends but we could never be friends."

"You mean you and your father?"

"Yes, Sir. As long as he was alive, he was a threat or a danger to my life. And I had more respect and never hit my father with a hand. I never hit him with a hand. He hit me. He did all the fighting. He's the one that beat me up. I never hit him back. I tried to wrestle and hold him. I ain't never punched the man."

"Why was he a threat to your life?"

"The man told me he was going to kill me."

"Your father told you?"

"Yes, Sir. He told me he was going to kill me. He told me he had a silver bullet in his gun and he was going to blow me away. My mother told me she was going to get me. My sister is with these knives, running around the house. I broke up a fight. . . . Once this happened: My sister had a butcher knife, trying to kill my father with it. My mother is trying to pull my

171

sister off. I go down and break it up. Who gets the worst end of the whole deal? I get a beating over the whole thing. I get my poor sister out of the house with the knife. I'm deathly afraid of knives because I was stabbed in the back with a knife when I was thirteen or fourteen years old. I'm afraid of them knives. Anybody points a knife, I'm afraid of the knife. As soon as a person does that, that's it."

Finally, said DeFeo, he told his family that he couldn't live at home any more, or he would wind up killing everyone. "And I told everybody in that house that I would kill them. A number of amount of times I had told my friends in the street that I could not take no more of them. They are—my old man, I'm going to wind up killing them all. And they were warned and warned and warned. Now, what I tried to do to prevent this is I left my house. I got—and I just packed up and I left."

This was several weeks before the murders, Butch said, and he moved in with a girlfriend. He had left home before but his parents always made him return by applying financial pressure. "And this time, right, I wasn't coming back," he told Dr. Zolan. "This was it." But two or three days later, he came out of his girlfriend's apartment and couldn't find his car.

"Now, I thought somebody stole it. So I was going to call the police. Good thing I didn't. I took my girlfriend's car. I found my car in the driveway. And now I had my keys and I went to take it. I got in the car. He pulled all the spark plug wires and coil wire. So I said to him, 'What is going on? You took my car.' He said, 'I want you to come home. If you don't want to go to work, you don't have to go to work.' You know, but he wanted me home. Now he told me he wasn't going to give me any more money. He took my car, took everything. So I still didn't come home. I went back there and I used my girlfriend's car."

"You were working at your grandfather's place in Brooklyn?"

"Yes. Then he stops my salary. He wouldn't give me any more money."

"Excuse me. How much were you earning a week there?"

"Well, Doc, there is a little more to what the Buick dealership is. I honestly—for the last two years, every Friday, Doc, there is some weeks the least I had was five hundred dollars, some weeks I had two, three thousand dollars every week. . . . Money, I never had any problems with money if I wanted money. I could be—be home and ask my father for five thousand dollars, and bingo, it was there. I have done it many times."

DeFeo gave in and returned to Ocean Avenue. "'I don't care if you come to work or not,'" he said his father told him. "'You could have your car back. You can have everything back. Just come home and live there.'" And I told the man, 'I can't live in the house with you people. I'm going to wind up killing you all.' He thought it was a big joke. As bad as I was getting, every night something was happening. There was trouble every night. And he still wanted me to come home."

"Why do you think he wanted you home so badly?" asked Dr. Zolan.

"I don't know. I honestly don't know."

"Well, is it conceivable that in spite of all the quarrels and the fights that you are his son and he loved you and still wanted you at home?"

"I thought about that, but I don't know. I think they wanted me in that house so they knew where I was so I couldn't get them. That's what I started thinking about but it doesn't make no sense."

Dr. Zolan was leading up to the crime, but DeFeo wanted to tell him about something else first. A death list he had jotted down in jail. He had given the list to Dr. Schwartz.

"Can you give me the names on the list?" Dr. Zolan asked.

"I had my grandparents, not my grandmothers, my two grandfathers; Peter DeFeo; my uncle, Vinnie Procita and his wife, Phyllis Procita; one or two of my sister's girlfriends; some of my friends. There was a lot of names on it, a good fifty. Took me a long time."

173

DeFeo said that people on the list, which included Louis Falini and a couple of police officers, wanted to get him. "Why do they want to get me? I imagine because of what happened, just to start with. Because maybe they feel that I got it in for all them, too. If they don't get me, I'm going to get them, or vice versa. To be truthful, I told Dr. Schwartz exactly what I'm telling you. I told him if I got out of here, my aunt's own daughter—and she was on the list—I have full intention of killing every one of them. . . ."

Then Dr. Zolan took DeFeo over the murders. Apparently, his memory had improved. Not only did he furnish details of the crime, but he produced a brand-new version—which he would repeat at the trial. The beginning was the same—he stayed home sick that Tuesday with stomach problems. After that, the story changed. He heard his family fighting at dinner. "They were all fighting again. My sister again with the knife. Every time with the damn knife. I went down there."

"Was she attacking somebody with the knife?"

"Yes, Sir. She was trying to kill my father. Honestly, I wanted them to kill each other . . . but I couldn't take the noise. So I went down there and tried to break it up. I got my sister out of the house. She got in the car and left."

Shortly before 11 P.M., Dawn returned. She went to her room, and Butch watched *Castle Keep* in the sitting room. The rest of the family went into his parents' room, where at some point, he stood by the door and heard them plotting against him. "They were all going to get me that night."

"What were they saying?" asked Dr. Zolan.

"They were saying, 'We'll wait until he goes to sleep,' this and that. You know, I couldn't hear too good because of the war picture. I was hearing, you know, words."

"Now I was watching the war picture," DeFeo continued. "Dawn, if I remember correctly, came down the stairs and said something to me. She said, 'I'm going to get him. I'm going to get Mommy. I'm going to get you. I'm going to kill everybody in the house.' I said to her, 'When you kill everybody in the house, you let me know. I want to get out of here,' or something like that. And then she went back upstairs."

After the movie ended, he either blacked out or fell asleep on the floor. He believed Dawn woke him up. "It must have been her. The light now in the TV set was off. I know I didn't shut it off. I imagine—I believe it must have been her. When she came down the stairs and kicked me and woke me up, she had the .35-caliber Marlin in her hand. And there was a strange thing about her hands that I told Dr. Schwartz that I didn't understand. Her hands seemed to be black to me."

"Black?"

"Yes, Sir. I believe they were gloves. And she had this gun and gave me this gun. She put the gun in my hands. And I don't remember what I said or what I did. But I wasn't angry or mad. I was calm. Just very, very, very calm. And it was sort of like she disappeared and went somewhere."

DeFeo said he took the gun and walked to his parents' bedroom, opened the door and shot his father and then his mother. "I remained calm. But the thing that bothered me. I fired the gun but the gun didn't make any noise when I fired it. And then I dropped the gun—I didn't throw it—just dropped it and left it there." He returned to the sitting room; then he heard shots and saw Dawn come out of his brothers' room with a rifle. And he thought he saw a second person.

"Who was the other person?"

"I don't know. This is what I'm trying to explain to you. I thought I saw two people. I figured it was my own mind."

"Could it have been one of your brothers?"

"I don't think so. Because when I heard the shots the only light that was on—none of the lights were on in the house but the bathroom light on the second floor. There was enough light between that light and the candle that my mother and father had under the statue in their room to see . . . I heard shots. And then when I went and got up I seen my sister, the person I

175

believe to be my sister, running up the stairs with the gun."

"You say the person you believed to be your sister?"

"Dr. Schwartz seemed to be telling me that it couldn't have been my . . . You know, it was my imagination. But I don't believe any of this to be in my imagination."

"Dr. Schwartz told you it was your imagination?"

DeFeo changed his mind. "I don't think it was Dr. Schwartz. I think it was Mr. Weber that might have said that to me."

"It couldn't have been your sister?" Dr. Zolan said.

"Yes, because he said to me that he knew personally that I had a great hate for black people. I felt, you know, all my life I hated niggers all the—"

"Your sister was not black?"

"No, Sir. He and a doctor, he was saying something about the gloves . . . they weren't gloves, they were black hands. I don't know what he was talking about."

They returned to the murder chronology, and DeFeo said he went to Allison's room and his brothers' room and saw shell casings on the floor. After that, he walked up the stairs to Dawn's room. "When I got to the top of them stairs and I looked at my sister, she was putting a shell in the gun. I took the gun away from her, and I don't remember . . . What I believe is I wanted—I told Dr. Schwartz I wanted to throw her out the window."

"Throw her out the window?"

"Yes, Sir. I wanted to throw her out the window. Even though in my own mind I felt my whole family was a threat to me, I felt what she did wasn't right. Now I felt that she was a threat to my life and that she was going to kill me in fact with this gun that she just killed them kids with. . . . I pushed her, and I pushed her face down into the bed. . . . And I remember taking the gun away from her when I pushed her down, and I shot her. But again the gun didn't make no noise."

Dr. Zolan summed up. What DeFeo was saying was that he killed his parents and Dawn? Yes, DeFeo said.

"But that Dawn in turn killed your two brothers and Allison?"

"See now, another funny thing, too, Doc," answered DeFeo. "When we had this argument, I did kill Dawn. I'm telling you I heard footsteps and when I turned around I didn't see nobody, but somebody ran down the stairs because I heard all these footsteps . . . and when I got down the stairs the front door was wide open and the screen door, and I seen somebody running across the lawn."

"Could you recognize him?"

"No, I didn't know if it was a girl or a guy," DeFeo said, and he offered a rationale that took him partially off the hook. "What I believe in my own mind is that my sister and another one of her friends had this whole thing planned. . . . Maybe they were going to try to get me to help them. I honestly don't know. I do know how they were going to pull this whole thing off was that if I didn't kill Dawn—that's why I say there was another person—if I didn't kill Dawn, she in turn was going to kill me. She was going to kill me and tell the police he was drunk or stoned on dope or something and he killed everybody and we had to kill him."

Later that morning, said DeFeo, he cleaned up the house and went to work. Although he suffered from a whistling noise in his ears, he was not unduly upset. "I felt good that they were dead. I might have felt a little bad, but I felt good that they were dead."

In the little more than two weeks that had elapsed since the first examination, DeFeo had made a complete turnabout when it came to the nature of his act. "I didn't believe there was nothing wrong with it," he said. "As far as I'm concerned . . . what I did was self-defense because if I didn't kill them they were going to kill me. It's just who got who first."

DeFeo seemed to think it was important that he cleaned up the house after the murders. "Everything was thrown all over the place. It looked like a shithouse. Shell casings all over the place. It was a big mess. So rather than not be a pig, because

I'm not a pig, I cleaned the place up. I picked everything up, nice and neat."

He told about removing evidence, but denied that he was trying to hide anything. "I just put the stuff in a place where I felt in due time I would tell the police . . . I was going to, in fact, tell the police what had happened."

DeFeo said he knew exactly where he had thrown the gun, and Dr. Zolan pointed out that in the first examination he said he didn't remember where he dumped it. Butch claimed that he hadn't been able to say what he wanted to say because of my presence.

But he actually knew exactly where he put the gun?

"Yes, Sir. See, the police asked me about a lot of other things; where the gun was. You know, I got on the stand (at the pretrial hearing); everything I said was the truth. I didn't lie about anything. Mr. Sullivan got me mixed up, you know, with words in themselves. I think that's the only thing I'm really afraid of in life is words. You know, people get me mixed up."

He said he left the gun where it wouldn't be found right away so that he would have time to bury his family. "All the police needed against me was the gun to prove this gun killed everybody through ballistics. As far as the rest of the stuff went, it was just garbage to me. It belonged in the garbage can. . . . When I did stop at the corner (in Brooklyn), there wasn't a garbage can, so I saw the sewer, I took it out and just threw it in there rather than litter the goddamn streets up like an animal, like the rest of the people out there.".

Dr. Zolan asked about the cash box. DeFeo said his father had ripped off his grandfather for two- or three-hundred-thousand dollars just before the killings. He claimed that his father was worried about being under surveillance by the FBI, and asked Butch to bring him one hundred thousand dollars that he had been keeping alongside the cash box. His father went to work, and then Butch brought him the money. If the one hundred thousand dollars was still around, DeFeo said, it was in a safety deposit box or somewhere in Brooklyn.

As for the cash box, that was empty. He had taken money from the box, but always reported the amount to his father. But Dawn was less honorable. "Dawn was going down there and she was taking money out of this cash box and not telling nobody—just taking. Dawn was starting to use drugs, and we knew this. And, in fact, I tried to stop it. One time I went to the school, St. John the Baptist, a couple of years ago and I threatened somebody to do physical harm if he didn't quit selling the kid drugs."

It seemed to me that DeFeo was setting up his defense. The cash box was empty, and money wasn't a motive. "If anything, to be truthful with you," he told Dr. Zolan, "I had too much money. Because the more money I had in my pocket, the more I spent. And I believe two weeks before they were killed, on a Friday night, I had eight thousand dollars . . . And boy, I went through that quick—one, two, three."

"What did you do with all of it?" Dr. Zolan asked.

"I went out and bought, I don't know, clothes. I gave money to my girlfriend, this other girl I was going out with. It was all over. I gave Dawn money. . . . I was drinking a lot of booze, a lot of booze. I was spending like, without exaggerating, on myself fifty dollars, and I used to buy the whole bar drinks."

"Fifty dollars a night?"

"Yes. It was coming to a hundred dollars a night, the whiskey bill, when I got through buying everybody drinks."

Dr. Zolan went after DeFeo's inner feelings. "My feelings," DeFeo said, "it's like my feelings got out of my body and left. Crying—I could never cry. As far as hurting somebody and feeling bad, I can't feel bad. As far as having a conscience, I have no conscience."

"To this day," DeFeo told Dr. Zolan, "I honestly believe—you might laugh about it—I honestly believe sometimes that I'm a secret agent for God. . . . So I feel with a gun in my hand, the way I was going lately, I feel that I am an ultimate supreme being. I was God when I had a gun in my hand."

"You thought you are an agent for God in what way?"

"Them voices, they were voices always talking to me."

"Whose voice would it be?" asked the doctor.

"I don't know. I told you in the beginning I used to turn around and look—who the hell is calling me?—and there would be nobody there. Later on, I realized it was a voice telling me what to do sometimes. Like one night, I took this girl out, I took her to the movies. I left the movies. I stopped down in the bar. It was about three o'clock in the morning. I wasn't drinking. It was a Saturday night. I said hello to a couple of my friends and I left. Right after I left the bar, a voice told me to go crazy, go on—like I don't remember the exact words. . . . I then found myself with my car on people's front lawns, ripping down stop signs in the neighborhood, and this kept going on. I ripped the woman's stoop off. Just about half the side of her house. Not crazy or mad, just that I kept doing all of this. Then finally the police got somehow involved in it, and they were chasing me all through the neighborhood. I was going through backyards, all this, all that.

"Maybe in my own mind," said DeFeo, "I believed that God was trying to tell me to go out there and clean up this earth and get rid of all the bad people. . . . As far as I'm concerned, all them out there are animals."

The interview was almost over. "Anything else that you know you might feel would help me understand you better?" Dr. Zolan asked.

"I don't think so," DeFeo answered. "Just that like I told Dr. Schwartz, the main thing that I felt, that people were becoming a danger—some people became a danger and a threat to me, and that's why I did certain things. As far as I know, I could have killed ten people before out in the street and not known it. Not that I ran or tried to hide anything. It's just that I—if I might have shot somebody, I might have left them there to die. I don't know."

"You mean you think there is a possibility that there are other people that you may have killed that you don't remember?"

"Yes, Sir."

DeFeo elaborated on his feelings about me. He referred to an incident that had occurred a couple of weeks before in the courtroom, when I had tried to talk to him. We were early; neither Weber nor Judge Stark were there. We said hello, and a few minutes later, I turned around slowly and asked how he was doing. DeFeo stared at me, and answered: "Okay. How're you doing?"

I said I was fine, and made a comment about how we had to spend a lot of time waiting for people to assemble. But DeFeo was through talking; he just kept staring at me.

DeFeo gave Dr. Zolan this version of the incident: "Now, like in the courtroom Mr. Sullivan says hello to me. He says, 'Hello, Ronnie,' to me a couple of weeks ago. Now, how can he say, 'Hello, Ronnie,' to me and then turn around and put me on the stand and try to rip me apart in words and try to make me look like the scum of the earth? I don't understand how he could do all this and say hello to me. He can't be my friend and be my enemy. And he can only be one. In my mind that man just has become a threat to my life, like the rest of them people that wanted to do some harm to me, physical harm to me."

"Well, you got on the stand then. You can understand as a prosecutor he would be trying to get you convicted of a crime."

"Yes, Sir. But the attitude and the way he lunges at me. He starts to put a little fear in my own mind and starts making me feel like he's now becoming a danger or a threat to me and wanting to kill me."

"You think Mr Sullivan wants to kill you?"

"Yes, Sir. I honestly believe that."

"With a gun or a knife?"

"I don't know what he wants to do it with, but I believe in some way he is trying to make an attempt for my life."

"You mean personally?"

"Personally. Yes, Sir."

"In the courtroom?"

"I don't know. I keep my eyes on him all the time in that courtroom."

"Why would he want to kill you?" Dr. Zolan asked a minute later. "What's so important about Ronald DeFeo?"

"I don't know what," DeFeo said. "That's what I'm trying to find out myself. I'm not sure if I'm Ronald DeFeo sometimes."

When Dr. Zolan asked who he thought he was, DeFeo brought up God again.

"You think you might be God?"

"I honestly think I have something to do with God. Yes, Sir."

"I mean, do you have more to do with God than any of us who believe in God or pray to God?"

"I think I am a little closer to God than anybody else."

"In what way?"

"I personally have talked to Him before."

"How?"

"Not kneeling down and praying, but I just sat and spoke to Him, held a conversation with the person I believe to be God. I haven't seen Him."

"How do you know it was God who was talking?"

"I believe it's God because I can't see who else it could possibly be," explained DeFeo.

The prisoner discussed jail. "I want no part of the world out there," he said. "As far as I'm concerned, out there, there is nothing but trouble, disease, animals. I want no part of the world. In here at night when we lock in, they lock us in the cells. I feel safe, that nobody is going to get me. I feel fine. I really like that. . . ."

At the interview's conclusion, Dr. Zolan thanked DeFeo for coming in.

"Right," said DeFeo. "Okay. Take care of yourself."

"You, too," said the psychiatrist.

*　　*　　*

Tom Spota and I waited for Dr. Zolan to return to my office when we finished the examination. Although we knew his judgment was totally independent, we were smug with confidence. *Falsus uno, falsus omnibus.* Loosely translated, that comes out to "Once a liar, always a liar." If Dr. Zolan thought DeFeo was lying at their first session, how could he believe him at their second meeting? That was our reasoning. Unfortunately, we were thinking like lawyers. Dr. Zolan was not necessarily dealing with credibility. He was dealing with insanity, and its definition according to law.

It was early afternoon when Dr. Zolan arrived at our office. We were smiling until we saw that he wasn't. "How'd it go?" I asked.

"I don't know," he said. "I don't know."

We hurried to an inner office, where Dr. Zolan told us that DeFeo had given a bizarre but detailed account of how the murders took place. There had been overtones of paranoid psychosis and Dr. Zolan would not make any snap decisions. He wanted to study the transcripts of both examinations. And he would need to see whatever information we had that would corroborate or contradict what DeFeo had told him.

I drove home that night thinking that nothing was easy in this one. Here we were, into the trial itself, and our whole case could evaporate like drops from a sun shower. There had to be something wrong with a system that allowed a mass-murder trial to hinge on whether an adroit liar could con a psychiatrist into believing his cockamamie story. Goddamn it, that wasn't going to happen to my case. Not if I could help it.

I got into the house, greeted the kids and was hanging up my coat when the phone rang. Tom Spota felt the same way. We agreed to spend the coming weekend collecting every pertinent scrap of information for Zolan. Jail logs, DeFeo's letters, statements obtained by police, synopses of prospective testimony, school records. Everything we had on the phony holdup and the hidden cash box. By 10 A.M. on Monday, a detective delivered an eight-pound package to Zolan's office.

On Wednesday evening, I received a call at home from Dr. Harold Zolan. He had some news he thought I wanted to hear. Really? I said. What about? What case was he talking about?

I was masking anxiety with flippancy, and then it wasn't necessary. "Malingering," Zolan said. "The guy's a liar, and not a bad one. My diagnosis is antisocial personality. And you can take that to the bank—that's solid."

Dr. Zolan's diagnosis had started to coalesce almost from the beginning, but he wanted to be absolutely positive. The material we sent him had cinched his decision. DeFeo was an antisocial personality—someone who has not been socialized into his society. Such a person is immune from guilt, and his sole concern is self-gratification. This is a personality disorder as opposed to a mental illness. The bottom line was that Ronald DeFeo, Jr., was legally sane when he committed the murders.

Years later, during a discussion of the case, Dr. Zolan would recall his thinking: "It would have been very simple for me to say, 'Oh yes, this guy is a phony, period, and that's the end of it.' But I do not see myself making a commitment as to a finding unless I am absolutely sure in my own mind, and at that time I suspected it, suspected it strongly, but I still wanted to make sure. I would not make a final decision until I had read everything."

Dr. Zolan would explain that he began to suspect antisocial personality when DeFeo talked about his schooling: "Antisocial personality does not begin at an advanced age. It begins in childhood. Here's a guy getting into fights with everybody in school, getting kicked out of one school after another, destroying books—that began to make me suspect. But the one thing that made me more convinced than anything else was his credo. And his credo was that he wanted what he wanted, how he wanted, when he wanted, and he was going to get it no matter what he had to do to get it."

In this instance, Zolan would reason, DeFeo wanted money.

For most of his life, Butch lived in what the psychiatrist described as a "sociopath's Garden of Eden" where there was nothing he wanted that he couldn't have. But in the weeks preceding the murders, his father showed that he could stop the cash flow. And in any case, said Dr. Zolan, DeFeo could never really have enough money. So he killed to get it.

We did not go into all of this that Wednesday night in October, 1975, when Harold Zolan called me. "Antisocial personality," he said over the phone, and the words sang. In the context of the law, Ronald DeFeo, Jr., was a sane murderer.

All I had to do was prove that to a jury beyond a reasonable doubt.

PART THREE

Hearing

15

USUALLY, I SET MY RADIO ALARM to go on at 7 A.M. The first day of the suppression hearing, September 22, 1975, I was at my desk by that time. Otherwise, I followed my regular trial routine. I ignored breakfast, and I drove Clementine to the office with the volume turned up on the tape deck. My selections were consistently classical—Beethoven, Wagner and sometimes Mendelssohn. If anything revved me up for trial, it was Mendelssohn's *Hebrides Overture*.

In my office, a cubicle on the fourth floor of the still-new criminal courts building, I made coffee—my secretary had left the machine set up; all I had to do was push the button—and went over the questions I had prepared for my opening witness, First Squad Car Detective Gaspar Randazzo. My cardinal rules include never putting a witness on the stand unless I have already talked to him, and writing out everything I want to ask. But I never read from these notes in court unless I'm asking a technical question or one for which the law requires a set form. For all other purposes, the act of putting questions on paper locks them in my memory.

I studied the written-out examination for more than an hour until Tom Spota came in to discuss strategy, and Randazzo arrived for a final review. Then it was time and we went down the back stairs to the courtroom one floor below. There was an elevator, but I never used it during a trial. The elevator was too public. And when I was this close to conflict, it was too slow.

I performed one last ritual before entering court. I went inside the men's room, splashed water on my face, straightened my tie and jacket, checked the buttons on the collar of my buttoned-down shirt, took several deep breaths and slammed out of the bathroom. I strode into the courtroom, pushed the door open and didn't just say "Good morning" in a quiet voice. "How ya doing?" I boomed. I could hear the *Hebrides Overture* swelling in the background.

My setting was the white stone criminal courts building, whose five stories made it the tallest structure in the county complex at Riverhead. I had prosecuted the first murder case held in the building; the DeFeo case was only the third or fourth. It mattered that the suppression hearing was taking place in the same courtroom in which the trial would be held. For more than eight weeks, the room would be my arena.

The room seated about sixty-five spectators in black-backed, red-cushioned chairs. It was red-carpeted and paneled in teak except for the wall behind the judge's bench, which was faced with beige-colored Italian marble that bore the gold-lettered legend, "IN GOD WE TRUST." Recessed light shone through small circles above the well of the courtroom. The jury box lined the left wall, and a rail sectioned off the prosecution and defense tables and the bench. A lectern for attorneys stood at the left of the counsel tables facing the witness chair. At the head of the room was the teak bench, flanked by the flags of state and nation.

The suppression hearing was a dry run for the trial. But the fact that Judge Stark would preside over the hearing without a jury made our job simpler, but not easier. Juries can be persuaded in ways that judges cannot. Oratory wouldn't work with Judge Stark, and neither would any attempt at dominance. You can steamroll over some judges and own the courtroom. But don't even dare with Tom Stark. He has territorial rights to every square inch of the room.

The defense's motion struck at the heart of our case. Weber was asking Judge Stark to suppress from the trial all written and oral statements that DeFeo had made to police after the murders, including his confession. If Stark upheld the motion, we couldn't submit the evidence that police recovered as a result of DeFeo's admissions. We wouldn't be allowed to produce the murder weapon. To tell the truth, I didn't see how we'd be able to go to trial.

Weber's grounds were police brutality and rights-violation. Specifically, the defense claimed that DeFeo was held in custody for more than thirty-six hours, intentionally deprived of his rights to counsel, severely beaten, put under mental duress and denied due process of law. I foresaw few problems in handling the police brutality charge. I had talked to the officers involved, and was convinced that nobody had pushed DeFeo around. And I had John Donahue, the youngster who had seen the fight between DeFeo and his father, which accounted for Butch's bruised lip. But the rights issue would be tougher. This hinged on the believability of attorney Richard Wyssling, who would be the defense's star witness. Wyssling, whose wife was DeFeo's second cousin, had appeared at 112 Ocean Avenue shortly after 11 P.M. the night the murders were discovered, and asked for Butch. The key question was whether he asked as an attorney or as a member of the family.

According to the officers who saw Wyssling that night, he never represented himself as DeFeo's lawyer. Three weeks before the hearing, I had phoned Wyssling to get an idea of what to expect in court. He told me that he most definitely appeared as an attorney, and was given a run-around by police. But he seemed unsure of his recollections. And it was pertinent that Wyssling had trouble of his own. The attorney had served as a Suffolk County personnel director, and was facing a perjury indictment stemming from his actions as a governmental employee. Our office had secured the indictment, and I figured that he felt more than a little hostility towards us.

The prosecution went first. I opened with Randazzo, the first county detective to whom Wyssling had spoken at the murder scene. Randazzo had told me that Wyssling never said he was acting as a lawyer, but identified himself as a relative. And despite the confusion at the scene, Randazzo had watched carefully when Rocco DeFeo, Butch's paternal grandfather, used the kitchen phone early in the evening. The detective noted the number and had it checked. In less than an hour, he learned that Rocco had called a relative thought by police to be connected to the underworld. Organized-crime overtones in the case had been stirred by Butch's references to a hit-man, and now they were heightened. The possibility of Mafia involvement in the killings had made Butch's safety an important consideration. DeFeo wasn't under arrest that night; he was under protection. Randazzo's testimony about the call would help make the point.

Randazzo was an excellent detective who conveyed sincerity. His appearance was a logical starting point for the hearing, and I figured he would do well on the stand. But his testimony gave us unexpected problems.

I became apprehensive as soon as I started questioning him. Randazzo was so tense he wasn't even sure of the name of Patrolman Greguski, the Amityville cop who greeted him at the scene. I suspected that he was overwhelmed by the importance of the case. I had seen this sort of reaction hit experienced cops before, not to mention a few prosecutors, and I halted my questions after we got past Rocco DeFeo's phone call. When

Weber rose to cross-examine, I was worried. He had to sense Randazzo's nervousness.

Near the start, Weber brought out the fact that DeFeo was sobbing when police arrived and that he was consoled by a priest. I was repelled. I thought about Butch DeFeo sitting in the house where he had violated the Fifth Commandment, sitting at the kitchen table with heroin in his veins and accepting consolation from the priest who had just given the last rites to the souls of his victims. I glanced at DeFeo, who had shaved his beard and dressed up in a plaid jacket and light-yellow shirt, and I detested him.

Under cross-examination, Randazzo remained firm in denying that DeFeo was in custody at the scene. But he faltered on Wyssling.

"Officer," asked Weber, "at about eleven or eleven-thirty, were you approached by an attorney at the premises?"

"I was approached by a man who said that he was a friend of the family, and he had said that he was an attorney."

"So the answer to the question, officer, is that about eleven o'clock you were approached by an attorney; is that correct?"

Randazzo answered yes, and went on to testify that Wyssling wanted to know DeFeo's whereabouts. The detective learned that DeFeo was at a squadroom in the First Precinct and told Wyssling he would call there.

"To tell them that an attorney was looking for Ronnie DeFeo?" Weber persisted.

"That somebody was looking for Mr. DeFeo, right."

"An attorney was looking for him, or just someone?"

"That someone—" Randazzo started to answer, and Weber interrupted. I objected, and Judge Stark sustained me. But Weber saw the jugular and he was going for it. "He identified himself as an attorney?"

"As an attorney," Randazzo answered.

Minutes later, Weber scored more heavily. He was pressing Randazzo about police moving DeFeo from the Ireland house to a precinct. "So somewhere between eleven and eleven-thirty, Detective Barylski told you that DeFeo was taken away from the Ireland house?"

"No, Sir," answered Randazzo. "When I made my phone call I found—when I—when Mr.—when the attorney asked to see Mr. DeFeo, I went inside and he was gone. And at that point—"

Without prompting, Randazzo had referred to Wyssling as "the attorney." All I could do was try to repair the damage on redirect. Deliberately, I changed my approach. I held my breath to redden my face, slammed my notes down on the lectern and virtually shouted my first question. Randazzo looked shocked. But he sat up, leaned forward and told me what I wished he had told Weber.

"Detective Randazzo," I asked, "this individual who was looking for Ronald DeFeo between eleven and eleven-thirty, would you tell us to the best of your recollection what words he used in identifying himself?"

"Yes," Randazzo answered. "He said he was a friend of the family's and he says he was a lawyer, and he says he would like to speak to Mr. DeFeo."

"Did he ever tell you that he was representing anyone?"

"No, Sir. He did not."

"Did he ever tell you why he wanted to talk to DeFeo?"

"He wanted to ask him what happened, period. And I told him he could speak to him if he wanted to, and I told him where he should go."

I had an extra patch to apply. "At that point in time," I asked, "was Ronald DeFeo a suspect in any criminal activity?"

"No, Sir."

"Did this individual ask you whether or not he was?"

"No, he did not."

Randazzo stepped down. I turned to Tom Spota with a look of relief on my face. Tom responded with an exaggerated sigh.

The detectives who followed Randazzo to the stand— Gozaloff, Harrison, Rafferty and Dunn—made up considerable ground. Gozaloff came on first. A street-wise cop who scored near the top of every police exam he took, Gerry Gozaloff didn't let anybody put words in his mouth. On cross-examination, Weber asked him about DeFeo's transfer from one police facility to another. "So in other words, it would be normal police procedure to take any suspect back to the squadroom; is that correct?"

Gozaloff's answer was quick as a Ping-Pong return. "I didn't say he was a suspect."

"Was he in your protective custody?" Weber asked later.

"No, Sir," Gozaloff replied. "He wasn't in custody. He was there of his own free will."

Harrison followed Gozaloff, and their combined testimony was like a one-two punch. They emphasized that nothing inadmissible occurred while DeFeo was in their presence, that he was not pushed around and that in no way did he become a suspect until the morning after he went to sleep in the file room. Throughout the night, he was treated as a prime witness whose safety was paramount. He did not ask to talk to a lawyer or to any of his relatives. His attitude was that he wanted to help police find whoever killed his family.

This was exactly what I was after. I wanted a picture of DeFeo to evolve through testimony. I wanted to set the scene for his confession. Gozaloff and Harrison provided a bridge between the sobbing DeFeo described by Randazzo and the mass-murderer who would be depicted by Rafferty and Dunn.

The latter pair came next, and they were beautiful. I had spent many hours going over Rafferty's testimony; I knew it almost as well as he did. I expected a rat-tat-tat of objections from Weber, but there were only three brief interruptions during the three hours of Rafferty's direct testimony. I suspect that Bill Weber was no different than anyone else in the courtroom. He was held silent by the narrative.

Then I called Dunn. A handsome, well-educated man with a booming voice and strong presence, Bobby Dunn sits forward, folds his hands on the rail and looks directly at the lawyer questioning him. There was one moment when the emotion in Dunn's voice chilled the courtroom. I asked him why he had left the file room before Rafferty finished obtaining the confession. "I was awed by the horror of it, to be perfectly candid," he answered.

Although I knew we were racking up points with the four detectives, I was preoccupied. My main concern was the Wyssling issue, which would not be resolved until I had my shot at him on the stand. Meanwhile, there was a lesser problem, which I dealt with near the end of my direct case—a mysterious spectator who showed up in court each day.

The stranger could have been invented by Damon Runyon. He looked in his early sixties (actually, he was several years older), and had silver hair, heavy-lidded dark eyes and a voice of purest gravel. He wore jackets and ties but leaned to colors like yellow and lime-green. I sensed a touch of New York flash, and it bothered me that nobody knew who he was.

I had my suspicions. Witnesses were banned from court prior to their testimony, and I had the guy made as a spy for Mike Brigante, who was due to be called by Weber. To make sure, I put a detective on him. "Watch him in court," I said. "Follow him when he leaves the room. If he makes any phone calls, get a make on the number."

My detective, Eddie Fitzgerald, kept the man under surveillance the next morning. At the first recess, silver-hair left the courtroom and Fitzgerald followed him. But there was no phone in the men's room. During lunch, we got lucky. Fitzgerald tailed the guy to a car in the parking lot and ran a check on the plate. We had to wait until the afternoon for the answer. I was examining a witness when Fitzgerald came to the rail and handed one of the court officers a folded piece of paper to give me. As soon as I got a chance, I pulled it open.

"Your 'spy,'" I read, "is George Glaubman, Wading River resident and confirmed court buff. He apparently likes watch-

ing mass-murder trials more than raking leaves in his retirement. Congratulations on your sixth sense, Sherlock."

I folded the note and slipped it into my pocket. I refused to
look at the detectives in the spectator seats. I knew they were
all grinning at me. Trouble was, I couldn't keep from smiling
myself. Later, I became acquainted with George Glaubman, one
of the nicest court buffs I've ever met. I was right about one
thing. He did have a New York background—he grew up on the
East Side.

The police officers completed my direct case, and it was
Weber's turn. As I expected, his witnesses included Michael
Brigante, Sr., who had watched the bodies of his daughter and
son-in-law and four of his grandchildren being carried out of
the house in Amityville. The sympathy Brigante evoked and his
run-on speaking style made it impossible to keep his testimony
admissible. Brigante was a learning experience—I knew that
when we went before a jury, I would have to hold his cross-
examination to a minimum.

His style showed in direct testimony as the hoarse-voiced
man in the dark suit, white shirt and silver-gray tie described
the phone call in which he heard about the murders: "There
was a police—the man said he was a police officer out in Suffolk
County. He said, 'Your daughter just had a terrible tragedy.' I
said, 'Now wait a minute. What is it?' He said, 'I can't tell you.
You have got to come out here.' We were watching I believe it
was 'Adam 12,' which was on about eight o'clock or somewhere
in there. I said, 'Look, I lived with cops all my life. I'm pleading,
asking, begging you. I want to know . . . Please let me face it.'
He said, 'Your daughter and your family are all murdered. They
are all dead. Will you come out?' I said, 'Yes, I'll be out.' And my
son drove us out there. . . ."

When I began my cross-examination, Brigante seemed upset
and I asked if he would like a recess. I shouldn't have. "No, no,"
he answered. "Go right ahead. If I want to die, I'll die right here.
Don't worry about it. This is hell in heaven, but go ahead."

It wasn't easy. For instance, I wanted to convey his personality by showing how he had flashed police shields at the murder scene. Before we were through, the witness pulled out his wallet and unslung an accordion insert crammed with cards. Looking at the display, I wondered if there was any place in the United States where Mike Brigante could be stopped for a traffic violation without having an appropriate police card to show the officer. Our dialogue smacked more of Abbott and Costello than it did of Blackstone. I asked Brigante if he would identify the cards, and he replied, "Sure. Why not? It would be a pleasure. Do you want to see them?"

"Would you just tell us for the purposes of the record what shields they are?"

"Yes, I can tell you in two minutes. One was given to me by the assistant chief inspector who is now dead, and that's not Tom Conolly, but he's an A.C.I. His daughter is a policewoman right now, anyhow. Anyhow, this is the chief inspector. And I have a deputy commissioner shield belonging to Lieutenant Stutman, which I never mentioned his name. Former deputy police commissioner of the City of New York. I never used the name. And this here is Detective Endowment Association shield, which I'm a member of for life of the City of New York."

"Now, did you tell us that you did exhibit those at the scene in an attempt to get into the crime scene?"

"I didn't exhibit them," Brigante said, "except to try to give somebody my card. I didn't make a spectacle of myself trying to be a big shot or something like that, no. If that's what you're trying to say."

"Did you tell some police officers that you were a very active participant in the Policeman's Benevolent Association in New York City?"

"No, I said I was active. Sure, I'm active in all the police reserves, that's correct, buying police ticket dinners for various affairs and things like that for Nassau, Suffolk, Westchester, Putnam County or New York City, wherever it may be."

"My question, Mr. Brigante," I said, "is whether or not you recall making that fact known there at this crime scene?"

"Well, I made that known, but I said, 'Look, you got to help me, Randazzo. I want to find my grandson, see where he's at.' I said, 'Look, I'm active with many police associations. You got to help me. I'd appreciate it. I am trying to help policemen or somebody else. So please help me.'"

Brigante claimed that he spoke to Richard Wyssling twice at the scene and asked him to find Butch. At 3:30 A.M., Wyssling called him at home and reported his lack of success. Brigante said he told Wyssling he would contact Richard Hartman, a well-known Nassau attorney, and see what he could do. But on cross-examination, Brigante used the surname Richard without explaining whether he meant Wyssling or Hartman. And he seemed confused as to when he first learned that his grandson had been arrested and needed an attorney. I asked if he could have gotten the news on the evening of the 14th, which was the day DeFeo was booked. This was important because Brigante seemed to be saying that he didn't realize the need to retain a lawyer for his grandson until a day after his contact with Wyssling at the crime scene.

His answers were vague, and Judge Stark joined the search for clarity. Turning to Brigante, the judge asked when he had the conversations about a lawyer for DeFeo. "Was it after you learned he was accused of the murder?"

"As far as I can recall," Brigante answered, "they had said that you have got to get a lawyer, somebody to represent him. After I told Richard, 'Richard, you are not a trial lawyer. You better not handle this. You better get somebody else.' Now, I don't even know. It might have been even Richard might have asked—Richard Wyssling might have asked Richard Hartman. I don't know, see? I said, 'Richard, this is not a case for you. You are in the family. I don't think you better try this case.'"

Judge Stark tried again. "Is it a fair statement that this took place after you learned your grandson had been accused?"

"I would think so, Your Honor," Brigante said.

The point had been made. "I have no further questions," I said.

It was Weber's turn to do some patching on redirect examination. He asked if Brigante had asked Wyssling to act as a lawyer for Butch. Yes, Brigante said. Then, as he left the stand, Brigante provided the hearing with its most dramatic moment. "Your Honor," he asked, "have I got permission to kiss my grandson?"

Stark assented. Years later, he would explain that he gave permission because it was a nonjury proceeding; he felt it was a matter of letting a grandfather communicate with his grandson.

I had reservations. I got up from the table and quickly walked to the back of the courtroom. Tom Spota did the same thing on the other side. The deputy sheriffs assigned to the hearing stood up and unbuckled their holsters. Brigante came off the stand and walked behind the defense table to where DeFeo was sitting. They stood and embraced each other for several seconds, and I could hear sobbing. Brigante pulled back and kissed Butch on the face. He said something in Italian in a low voice, and then he changed into English.

"Tell him the truth," Mike Brigante told his grandson, "and the truth will set you free."

There is some disagreement among observers as to DeFeo's precise answer. But what I heard was: "The truth will get me life."

Outside the courtroom in the lobby, Brigante walked up to me. "Hey, Sully," he said in a loud voice. "I just want to let you know I'm going to say good things about you to your boss. I know Harry. I know Harry."

Brigante reached out. I said something innocuous and we shook hands. A few witnesses later, Weber called Richard Wyssling.

16

THE MAN IN THE WITNESS CHAIR was obese, round-faced, prone to perspiration. When I rose to examine him, I spread so many legal documents, transcripts and cassettes over the lectern that they overflowed onto the front rail of the jury box. For the next two hours, Richard Wyssling kept stealing glances at the mass of paper. He couldn't know that much of it had nothing to do with him.

I was geared up for Wyssling; I wanted him to worry. And a little pizzazz wouldn't hurt. Every good trial lawyer has his own style. For instance, counsel is supposed to stay at the lectern but I find that confining. Moving up to a witness is a way of emphasizing what's being said. I believe in eye contact with the witness, and in hand motions such as rapping my ring on a table if his attention wanders. A ring, incidentally, is handy with juries as well as witnesses. Wham! Nothing beats banging your ring on the jury rail to call the panel's attention to your next question.

I would use it all on Wyssling, plus any extras that came to mind. I was convinced that the linchpin to Wyssling's testimony was his hostility toward the Suffolk district attorney's office. After a long grand jury investigation by our office, the former county personnel director was indicted on eight counts of perjury, one count of contempt of a grand jury and two counts of offering a false instrument for filing. The charges stemmed from allegedly denying that he had conducted his private law practice on county time. I had pored over the case, and I was ready to wash Wyssling's dirty linen in the courtroom and exhibit the grime in a glass bucket.

I had taken a cram course on Wyssling from Chief Assistant District Attorney Sam Fierro, who had examined him before the grand jury that brought the indictment. Give Wyssling enough rope, Sam told me, and he'll hang himself. Let him talk. I nodded. In general, lawyers make lousy witnesses. They rarely follow their own advice, which is to answer questions succinctly without volunteering information. Put a lawyer on the stand, and he has to flaunt his knowledge of the law.

Wyssling was well prepared for his direct testimony. He radiated conviction as he told Weber that he had identified himself to Randazzo as DeFeo's attorney at 11 P.M., and made a similar declaration at midnight to the desk officer at the First Precinct. He said he continued to get nowhere at 12:50 A.M. at the Fourth Precinct, where he talked to two patrolmen and a lieutenant. To bolster his account, he displayed a phone bill showing that he called his wife from the Fourth shortly after midnight. The sense of his story was that police gave him a runaround.

Weber questioned Wyssling for only a half-hour. The defense attorney looked confident as he turned the witness over to me. Judge Stark declared a recess, and before we went out, I asked if I could bring in a tape and a recording machine. "I'd like to have it as of the time the Court comes back," I said, "because I intend to use it upon cross-examination. There is also an internal speaker system within the courtroom, and I think we can pipe it into the courtroom so the audibility will be improved."

Judge Stark asked if the tape bore on the credibility of Wyssling's testimony. "Yes, Sir," I answered. I noticed that Weber was looking a little less secure and Wyssling was starting to sweat.

I was bluffing. The tape talk was designed to psych out the defense. I had taped the phone call I made to Wyssling in early September, but I had no burning desire to play it. I preferred to read from a transcript I had made of the twenty-minute conversation. That way, I could put my own emphasis on particular words and phrases. During the recess, Tom Spota and I hurriedly listed contradictions between the phone call and Wyssling's direct testimony. When we returned, I spread out my paraphernalia. The tape was ready in a playback machine, but I hoped I wouldn't have to turn it on.

Minutes into the cross-examination, I hit Wyssling with the charges of unethical conduct that were facing him. Within fifteen minutes, Wyssling took the Fifth Amendment against self-incrimination twelve times. Meanwhile, I pressed the issue of his hostility toward our office. "Do you have any hostility or animosity toward the party against which you are giving testimony on this date?" I asked.

"Who am I giving testimony against?" Wyssling responded.

"You appreciate that the district attorney of Suffolk County is the prosecuting agency for the People of the State of New York, do you not?"

"Do I appreciate that? That's a fact. Yes, Sir."

"As against the district attorney of Suffolk County, do you harbor any hostility or resentment as you testify here today?"

Wyssling couldn't let the chance go. "Not against the district attorney's office, but against some of the personnel. Yes, Sir."

"As a matter of fact, your feelings of hostility and resentment run very, very deep, do they not?"

"Against certain individuals in the office. Yes, Sir."

Wyssling denied that his testimony was colored by this hostility, but I continued: "Do you feel that you are being persecuted by the office of the district attorney?"

Instead of answering, Wyssling took the Fifth. I asked if he were under indictment, and he took the Fifth again. It was time to get specific. "Are you not in fact under indictment for eight separate counts of first-degree perjury in Suffolk County?" I asked.

"Yes," Wyssling answered.

"And isn't it true that you are also under a separate charge of criminal contempt of the Grand Jury in the first degree?"

"I believe I am," Wyssling said this time.

"And isn't it also true that you are charged with offering a false instrument for filing in the first-degree."

"I believe I am."

"On two separate counts?"

"I believe I am."

"Aren't you finally charged with the crime of taking security upon certain property for a usurious loan?"

"I believe I am."

You didn't have to be an expert in body language to know that Wyssling was upset. He was putting his hand over his mouth, rubbing his brow, pulling at his tie. He had reason; I had raised serious doubts about his impartiality. Now I set him up for the phone-call transcript. Did he want time to rethink any of the answers he gave Weber?

No, Wyssling said. Seconds later, he was stumbling over a question as to when and where he spoke to Randazzo. Judge Stark interrupted. "Is it your testimony that you made an inconsistent statement in your telephone conversation with Mr. Sullivan?"

"Yes, Sir," answered Wyssling.

In short order, I caught Wyssling in ten inconsistencies. In each case, he either admitted making the statement and tried to explain away the contradiction, or said he did not have a clear memory of what he told me. Not once did he deny making a particular statement—which would have forced me to play the tape.

I felt we had scored the go-ahead touchdown when I had Wyssling insisting that after arriving at the murder scene at 11 P.M., he learned that Butch DeFeo was under arrest for the six murders. This was patently impossible. DeFeo had not even become a suspect until the following morning. And Wyssling said his source was Mike Brigante. But Brigante had already testified that he did not know about his grandson's arrest until the next day.

My feeling was reinforced when Judge Stark took over the questioning: "At what hour of the evening did you come to the conclusion that Ronald DeFeo is charged with these homicides?"

On direct, Wyssling had been a forceful witness. Now he was rambling. "After—when I got to the Ireland house and talked to the DeFeos, at that point—I'm sorry, not the DeFeos," he said. "The Brigantes at this point. It was my understanding—no one physically said it, I don't believe, that he was under arrest. They may have. There was no impression that he was not arrested. And I either assumed it or Mr. Brigante may have said that he was arrested, or he didn't remember, but certainly by the circumstances it was very clear in my mind that he was arrested earlier in the evening for these—for this case. When I talked to—when I mentioned—I gave my card to Mr. Randazzo, he didn't seem surprised or he didn't say, 'Gee, he's not under arrest,' or 'We are only holding him.' There was no response in any way at any time either at the First Precinct or at the Fourth Precinct for any reason why I wouldn't have continued upon the fact that he has been arrested earlier in the evening and he was charged with these murders. No one specifically said that he was arrested to me either at the First or Fourth Precinct."

Judge Stark's voice was edged with incredulity. "Did you at

any time convey your impression or thoughts to the boy's grandparents that you thought or were impressed that he was under arrest and charged with these homicides? Or was this an impression you kept to yourself, what?"

By this time, Wyssling was sweating heavily. "What I said was when—I said that he should have an attorney if he's being questioned by the police at this point. And I'm trying to recollect—trying to do it as the words went so that I'm not trying to mislead the Court here."

I continued to bang away at the inconsistencies between the transcript and Wyssling's testimony. And I had a surprise for him. Earlier, Wyssling had testified that he had become a "little boisterous" with a desk officer at the Fourth Precinct while demanding to see DeFeo. I asked how much time he had spent in this particular officer's presence.

"How much time I physically spent with him in his presence?" Wyssling asked back.

"Correct."

"Approximately a half an hour, but I could probably tell you— you know, this may sound silly to you—but I could probably tell you some of the posters that were in the precinct better than I could tell you what the people look like."

I pounced. "Mr. Wyssling, do you know that you rode down an elevator with this man today, no more than one foot from him?"

"The patrolman that was in front of me at the time?"

"That's correct," I said.

Weber asked for the officer's name, which I had not yet given. I said it would be placed on the record, but Judge Stark was directing himself to Wyssling. "Just answer the question," the judge said. "Did you have this realization?"

"No, Sir," Wyssling answered.

Minutes later, I was finished. Weber took redirect and elicited the fact that I hadn't told Wyssling I was taping the phone call. Perhaps I hadn't been a perfect gentleman, but we weren't dancing the minuet. The tape had helped expose the truth.

And the truth was not about to set Ronnie DeFeo free. Not if I was correct in my conviction that I had chopped Wyssling's testimony into confetti—shredding it even more than I had hoped. After court, Spota and I celebrated by adjourning to Mike Esposito's, a watering spot in Riverhead, where we each put ten dollars on the bar and started drinking Scotch. We kept drinking for a couple of hours, and we must have been more wound up than either of us realized. When we left, both of us were absolutely sober.

At home that night, I stayed up until 2 A.M. going over my game plan for what was left of the hearing. After Weber rested his case, I would call Tom Muratore and Dave Menzies. Muratore was the officer who had ridden in the elevator with Wyssling. Menzies, now retired, had been the lieutenant in command at the Fourth Precinct when Wyssling showed up looking for DeFeo. And I would finish off the brutality issue by calling John Donahue, the child who had been stirred by the story of "The Prodigal Son." I was over the hump; I anticipated no problems.

At 10:30 A.M., Weber surprised me. "The defendant will take the stand, Your Honor," he said.

Only weeks later, would I understand why Bill Weber called Butch DeFeo. In a suppression hearing, the odds were against a defendant's own testimony making a critical difference in his behalf. And in putting DeFeo on the stand, Weber was giving me a chance to preview him as a witness. What I would realize in retrospect was that Weber may not have had any choice. If DeFeo insisted on testifying and Weber failed to call him, the assigned counsel might be leaving himself open to later charges of ineffective representation. Even more important, perhaps, was the insanity issue. That morning, Weber had announced in court that he had not been able to contact the defense psychiatrist who had examined DeFeo, and therefore could not yet say whether he would rely on a psychiatric defense at the trial. I think Bill was playing his cards tight to his vest—that he was all but counting on a legal insanity case. The defense would produce its own psychiatrist, but DeFeo could turn a jury by selling insanity himself from the witness chair. I think Weber wanted to give Butch a practice run.

At the trial, attention would be a constant companion for Ronald DeFeo, Jr., who was accused of a crime beyond the imagining of many people. His appearance on the stand would be a dramatic climax. But that was not the case at the hearing. The issue at the hearing was not whether Butch DeFeo had committed murder; the issue was whether he had been deprived of his rights by police. That issue revolved around Richard Wyssling, and it was Wyssling whom I considered the major witness. DeFeo was an actor for whom the stage was not yet set.

I don't know how Weber rated DeFeo, but I thought he flopped. DeFeo would not have impressed a jury as crazy. He was too street-wise, and his testimony was too obviously self-serving. Nor did his manner do much for his image. He was brash, preening; he walked into court with a swagger. He smirked at the young women who came into the courtroom; most of them county employees on breaks. Whenever he heard a rustle in the spectator seats behind him, DeFeo would turn halfway around in his chair. The grin and the unbuttoned shirt would be in evidence, and he would stare at one of the new arrivals until she dropped her eyes or turned away.

As I watched DeFeo on the stand, I could visualize him in the South Shore bars, strutting and bragging. All that was changed was his appearance. His hair was trimmed, and he had reduced his beard to a neat mustache. Instead of wearing denims, he was sporting a new outfit, which had been purchased by his aunt—brown shoes, green bellbottom slacks, a yellow-on-white sports shirt and a muted-green houndstooth jacket.

In his direct testimony, DeFeo did not go into the commission of the murders. He described finding the bodies and told about the rest of the evening. He asserted that at both the First and Fourth Precincts, he asked about contacting a lawyer and returning to his relatives. He claimed that when he was taken to homicide, he thought he was going to the home of his paternal grandfather, Rocco DeFeo. According to Butch, Gozaloff and Harrison had agreed to take him there after he signed his original statement.

As he testified, DeFeo let out all the stops. At homicide, the police wouldn't let him eat, drink or go to the bathroom. Harrison told him he had better sign a statement saying he committed this crime or three detectives waiting outside the file room were going to come in and kill him. He refused, and the three detectives entered. One of them was six-foot-four and weighed around two hundred and sixty pounds, and all three punched him in the stomach and jumped on his foot until he fell to the ground.

"Will you continue describing what they did to you?" Weber asked, and DeFeo overdid the fantasy. The three cops began kicking him in the stomach. A few times he turned over, and they kicked him in the back. When he got up, they told him to sit in the chair. They put a phone book on his head and got a blackjack and kept slamming it on top of the phone book. Then they put a paper bag over his head, and banged his head into the filing cabinet or the wall. After all that, the three detectives left the room, and Rafferty and Dunn entered. They expressed concern, but Dunn pushed him into a filing cabinet and Rafferty handcuffed him to a cabinet handle so he couldn't jump out of his chair. When they started poking him with their hands, he was crying and he couldn't take any more, and he said yes to everything they asked. At no time during the morning, he said, was he ever given his rights. George Harrison never read them to him.

I felt that the beating story was patently ridiculous. And I saw openings in the testimony that preceded it. Soon after starting my cross-examination, I caught DeFeo in a statement that caused snickering in the courtroom. I was going over his account of the evening of the 13th, and I asked if Gozaloff had questioned him as to who he thought killed his family.

"I'm not sure," DeFeo answered. "He asked me once or twice, Mr. Sullivan. I'm not exactly sure how many times he asked me in the house there."

"Do you remember what you told him?"

"I don't remember exactly. I started to tell him something, and I didn't. I started the first word of the name, but I did stop."

"You started what?"

"I gave—I said, like, 'Louis—,' like that, and I stopped. I did not give him the name."

I knew I was onto something. "Why?"

"Why? Because I just didn't."

"Why?" I repeated.

"Because I'm not a rat, Mr. Sullivan," answered DeFeo. "But under the circumstances at the time—"

"Wait a minute," I said. I went back over the question, and DeFeo reindicted himself. "I said in the house, you know, I was not a rat. That's why I didn't say the man's last name."

It was too damaging not to spell out. "In fact," I said, "it was Louis Falini that at the time you thought had killed your family?"

"Yes, Sir. It was."

"And you felt that quite firmly, didn't you?"

"Yes, Sir. I believe so."

"As a matter of fact, you still feel that, don't you?"

"No, not any more, Mr. Sullivan."

"And the reason that you didn't tell them the last name is because you didn't want to be a rat on the people who had killed your entire family?"

"At that time. Yes, Sir, Mr. Sullivan."

Just one more nail, I thought. "Is that what you want us to believe?"

"At that time," said DeFeo.

Later, I showed a diagram of his home that police had made with his help. DeFeo said he signed it but made no other marks. "Do you see the word 'BUTCH' written in one of the rooms?" I asked. Yes, he said, and I asked if it was his handwriting.

"No, Sir. It's not," DeFeo answered. "Looks like it, but I know I didn't put my name on here, Mr. Sullivan." Later, he claimed he knew nothing about "objects being taken to Brooklyn." He denied telling police about the storm drain. And he said he told detectives he threw a gun off the dock, but denied having anything to do with a diagram of the location. "I never saw that diagram until in this courtroom," he said.

I dealt with the beating story by breaking it down into details, which is a standard technique. Where was he hit first, in the face or the stomach? He didn't remember. Where did he feel the pain first? He didn't remember. Were all three detectives hitting him in the stomach? He didn't know.

"Was one of them holding you?" I asked.

"No, Sir," DeFeo answered. "Nobody was holding me."

"You were just standing there taking these punches from these three guys, correct?"

"Yes, Sir."

We got to the story about the paper bag being placed over his head, and I asked which side of his head was banged into the wall or cabinet. DeFeo indicated his right temple, but said he wasn't certain. "It was the side. I'm not sure if it was the right, left."

"It could have been your left?"

"Mr. Sullivan," he answered. "I'm not sure."

I felt that I had shown up the beating account for the nonsense it was. When DeFeo left the witness chair, I was satisfied that I could show a jury his macho posturing, his craving for self-importance and his lack of remorse. And in the immediate context of the hearing, I believed that I had impeached his testimony.

211

The defense ended its case with DeFeo, and I called several rebuttal witnesses, including officers Muratore and Menzies, and young John Donahue.

Patrolman Muratore made an extremely convincing witness as he described how Wyssling entered the Fourth Precinct around midnight, asking for Ronald DeFeo. Muratore was not aware of the murder investigation and could not find anyone by that name. The patrolman said Wyssling identified himself as "a friend of the family," and never said a word about being a lawyer. When I asked about their encounter in the court elevator, Muratore told how Wyssling, whom he referred to as "the gentleman who was in the precinct that night," looked directly at him.

We had flown Dave Menzies up from Florida, and the retired lieutenant fit the part in a light-blue leisure suit that complemented his tan. I suspect that he would rather have been in the sunshine than up north in Riverhead. He was less effective than Muratore, and I figured that it would not be worth bringing him back for the trial.

The gist of Menzies's testimony was that shortly before 1 A.M., he spoke to Wyssling, who had returned to the desk. Menzies knew about the homicide investigation and that detectives were talking to DeFeo in a squadroom. Wyssling identified himself as a lawyer, and Menzies asked if he were representing DeFeo. No, Wyssling answered, he was a friend of the family. Menzies said that DeFeo was talking to police at the moment, but Wyssling should contact homicide officers if he wanted to see him later on.

John Donahue was icing on the cake. I had asked him to wear his parochial school uniform, and he looked like an altar boy in his dark blue trousers, white shirt and plaid tie with the school's initials. John's only fear had been that Ronnie DeFeo would know he testified. I had told him that Butch was in custody and that when he took the stand, he should focus on me. Not once did the nine-year-old boy glance in DeFeo's direction. I knew he'd be fine when Judge Stark questioned him about what it meant to take an oath.

It meant to tell the truth, the boy said.

"And do you know what it means when a person swears to tell the truth?" asked the judge.

"Not tell a lie," John answered.

"Why do you think it's wrong to tell a lie?"

"Because you get a sin."

John testified in a loud, strong voice as he described the argument between DeFeo and his father. "Butch said to his father he wanted a new car and he wanted some more money, but then his father said no."

"What happened next?" I asked.

"So then Butch punched him."

"What happened after that?"

"Then his father punched him back."

I asked where the elder DeFeo's punch had landed, and John answered "right around here," and indicated his chin and mouth. Weber cross-examined him, but the youngster held to his account. I watched John Donahue, nine years old and in his school clothes, and my thought was that I couldn't wait to put him in front of a jury.

The hearing ended on September 30th, a Tuesday. It had taken up six court days in which nineteen witnesses were called and seventeen exhibits were offered into evidence. I felt that we had proven what we had to prove. If Judge Stark agreed with our finding of the facts, I thought, he would have to deny the motion to suppress. But any decision in the People's favor would have to be a strong one to avoid reversal by a higher court. Where a confession is concerned, there is no such thing as harmless error.

At 10:15 the next morning, Judge Stark read his decision from the bench. In his own mind, he had brought the issue down to what Mike Brigante, Sr., asked Wyssling to do, and what took place at the police stations. The judge had filled five pages in a red-bound, gold-edged book with handwritten notes on Wyssling's testimony. Now the hazel eyes burned behind the half-glasses, the baritone voice resounded through the courtroom. First, the judge reviewed the motion and cited the factors he considered in assessing credibility—such things as corroboration, the witnesses' bearing and conduct, the witnesses' ability to recall events and conversations, consistencies or inconsistencies and whether the witness had any reason to fabricate testimony or any hostility toward defense or prosecution. Then he listed the witnesses whom he found credible, and named all the police officers who had testified. As to the other witnesses, there were two exclusions—Richard Wyssling and Ronald DeFeo, Jr. When he mentioned them, Stark's decision was obvious.

Spectators didn't have to hear the judge to know what was happening. They could tell by watching the principals sitting in the well of the court beneath the light panels. Bill Weber was poker-faced, alternately looking at me and staring at the judge. Butch DeFeo was stony, his face muscles tight, his hand reaching up and stroking his mustache. Tom Spota and I were grabbing each other's knees; we were that ecstatic.

Judge Stark's ruling was clearly worded. He denied the motion to suppress. There was no violation of the defendant's constitutional rights. At no time was the defendant denied access to an attorney. All oral and written statements made by the defendant on November 13 and November 14, 1974, and the items of tangible property obtained as a result of those statements were legally admissible. They could be used as evidence at the trial.

It was not merely the ruling that had Spota and me elated. It was the way Judge Stark supported his decision. In a determination that contained a concise chronology of the events in question, he found that Wyssling never attempted to see DeFeo as his attorney, and that Butch was never abused by police or threatened with force.

The decision was like Tannhauser to my ears. "As to the hearing testimony of Richard Wyssling," read the judge, "I find that he gave truthful testimony as to his movements on the late evening of November 13, 1974, and the early morning of November 14, 1974. However, I find that his testimony as to the content of the various conversations between him and the defendant's grandfather, police officers at the scene, police officers at the First Precinct and the Fourth Precinct to be not worthy of belief. In particular, his testimony that by midnight on November 13, 1974, he had reason to believe that the defendant was somehow involved in the homicides, and that he had already been charged with six counts of murder, is incredible. No member of the defendant's family nor any police officer had expressed or even intimated such to Mr. Wyssling.

"My overall finding," the judge added, "is that Mr. Wyssling fabricated material portions of his hearing testimony. This witness' hostility towards and bias against the prosecuting authorities of this County was clearly evident."

Judge Stark was equally critical of DeFeo. "As to the hearing testimony of the defendant, Ronald DeFeo, Jr., I find many factors which demonstrate the unworthiness and fabricated nature of this interested witness' testimony. His claim that upon discovery of his parents' bodies he immediately suspected Louis Falini of killing his family but that he did not mention this to the police until seven and a half hours later, during all of which time he claims the police suspected and interrogated him, is incredible. His insistence that he never told the police of the location of an obscure storm drain in Brooklyn is also incredible. In view of the uncontradicted police testimony that they had located the drain solely from the defendant's directions and recovered evidence from the drain linking the defendant to the crimes by 4:30 P.M. on November 14, 1974."

Judge Stark had found DeFeo's testimony, as well as Wyssling's, not worthy of belief. As the judge read the decision, DeFeo remained impassive. Wyssling was contacted by the press, but kept his feelings to himself, saying that it would be improper to comment. Wyssling's own case—involving his actions as a Suffolk personnel director—would be settled in February, 1976, when he would plead guilty to one charge of attempted criminal contempt, a class "A" misdemeanor. On March 29th, he would be sentenced to three years' probation. Neither the plea nor the sentence would affect his right to practice law.

After denying the defense motion, Judge Stark ordered jury selection to begin the following Monday, October 6th. The process of picking a jury would not take place in Stark's courtroom, where the trial would be held, but in a larger room nearby. Meanwhile, our investigation was continuing, and I wanted to set up Zolan's second examination of DeFeo. That Friday, I worked late. The building was empty when I stopped downstairs at night to soak up inspiration. I looked at the silent jury-selection room and noticed a small white card outside the door. The card was slotted below the black sign that announced whether court was in session. "JUDGE THOMAS M. STARK," it said. But the name was scribbled instead of printed.

Hard-nosed professional prosecutors never become nervous. They just get a little frantic. To me, the card stuck out like a drooping toupee. The scribbled name was all wrong. It lacked dignity. It would make a bad impression on the jury we were about to select.

A good trial lawyer attends to details. I went right to work. I removed the offending scribble and returned to my office, where I blocked out letters with a ruler on a white card. I filled in the letters carefully with a magic marker. Then I went downstairs and put the new card in the slot. The result was neat and imposing. Bold and dignified:

M R. J U S T I C E T H O M A S M. S T A R K

I don't know if the anonymous work impressed anyone, but it stayed in place throughout the selection process.

PART FOUR

Trial⸺

17

"JESUS CHRIST, it's the DeFeo case!"

The exclamation broke from one of the one hundred and twenty men and women who filled every seat in the jury-selection room. They had come for jury duty that crisp, bright morning, driving to Riverhead past trees just turning color and farm stands decorated with Indian corn and pumpkins. Some of them had breathed in the morning from still-green lawns bordering development streets that led to highways. Others had caught the scent of sea air skittering across potato fields. Upon arrival at the courthouse, they had been sequestered from the central jury pool at Judge Stark's orders—he wanted them insulated from any gossip about the DeFeo trial. It was their first day of waiting and none of them knew what to expect.

Shortly before noon, they were led to the large courtroom on the third floor, where we were waiting—Tom Spota and I, Judge Stark, Bill Weber. And Ronnie DeFeo, glaring over his plaid shoulder. We stared at them; they glanced at us. They represented suburbia—engineers, housewives, salespersons, teachers, blue-collar workers. Some were retired; others were students. Watching their faces, I saw little beyond passive curiosity and the wakened social instinct of strangers thrown together in a new experience. It was not until the clerk announced the case that the reaction came. The exclamation broke from somewhere in the audience and crested on a rising murmur that was stilled by court officers as Judge Stark ascended the bench. "All rise," the clerk had intoned, "*People* v. *Ronald Joseph DeFeo, Jr.,* the Honorable Thomas M. Stark presiding." It seemed as if every one of the prospective jurors was staring at the back of Butch DeFeo's head.

Judge Stark asked if we were ready. "Your Honor," I said, "People are ready." It was a short opening line. Part of a litany. But I tried to say it with authority. I wanted to impress the prospective jurors with the seriousness of our business.

The judge did it much better as he introduced the trial. "At my direction, ladies and gentlemen," he said, "you have been brought from the central jury part to what is known as the Criminal Term of the New York State Supreme Court. My name is Judge Stark, and I will be presiding over the trial that is about to commence in this court. The trial that is about to commence in this court is a criminal action. The title of this case is *The People of the State of New York* v. *Ronald Joseph DeFeo, Jr., Defendant.*"

Judge Stark had asked his audience to pay careful attention to what he had to say, but the admonition was needless. The prospective jurors were rapt as he continued: "Now, the defendant, Mr. DeFeo, the gentleman seated at the rear table in the plaid jacket, is accused of committing six murders. In particular, the defendant, Mr. DeFeo, is accused of intentionally killing his father, Ronald DeFeo, Sr.; his mother, Louise DeFeo; his sister, Allison DeFeo; his brother, Mark DeFeo; his brother, John DeFeo; and his sister, Dawn DeFeo.

The defendant is accused of killing these six individuals by shooting each of them with a rifle in their respective bedrooms at the DeFeo home located at 112 Ocean Avenue in Amityville in this county between the hours of two and four A.M. on November 13, 1974."

Silence. Several people were shaking their heads, a few others were holding their hands to their mouths. As Judge Stark went on to identify me and Weber, I watched the men and women in the seats. They were acting as if this were the trial of the decade. Maybe it was, I thought. And it was mine. For a moment, the feeling about myself was more important than DeFeo and his conviction. Then it was gone, and I was concentrating on the business in front of me.

The judge was explaining that the trial would last upwards of five to six weeks, which would take it into November. Normally, jury service was two weeks, and Judge Stark would entertain excuses from people for whom the extended period would present financial or personal hardship. It was a measure of the trial's importance that out of one hundred and twenty people—most of whom probably looked forward to jury duty with the same enthusiasm they reserved for root-canal work—only thirty-two asked to be excused. Their reasons covered a cross section of everyday life. They included a housewife going day by day with her eighty-seven-year-old mother, who was near death in a nursing home; a woman scheduled for dental surgery; a food broker who had to run promotions for a popular brand of coffee and a well-known fruit punch; and a CPA who was putting together financial statements for an aerospace company.

After that, those of us left in the room were immersed in what I consider the most flawed facet of our system of trial by jury—the selection process. Even the most competent attorney only scratches the surface when he questions a prospective juror. It is ingenuous to think that anyone is going to reveal his or her inner passions and prejudices in a public courtroom filled with strangers while being interrogated by someone whose very presence forces a psychological defense.

Instead of facing the judge, I followed a habit of several years and sat at the far end of the prosecution table facing the jury box, to which members of the panel were called twelve at a time. This afforded me an overall view of the courtroom and enabled me to study the faces and body language of the prospective jurors as they were being examined by the judge and the defense counsel. Judge Stark apparently understood my reasoning, and made no objection. A less secure judge might have taken offense.

Bill Weber and I did our best to pry into the private lives and beliefs of the men and women in the box. We asked questions about their marriages and education, about any contacts they might have had with police. We asked about their reactions to firearms, and the sight of blood, and violence and death. We asked if any of them had ever been under psychiatric care or had biases against that profession. And we tried very hard to ascertain what each of them knew about the DeFeo case, and how they felt about it. And whatever we turned up, we pursued. We found a hypertension sufferer who believed he would become seriously ill if he had to sit through a trial. We learned that a woman's sister had been confined to a state mental hospital for thirty-five years. We discovered that someone else's mother had suffered a nervous breakdown when the would-be juror was a child. We heard about people's homes being burglarized, their cars ransacked. Or about their children being arrested. One woman who asked to be excused said that her son had been in trouble for gambling. "It's embarrassing for me," she said.

On the second day, Tuesday, Weber and I agreed on five jurors. Two would stand out. Mary Astromovich, a housewife who had five children and seven grandchildren, was the first juror chosen. As such, she automatically became the foreperson. We were fortunate. Mrs. Astromovich was a strong woman

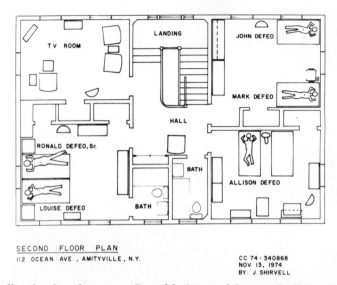

SECOND   FLOOR   PLAN
112 OCEAN AVE., AMITYVILLE, N.Y.

CC 74-340868
NOV. 13, 1974
BY: J. SHIRVELL

The killer fired eight times. Ronald, Sr., and Louise DeFeo each had been shot twice, and the children once. Ronald, Sr., had been hit twice in the lower back—one bullet exploding through the kidney and exiting near his right nipple onto the bed, and the other entering at the base of the spine and burying itself in his neck. Bullets had pierced Louise DeFeo's right flank and chest. One bullet landed on the blood-soaked mattress; the other came out the middle of her chest and reentered her left breast and wrist. The bullets shattered her rib cage, and the splintering bone destroyed most of her right lung, diaphragm and liver. Both Mark and John were shot in the back at close range—examination of the wounds disclosing that the murderer stood between the beds less than two feet away from each boy. The killer remained in the same spot while turning to fire the second time. The bullets penetrated the liver, diaphragm, lungs and heart of each victim and burrowed through the boys' mattresses into the box springs. In John's case, his spinal cord was severed, which may have caused involuntary twitching in the lower part of his body. Allison DeFeo apparently had awakened and turned around in time to stare at the muzzle of the exploding gun less than two feet from her face. The bullet smashed upward from her left cheek through her right ear, lacerating her brain and damaging her skull. The slug tore through the mattress, hit the back wall of the bedroom and bounced to the floor. Dawn's wound was the most terrible to look at. The killer stood about two and a half feet away and fired at the back of her neck, the bullet entering just below the left ear and slamming through the left temple into her pillow. The left side of her face had collapsed, and brain particles mixed with the blood saturating her pillow.

Outside the house, the curious gathered—not just neighbors, but the emotional scavengers who materialize at crime and accident scenes with the mindlessness of slugs in the midst of something rotten. They swayed and surged beyond the police line, alert to rumors, excited by comings and goings and staring ever-avidly at the shrine to the Baby Jesus and the jack-o'-lantern windows and the sign affixed to the lamp post by the front path. The sign, consisting of black letters on a decorative white board, was as much a status symbol as the three Buicks lining the driveway. The sign gave the house a name: HIGH HOPES, it said.

The police came in waves. Through the night, they snapped photographs, took measurements, searched for expended bullets. They walked through the living room and around the baby grand piano and the alabaster fireplace and looked about the dining room where a gold-and-crystal chandelier glittered above artificial roses on a damask tablecloth. They stood on the wide patio that was raised five steps above the ground. They walked along the driveway pocked by fallen brown leaves and past the swimming pool to the boathouse that opened onto the canal.

There were eight shots, but no one in the neighboring homes on Ocean Avenue in Amityville heard them. The best explanation anyone could give for this was that the three-story home muffled sound like a castle.

Ronald DeFeo, Sr., had been turned on to religion a few years before his death by a Canadian priest, with whom he exchanged gifts and letters. His religious rebirth began shortly after a family quarrel in which Butch clicked a rifle at him and the gun failed to go off. The elder DeFeo decided he was similar to Brother André, because both had been saved by miracles.

Ronnie, Sr., and Butch DeFeo. Ronnie, Sr., referred to Butch as the devil, that he had the devil on his back and he had to get rid of him. Later, after he was imprisoned for the murder of his entire family, he wrote his grandfather, "My father the bigest theif and con man had you's all fooled. My father is fulley responsseble for the death's of the family. Its a shame that the kids had to die for them."

John Donahue, a nine-year-old student at St. Martin's Catholic School, told his teacher that he had witnessed a fight between Butch DeFeo and his father. One day, John and Butch's youngest brother, John, played games in John DeFeo's room, then went down to the finished basement, where they played pool and constructed models. They were working on the models when Mr. DeFeo and Butch came downstairs. Mr. DeFeo told the boys to leave, but instead they sat on the steps leading to the first floor and watched what was happening. The two DeFeos started punching each other near the pool table. Mr. DeFeo hit Butch in the face, and blood ran from Butch's mouth.

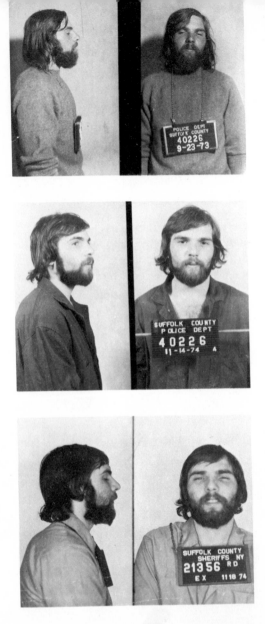

Ronald Joseph DeFeo, Jr., was 5'8", about 175 pounds, hairy-chested and huskily built without looking like someone who had weighed 250 pounds as a teenager. His face was fair-complexioned with long, curving brows, wide-set brown eyes, a broad, straight nose and a spade-shaped beard that connected to a mustache and sideburns. His brown hair was collar-length, worn over his ears and brushed to the right side without a part. His most arresting feature was his eyes. He was adept at direct stares, and he could grin by relying on his eyes and barely moving his lips. (The middle photograph was taken the day after his arrest.)

who would become a matriarchal figure to the other jurors.

The second juror to be sworn in would become focal months later. She was Rosemary Konrad, a twenty-nine-year-old supermarket cashier. Mrs. Konrad was a licensed hairdresser who gave up her profession to care for her three daughters. She worked part-time in the supermarket. During her first day in the selection room, she had watched Butch DeFeo and thought that he seemed expressionless, almost as if he didn't care about anything. That night, she told her husband, Dennis, a postal employee, about the proceedings. "I'll be questioned tomorrow," she said.

"You'll be picked," said Konrad.

During the trial, Mrs. Konrad would have a small surprise. This would occur when the photo of the corner where DeFeo dumped the pillowcase would be shown to the jurors. Mrs. Konrad's husband grew up nearby, and they used to go to the delicatessen in the picture. "That's Joe's Deli," she would say to herself as she stared at the piece of evidence.

By the end of the third day, we had chosen eleven jurors but we had used up the pool. Forty-three more persons had to be called, and it was not until 4:10 P.M. Thursday that the twelfth juror and four alternates were sworn in. Usually, two alternates sufficed, but Judge Stark insisted on four because a long trial increased the risk of jurors having to be excused because of illness or other reasons. About halfway through the trial, juror number three, Marie Burns, would ask to be excused because her two-year-old daughter had been hospitalized with nephrosis. She would be replaced by the first alternate, Amelia Franza, a former teacher whose husband was a high school English department chairman.

The jury consisted of six women and six men, and they ranged across the world that had produced Ronnie DeFeo. Robert Capobianco was a checker for a jobbing outfit, who fished from his own boat and belonged to the Knights of Columbus and the Sons of Italy. Charles Vetter worked the

3:30-to-midnight-shift at Grumman, where he ran an aircraft assembly crew. Jesse Skelton was a production-control expediter for Sperry Gyroscope and played softball in the summer and bowled in the winter. Harry Weaver was a Grumman engineer who sang bass in a barbershop quartet. Joan Rowe was a project coordinator for a company in Farmingdale. She belonged to the PTA and she showed and bred Irish setters and English bulldogs.

Dorothy Grennan had eight children—they ranged in age from eight to twenty-five, and six were still living at home. She didn't have much spare time, but occasionally, she relaxed by going to garage sales and looking for antiques. During the screening, she reported noticing a headline in *Newsday* about the jury selection, but said she didn't read beyond it. "I went on to Ann Landers," she explained. Margaret Giambra, who was a few years younger than Mrs. Konrad and qualified as the jury's junior member, also perked us up during the questioning. She said her husband managed carrier boys for the now-defunct *Long Island Daily Press*. "He has nothing to do with the editorial staff of the paper?" asked Judge Stark.

"He doesn't even read the paper," she answered.

The other jurors, Patsy Capasso and Joseph Cordaro, were interested in guns. Both owned .35-caliber Marlins. Capasso, a retired mechanic who was only twenty-eight months past open-heart surgery, used his rifle for target shooting. Cordaro, a construction inspector for Consolidated Edison, had used his for deer-hunting. Both agreed not to discuss their knowledge of the weapon with their fellow jurors. "I don't know what kind of information I could give other than it's a rifle," Cordaro said.

I watched the jurors glance at each other. They were strangers who would establish a group dynamic. Each weekday over the next several weeks, they would see each other in the jury box, or in a deliberation room located along a corridor in back of the court. It was a narrow room with gray-blue walls, a long, imitation-wood table and a window that faced west. From the window, one could see power-line towers to the south and the county jail straight ahead. The jail was a clean-lined building with brown-and-green panels in its windows. There was a grassy yard around the jail, and a basketball court. Sometimes, despite the season, the jurors would see prisoners playing on the concrete court.

I wanted the jurors to know one another, to be able to work together. I wanted collective thinking, unanimity. I wanted to convince all of them that Ronald DeFeo, Jr., was guilty as charged beyond a reasonable doubt. I had to convince all of them. There could be no dissenters—one person could hang a jury. I looked at the people in the box carefully. Who, I wondered. Who would require extra convincing?

After the jury was completed, Judge Stark explained that a previous commitment made it impossible for him to hold court the next day, Friday, and that Monday was Columbus Day, a legal holiday. The trial would resume on Tuesday, October 14, 1975, when Assistant District Attorney Sullivan and the defendant's attorney, Mr. Weber, would make their opening statements. Nothing either lawyer said would constitute evidence. The basic evidence upon the trial would consist of exhibits and the testimony of sworn witnesses.

18

"One of the first things Mr. Sullivan said was
that this thing would stay with you the rest of
your life, and it does."

Rosemary Konrad,
DeFeo murder-trial juror,
February 4, 1980.

I SPOKE SOFTLY, dispassionately. The facts were chilling; they
carried their own drama. I wanted the facts to impress the jury,
not theatricality. But I was making my opening statement, and
I wanted to set up the facts so that they burned home.

"Ladies and gentlemen of the jury," I said, "each of you will
be changed to some degree by this case. You will leave this
courtroom after rendering a verdict perhaps a month from now,
carrying with you an abiding memory of the horror that
occurred in that house at 112 Ocean Avenue in the dead of
night eleven months ago. Before this case concludes, and your
purpose here is fulfilled, the first anniversary of those horrors
may come and go."

Bill Weber objected, and the judge admonished me to limit my remarks to "a statement of what the people intend to prove." But I could tell from the jurors' faces that I had made an impression. Now I could let the facts of the case speak for themselves. Although there were some questions that would never be answered, I said, the direct and circumstantial evidence showing Ronald DeFeo guilty of six separate crimes of second-degree murder would be "clear, convincing and persuasive beyond a reasonable doubt."

I described this evidence as consisting of physical evidence gathered at the scene, the murder weapon, the articles found in Brooklyn and DeFeo's own statements to police. "You will see," I said, "that DeFeo, through the course of relating successive differing versions of what had happened, eventually revealed his guilt for these murders. These admissions occurred in stages, each stage becoming increasingly more incriminating and closer to the truth."

I wanted the jurors to sense as well as know what Butch DeFeo had done. I wanted to put their imaginations at the scene early in the morning of November 13, 1974. I established Butch's ownership of the Marlin rifle and outlined the events immediately preceding the crime. Then I reconstructed the killings as carefully as I knew how—one by one, murder by murder. I did not forget the barking dog.

"At about 3 A.M., Ronald DeFeo, Jr., went to his bedroom, where the Marlin rifle was kept, as his family slept. There he loaded the rifle to capacity, and, leaving his bedroom, set out to end the life of his father. Evidence will also establish that the DeFeo family owned a large English sheepdog which was ordinarily kept leashed behind the back door leading from the kitchen to the outside portion of the house.

"At 3 A.M. on November 13th, a fifteen-year-old boy who lived two houses away from the DeFeo home—the house in-between being unoccupied—was awakened out of his sleep by the noise of the DeFeo dog howling and barking loudly from somewhere outside the DeFeo house. The noise, he will testify, lasted about fifteen to twenty minutes. There will be clear evidence that this dog was put outside the house by DeFeo and remained there, confined in a shed attached to the house as the defendant spilled the blood of his family. When it was over, the animal was quiet.

"Members of the jury, the People will prove that sometime after 3 A.M. on November 13th, Ronald DeFeo pointed the death weapon at his father's back and fired it. It took Ronald DeFeo, Jr., two shots to kill his father. One of these entered his father's back and passed through his body, destroying his heart. And there is no definitive proof as to where precisely Ronald DeFeo, Sr., was at that point in time when his son fired the first shot into his back. That bullet, you may infer, stopped inside of his body.

"Testimony by the deputy chief medical examiner will show that the trajectories of each bullet which entered his back were different. The difference in the angles of these bullets entering the body, combined with certain other evidence in the case that you will learn about, may cause you to conclude that this defendant first shot his father after he had gotten up from his bed, and thereafter the body of his father was placed back into bed to be found later by police. You will find proof tending to show that the body was pushed or moved along this bed after DeFeo, Sr., was shot.

"Now the proof will further show, members of the jury, that Ronald DeFeo's mother awakened, and as she was just raising herself up from the bed and looking back in the vicinity of the doorway into this bedroom, Ronald DeFeo fired into her body, ending her life. And we will show that he intended her to die. He shot her twice. And death to this woman was almost instantaneous. Here, too, we will offer testimony of experts as to the trajectory of the bullets, the position of Louise DeFeo when she was hit for the first time and when she was hit for the second time, and how these bullets in fact caused her death.

230

"This defendant then quickly ejected the spent cartridges and turned his weapon on his younger sister, Allison, lying in her bed just across the hallway from the room in which his parents had just been murdered. DeFeo stood almost next to her and placed the muzzle of his gun less than two feet from her face. The proof will show that Allison DeFeo had awakened and raised her head toward the door, where her murderer stood at the moment of her death. He fired into her head, and the bullet destroyed the girl's brain before it passed through the opposite ear, through the bedding, bouncing off the wall at the head of the bed, coming to rest on the floor beneath it. Her death, too, was instantaneous. And the position of her body in death, as you will observe, suggests that she died as she was awakening from her sleep.

"Ronald DeFeo then ejected the spent cartridge into a spreading pool of his sister's blood and turned toward the bedroom of his sleeping brothers, Mark and John, just steps away on the same floor. Each boy occupied a bed on opposite sides of the bedroom, and they lay parallel to one another. We will offer evidence that Mark, the eleven-year-old boy, suffered from a football injury to his hip and could only move about with a wheelchair or crutches, and that this same injury limited his ability to move about in his bed. He needed assistance to turn over in his bed, and indeed was most likely to have slept on his back. When this corpse was found by the police he lay on his stomach, his head buried in a pillow. Ronald DeFeo fired almost point blank into both boys' backs from a position standing alongside, somewhat to the rear of their beds. Later, DeFeo described to homicide detectives how he watched as his brother's foot twitched, until it stopped.

"Here again you will find no definitive evidence indicating whether either or both of these boys awakened prior to being murdered by DeFeo—only the inference that may arise upon considering the limitations of Mark's injury and the evidence that these victims, four and five, were also found lying face down in death. We will, however, offer proof indicating that the last victim, Dawn DeFeo, may very well have awakened in her third-floor bedroom as the defendant moved toward the stairs. Testimony concerning the gun will establish that at a point, before going to Dawn's bedroom, Ronald DeFeo reloaded the weapon. In all, eight shots were fired in that house that night, each shot striking a victim. The rifle held seven and required reloading.

"Testimony by homicide detectives concerning statements afterward given by Ronald DeFeo will attempt to show that there were some words spoken between the defendant and his sister, Dawn DeFeo. She, too, lying face down in her bed, was murdered by this defendant when he fired into the base of her neck, and at a range close enough to leave powder burns on the shoulders of her nightgown. The power of the shot caused extensive and immediate destruction of the girl's brain matter, spilling these tissues from her head into the pillow and leaving a marked distortion of the girl's head. The defendant, you will learn, described to the police his impressions as he watched his sister's head react to this gunshot. Death in her case, too, was immediate."

I had told the jurors how and what. I also wanted them to know why. Newspaper reporters in the room made notes as I discussed motive. First, DeFeo's relationship with his family. "There were periodic altercations and episodes of violence between father and son as a result of a variety of problems," I said. "In fact, on November 13, 1974, Ronald DeFeo, as he afterward told police, in a most vile and hatred-filled language, had come to despise his parents, his eldest sister, both of his brothers. And on November 13, 1974, Ronald DeFeo had an affinity for firearms."

Further along, I discussed money: "Members of the jury, there will be evidence offered that there was another separate and distinct reason that motivated DeFeo through these murders—a thirst for money. There will be indications that the defendant stole a large sum of cash from a place where his father had for years hidden money and valuables within his bedroom. You will find that there is some evidence also to support an inference by you, the triers of the facts, that this defendant was actually in the process of looking for that money when his father awoke and interrupted him. We will show you through testimony and photographs where that hidden place was, how police found it based upon what the defendant told them, and that this metal cash box that contained the valuables was found by them to be empty and wiped clean."

I went into the manner in which DeFeo tried to conceal evidence, starting with his retrieving cartridge casings from the victims' bedrooms. "In picking up the spent casing from his sister, Allison's, room," I said, "Ronald DeFeo found that he wet his fingers in his sister's blood and wiped his fingers off on his pants. He described how he removed all of his clothing, how he showered, how he put on clean clothing, and he told police how the garments that might incriminate him he put into a pillowcase, and he even put in the pillowcase the towel that he used to dry himself. And the spent cartridges—of course, eight of them—into the pillowcase also.

"Ronald DeFeo went so far as to throw two unused .35-caliber rounds into the pillowcase," I added. "Anything that he thought could connect him or his rifle to the murders. And in this proof, you will find perhaps the clearest and most convincing evidence that this defendant knew exactly the nature and consequence of his acts in that house that night, and that his acts were wrong."

If the reference to the sanity issue was brief, I did not go into much more detail when I mentioned it near the end of my statement. Only after the defense claimed legal insanity would I call Dr. Zolan as a rebuttal witness. "This," I told the jury, "what I have revealed to you in an opening statement, relates only to the proof that you will hear on the People's direct case. Bear in mind that the evidence establishing and bearing upon how these crimes were carried out is as important to your verdict as the proof bearing upon who carried them out. Much of the evidence of 'How?' will bear upon the issue of whether you will excuse the defendant for his action by reason of some mental disease or defect. And that, as you have no doubt perceived, members of the jury, may at some point in this trial be thrust upon you as a third alternative."

I concluded by asking the jurors to remain objective. "If you will do that," I said, "if you will keep your minds open, carefully evaluate and assess all the proofs, I'm confident that at the end of the case you will come back into this courtroom and find Ronald DeFeo, Jr., guilty of six counts of murder in the second degree."

Weber's opening statement was brief. He started with the principle of presumption of innocence. Because the defendant was presumed innocent, he did not have to testify in his own behalf, nor did he have to produce witnesses or evidence. Then Weber raised the issue he had failed to win at the preliminary hearing. He asserted that the prosecution's evidence "admittedly came as a result of certain alleged oral statements made by Ronald DeFeo approximately twenty to thirty hours after he was held by the police in custody, intentionally deprived from consulting with an attorney, intentionally deprived, in essence, of his constitutional rights."

Witnesses would testify on DeFeo's behalf, said Weber, and the defendant would take the stand. This would constitute the first portion of DeFeo's defense. Legal insanity was obviously the second portion, but Weber was still playing it tight. "There is another aspect of the defense to be produced which I would rather leave for yourselves to hear about in the first instance," he said. "But as I say, among the witnesses we will be producing will be expert witnesses at some stage in this proceeding. And I believe that after you hear all of the witnesses and you hear the cross-examination of each of these witnesses, that you will find as I feel right now that your verdict at the end of the case will be not guilty."

That was it, and Judge Stark asked if I was ready to commence the presentation of proof on behalf of the People of the State of New York.

"We are, Judge."

"Call your first witness," he said.

"The People call Police Officer Kenneth Greguski."

19

AMITYVILLE Village Police Officer Kenneth Greguski was a burly man who had been a cop for more than nine years. But when he took the stand and described what he had found in the DeFeo home eleven months before, his eyes filled with tears. It made him a good witness.

At the start of his testimony, Greguski, the first cop at the murder scene, had trouble recalling whether particular bodies were covered by blankets. To refresh his memory, I produced photographs taken at the house that night. As he looked at the first, Greguski's eyes teared and his voice almost broke. His distress continued as he examined photographs of each of the slain children and told how he phoned village headquarters to report "that I had four deceased persons at this location." And how he hung up the phone when DeFeo mentioned something about sisters and hurried back upstairs to find Allison and Dawn.

"It appeared that she had been shot," Greguski said in recalling his discovery of Allison. "There was blood on the floor; there was blood on the side of her head. She was laying face down. It appeared that it might have been around the area of the neck or just at the top of the back area. It was really hard to tell with all the blood there."

Greguski seemed overwhelmed by the tragedy as he testified. The jurors leaned on every word; the ones closest to him straining their necks to see the photographs. I suspected that everyone in the courtroom was empathizing with the upset cop—everyone except the young man who sat at the defense table, stroking his mustache. The young man whom the officer had tried to comfort as DeFeo sat crying softly in the kitchen of his home eleven months before. "Just prior to my sergeant and lieutenant coming," Greguski testified, "I believe I placed my hand on his shoulder one time and just told him to take it easy."

After a brief cross-examination in which Weber emphasized that DeFeo seemed "a little upset" as he sat in the kitchen, we recessed for lunch. Greguski came to me in the lobby and started to apologize for letting his emotions show. No apology was needed, I told him. The display of feeling had made him an effective witness. And he might have helped the police officers yet to be called. He had reminded the jury that cops were like other people. They were human.

Greguski understood. The scene at 112 Ocean Avenue came back sometimes, he said. When he left the DeFeo home that night, his thoughts had been about his own children.

In the afternoon, I called Detective Jack Shirvell, the former draftsman who had made diagrams at the scene and turned up the carton in which the murder weapon had been kept. Shirvell testified about that discovery, as well as about finding the bullet hole in the living room floor at the home of DeFeo's friend, Steve Hicks. He also described the sheepdog's continual barking and told how DeFeo put the animal in a parked car.

Shirvell's testimony made it possible for me to introduce

twenty-three exhibits that had to affect the jury. These consisted of photographs of the victims as they lay murdered in their rooms, and diagrams of each floor of the house. The photographs showed the carnage in flesh and blood, body by body. The diagrams were accentuated by clear plastic overlays that were clinically chilling—with geometric shapes denoting furniture, and doll-like figures drawn by a police artist depicting bodies. Small dots in each body indicated the bullet holes. As he testified, Shirvell used a pointer on photographic enlargements of the diagrams, which were set up on easels. "The TV room," he said as he described the second floor. "Two chairs, coffee table, another chair, TV. This is another chair with a footrest. Another table. Next, the parents' bedroom, the triple dresser, chest, chair, night table, night table, television set, bathroom is self-explanatory. The bedroom of the two boys. This is the bed of Mark. Wheelchair, crutches, another bed. This is a dresser, another dresser with a hutch on top of it. The bedroom of Allison DeFeo. Two twin-sized beds. A dehumidifier. This was a—I believe it was a trunk with a puzzle on it. A double dresser, and a single dresser."

Details on details. When we left court, Tom Spota and I were satisfied. Our strategy called for dividing our direct case into what happened and how it happened, and, secondly, why the jurors should believe DeFeo committed the crime. I wanted them to view his responsibility sequentially. The confession would come last, as a drawstring that would pull everything together. We had made a good start in impressing what happened upon the jurors. I knew how I had felt six months before when I took the DeFeo file into my office and looked at the crime-scene photographs for the first time. I figured the jurors were experiencing similar feelings.

The day had been interesting for another reason. It was clear from the few objections Weber made to the photos and diagrams that he was not taking a scatter-gun approach to the case. Apparently, he planned to follow the pattern of his opening statement. He would attack the confession and then concentrate on legal insanity. We had demonstrated at the hearing that we could deal with the former, and I felt positive about the latter. Dr. Zolan was holding his second examination the next day; both Spota and I believed that he would find DeFeo legally sane.

Everything changed when Dr. Zolan came to our office after the examination and told us that he didn't know and that he needed more information. Trial resumed a little before 2 P.M., and I went into court thinking that I had never been so intensely involved in a case and, at the same time, so uncertain about where it would go.

Over the following week, we waited for Zolan's diagnosis and pressed forward with the facts of the murders. One of my big guns was Dr. Howard Adelman, Suffolk's deputy chief medical examiner, who had examined the bodies at the scene and then worked into the next day at the morgue, conducting the six autopsies.

Dr. Adelman delivered his testimony in a subdued setting. In later weeks the courtroom would be filled, but now less than half the spectator seats were occupied; most of them by court buffs and students from a high-school law class. I was low-keyed in my questions; Dr. Adelman was matter-of-fact in his answers. And at the defense table, Butch DeFeo wore his stone mask, his eyes cast in their cold stare as the doctor described how Ronald, Sr.'s shorts had ridden up along his thigh with the waistband pulled downward and his left leg flexed as if he had tried to push forward on the bed. Nor did Butch's face change when Dr. Adelman testified that blood spatterings on Louise DeFeo's sheet showed that she had tried to move before she was shot, that she had raised herself up from the mattress and that the axis of her body was turned to the right. Butch's impassivity was noted by *Newsday* columnist Jack Altshul. "He sits mostly with chin cupped in hand," wrote Altshul. ". . . If there is a sign that the grisly nitty-gritty is getting to him, it is only in the movement of his hands." Altshul described Butch folding and unfolding his hands, playing with his mustache, pressing his index finger into his cheek. Butch touched his face when Dr. Adelman talked about Louise DeFeo's last moments.

It was powerful testimony for the jury. The medical examiner described death in terms of wound canals and hemorrhages, and reinforced his statements with photos taken at the morgue, as well as at the house. At 4:15 P.M., Judge Stark asked if I wanted to stop; he intended to dismiss court at 4:30. We had just gotten to Allison DeFeo, and I said I could cover her death in the remaining fifteen minutes. I had planned to close that way—I wanted the jurors to go home with the picture of what Butch had done to his thirteen-year-old sister searing their minds.

Quickly, we got to the wound. Dr. Adelman testified that the bullet had ripped through Allison's left cheek and out her right ear. And he described the stippling, or powder burns, left by the shot: "There was a prominent amount of stippling noted in the area. Virtually the entire side of the face revealed the small dotted areas of stippling caused by the burst of flame from the weapon."

"Do you recall now what features of the face were affected by the stippling?" I asked.

"The entire cheek and I believe the eyes."

I spelled out my point by asking if the features affected by the stippling would have been exposed to the muzzle of the gun. Dr. Adelman said they would have, and I asked about the position of the girl's face and head. He said her head would have been raised and probably turned to the left.

"And what portion of the room was immediately to her left?" I asked.

"The doorway."

There was only one conclusion. The child was staring into the rifle muzzle when Butch pulled the trigger. I wondered if any of the jurors took home the question that haunted me. Had Allison been awakened by the sound of gunfire in her parents' bedroom across the hall? If so, the girl had lain frozen in bed with fear as the footsteps sounded in the hallway. And then she saw the gun and her brother's face.

The mood continued the next day when Dr. Adelman returned to the stand, and we went on to Dawn DeFeo. "The entire head region was distorted," the medical examiner testified. "The front—the exit wound—the wound of exit was noted on the left temple area. There were considerable fractures in the area, and the whole portion of the left side of her face was concave, had collapsed under the explosive effect of the wound."

I wanted the terrible nature of the wound to envelop the jury box. "Can you tell us, Doctor, in what fashion a gunshot wound to the head will contort or distort the skull or the head area?"

"The skull is a very confined space," Dr. Adelman answered. "Unlike the other cavities of the body, which are bounded by soft and elastic, relatively elastic tissues, such as skin, the skull is a nonexpansile space. The confines are bony and very rigid. Consequently, any increase of pressure is communicated on all sides, and the pressure can increase very rapidly. When a gunshot—when a bullet is fired from very close range into a skull, the gases have a tendency to explode within the confines of this closed space, closed inelastic space, and cause a secondary explosion inside the head. This would tend to fragment the bones and push them outward in the direction of the blast."

When we moved to the boys' deaths, Dr. Adelman testified that John DeFeo's spinal cord was severed, which could have resulted in jerking or twitching of the lower portions of the body. But he said that such involuntary movements would only have lasted "a few moments." This would become important when the confession was introduced, and there was mention of

DeFeo seeing John's foot move. The only way Butch would have seen the twitching was if he had been present when the boy was killed.

During Adelman's testimony, a diagram of the wound canals in Ronald DeFeo, Sr.'s body was introduced. The diagram showed a ten-to-twenty-degree difference in the angles of entry. This variance, plus the fact that Ronald, Sr., could have remained alive for as long as ten minutes after the first shot, had prompted my conjecture that he might have been up when he was hit and then replaced in bed. On cross, Bill Weber shredded my theory with a single question. "Doctor," he asked, "in your examination of Ronald DeFeo, Sr., did you find a disparity in the angle of entry of the two bullets?"

"There was—they were virtually parallel," the medical examiner answered. "There was only a slight deviation between the two."

My feeling was that Dr. Adelman might not have answered as precisely as he intended—the problem being the degree of deviation. But I couldn't be certain, and I figured not to take any chances on redirect. I didn't ask.

I should have been as wise when Weber scored again. He asked if Dr. Adelman had told reporters on November 14 that he was "mystified as to how a single gunman could have killed all six victims."

"At that time, yes," the medical examiner answered.

On redirect, I took a shot in the near-dark, and missed. "Is your opinion any different now than it was at the time you said that?" I asked.

"No," said Dr. Adelman. This time, I let it go.

Before the day ended, I had introduced another expert to the jury—Detective Sergeant Alfred Della Penna, chief of the Suffolk Police Department's firearms identification section. Jurors liked to play amateur detective, and Della Penna was their meat; a sleuth who made scientific deductions on the basis of physical evidence. He was an ex-Marine completing a

Master of Science degree, and he was understated but authoritative in the witness chair. All that, and Della Penna was so
dapper that it was a running gag to ask him whether he
loosened his tie when he cut the lawn. As usual, he was
wearing a three-piece suit set off by a pocket handkerchief, but
I suggested that he change his tiepin, which was a gold replica
of a Thompson submachine gun.

During Della Penna's testimony, fifty-seven exhibits were
introduced, including the death bullets. (I would call him later
in the trial with the murder weapon when a proper foundation
had been laid as to its recovery.) The ballistics sergeant
described his retrieval of the spent bullets—telling, for instance,
how he opened Mark's and John's box springs with a scalpel.
His expertise was evident when I asked what produced his
preliminary determination that they were fired from a .35-
caliber rifle, probably a Marlin.

"The type of rifling that was left on the bullets," Della Penna
explained. "The rifling being the channels or grooves which are
transposed from the inside of the barrel to the bullet. These
channels and grooves are placed inside the barrel to give it
trajectory and flight and stability. And as the bullet passes
through the barrel, they are transposed onto the bullet."

In describing other material he brought to the police lab,
Della Penna told of finding hairs inside the garbage shed at the
back of the DeFeo house—where, I had told the jury, Ronnie
had tied the sheepdog during the murders. "On the inside of
the shed," added the sergeant, "there were two swinging-type
doors that led into the shed, and these doors appeared to have
been damaged or scratched similar to the type of scratches that
are produced by an animal."

I asked if he could tell how fresh the marks were. "They
appeared to have been fresh, as did the hair in that particular
shed," Della Penna answered.

By now, we had a mass of physical evidence. Each day, this
evidence was piled on the narrow rail separating the judge's

bench from the well of the court. Occasionally, something fell off the rail and had to be put back. The night after Della Penna finished testifying, Anna Johnson, the maintenance supervisor, found a blood-stained bullet in a little white box on the floor. Anna, a small, stocky woman, was a court buff who came to work before her night shift to watch trials. Not only had she been sticking with the DeFeo case, but she had insisted on cleaning the courtroom herself. And she didn't fool around with the bullet. She safeguarded it in her bosom—keeping it there until court convened the next day.

"Mr. Sullivan," Anna called in a whisper as soon as she spotted me in the lobby. She told me what had happened, and pressed the box into my hand so no one else could see. I walked over to John Roberts, the chief clerk. "Are you missing something?" I asked.

"No," he said.

"Really," I said, raising an eyebrow. "Have you checked the evidence lately?"

The clerk knew a canary-eating cat when he saw one. "How did you know?" he asked, and I returned the missing evidence. He told me he'd discovered the loss when he put out the exhibits that morning.

At this juncture in the trial, I had a small adventure. Our investigation was continuing; I had more than court to keep me busy. I was preparing witnesses, and we were working on the Brooklyn inquiry. One of the loose ends in which I was interested was the mysterious Louis Falini, who had been eliminated as a suspect soon after the crime. I didn't question Falini's innocence; the allegation against him had been another of Butch DeFeo's outright lies. But Falini had been close to Ronald DeFeo, Sr., and I figured he might have something we could use. I sent Al Rosenthal to see him, but the detective didn't get anywhere. At least I didn't think he had until I got an unexpected phone call in my Riverhead office. It was Louis Falini. He was willing to meet me, but there were conditions. I had to come alone, no one was to know of our meeting and it would have to be held in a public place. He did not want our conversation recorded. I could pick the rendezvous, preferably a restaurant. "I want to buy you dinner," Falini said.

I was a lawyer, not an undercover cop, and I wasn't exactly knocking down fences for a clandestine meeting with a character who had been described as a retired hit-man. But I had no choice; the guy could be a hell of a witness. I set up a meeting at the Red Coach Grill in Hauppauge—the same place at which we would meet Burt Borkan and the Brooklyn district attorney's men soon afterwards. But I took precautions. I called Joe Conlon, the biggest, toughest detective-investigator on the district attorney's staff, and told him to settle his two hundred and eighty pounds at the bar before I arrived. I didn't carry a weapon (I didn't even have a pistol license), but Conlon would be armed. And in spite of Falini's conditions, I went wired. I carried a small tape recorder in my coat pocket.

When I walked in, Conlon was well established. I took a seat and waited. I kept watching the door, looking for a tough guy. An hour went by, and there was no Falini. About all that happened was that a chubby little man with thick glasses and a cane periodically came out of the dining room, looked around and spoke to the maitre d'. The man looked like somebody's uncle in a conservative suit and bow tie. On his third appearance, I wondered if he could be Falini and decided that he couldn't. Not this round little man. But when he made a fourth appearance, his voice carried. He was asking if anyone was looking for him.

I got up. "Louis?"

"Yeah, Jerry," the little man answered. "How are you?"

Louis Falini had something in common with George Glaubman and Anna Johnson. He was a court buff. He had been following the trial, and he wanted to advise me on questioning witnesses. Apparently, he took it for granted that we had the right man. If I followed his advice, a conviction was in the bag.

245

For an hour, I nodded and said yes. Then we got around to the DeFeos.

I didn't get much. If he knew any secrets, Louis Falini was not about to give them away to a nice Irish prosecutor from Suffolk County. Falini said he had been close to the DeFeos, but the relationship had eroded in later years. He felt terrible about the tragedy. Ronnie, Sr., had been a wonderful father who loved his family, and Falini had never heard of him being involved in anything illegal. As to why Butch had tried to put the blame on him, Falini couldn't imagine. But he knew the kid was trouble. Ronnie, Sr., had referred to Butch as the devil. "I have the devil on my back," Ronnie, Sr., would say.

We spent a couple of hours together. "You're not recording this?" Falini asked. I assured him that I wasn't, and the recorder in my pocket began to weigh several tons. Then he got up to go to the bathroom, and I pushed the thing under my arm in case he tried to pat me down. I also assured him that he wouldn't have to testify. But I knew that I would have to call him if he had something important to say.

I'm glad he didn't.

20

BY THE END OF OCTOBER, I had become a ghost in my own home. More often than not, my wife and children were still in bed when I turned on Clementine's tape deck and left for work. During dinner, when my daughters were brimming with the day's events, I was likely to be preoccupied, and I hurried upstairs to my desk after dessert. At midnight, Betty would come into the study to say good night, and in the morning, she would ask me when I'd gone to bed. Betty was keeping busy with the new house—doing many of the chores I should have been attending to. She was also collecting clippings on the DeFeo trial.

At this point, the clippings all concerned my direct case. Detail by detail, witness by witness, I was building the circumstantial picture of what happened at 112 Ocean Avenue, Amityville, on the morning of November 13, 1974. Along with the police experts, my early witnesses included two civilians—

Deborah Cosentino, the barmaid who drove past the lit-up house on her way home from work, and John Nemeth, the teen-ager who lived two doors to the north and was awakened a few minutes after 3 A.M. by the barking dog.

I had referred to Nemeth in my opening statement, and I let him give his story to the jury firsthand. He told about walking to the window and almost calling the police, and then changing his mind. And about the dog howling for fifteen minutes and stopping, and then starting again.

"Were you able to identify the dog that you heard howling?" I asked.

"Yeah," Nemeth replied. "It was the DeFeo dog."

I double-checked for the jury's benefit. "Was there any other dog in the neighborhood that had a bark like the DeFeo dog?"

"No," said the teen-ager. He testified that the barking sounded as if it were coming from the north side of the DeFeo home, where the garbage shed was situated.

After Nemeth, I brought in the detectives who had taken part in the original investigation. Randazzo, Gozaloff, Napolitano, Harrison, Rafferty and Dunn enlarged the jury's picture of the murder scene and reported the sequence of events that led to DeFeo's confession. All six officers were effective; Randazzo was a different witness than he had been at the suppression hearing. He withstood a tough cross-examination, and on redirect, I made sure there was no equivocation about Wys-sling:

"Did Mr. Wyssling ever tell you that he was the lawyer who represented Ronald DeFeo, Jr.?"

"No, Sir."

"Did he tell you he was there that night in the capacity of a lawyer?"

"No, Sir."

Randazzo said that Wyssling never gave him a business card, never said where he practiced. He was there as a friend of the family. "He wanted to know what was happening, and where was Ronnie?"

Gozaloff, Napolitano and Harrison advanced the investigation from the murder scene to the police stations. All three emphasized that DeFeo was never threatened or abused. They described their conversations with DeFeo, and his accusation of Falini. They told about finding the metal box beneath the saddle of the master bedroom closet. They described the mark in Butch's arm and his account of shooting heroin at Junie Reimer's house before he reported the murders. They traced the rest of his actions that day, including his appearance at work, his visits with Sherry Klein and Bobby Kelske and the afternoon spent drinking vodka-and-7-Ups at Henry's.

I made sure the detectives provided the jury with hard looks at DeFeo's character. Gozaloff told about DeFeo's admissions that he had set his father's boat on fire for insurance money and looted the house next door. According to Gozaloff, Butch saw an advertisement for an antique sale at the empty house, and he and Kelske raided it the night before the sale. Later, detectives knocked on the DeFeo door and asked Butch if he had seen anybody near the burglarized house. He said no.

Gozaloff packed a lot into his answer when I asked about DeFeo's attitude toward the family sheepdog. "He told me that they had a dog in the house, that it was a sheepdog, that they kept it tied up inside the kitchen door. And he told me that several weeks prior to that, that the dog had bit him. And he said that he had been bringing his girlfriend, Sherry Klein, in the side door; that he was going down the cellar to get laid, and that he was sneaking in; that the dog jumped him and bit him."

George Harrison covered much of the same ground. His most dramatic testimony focused on the moment when DeFeo was awakened and accused. Harrison went through his reading of DeFeo's rights, and told how the suspect suddenly lashed out at his family—reviling his mother's cooking as "shit," and calling his brothers "fucking pigs." After Harrison finished, it was time to call Rafferty and Dunn and unveil the confession.

For two sessions, Dennis Rafferty held the jury spellbound as he relived the long morning that turned into late afternoon in the small room at homicide. I asked, Rafferty answered and the testimony took on its own rhythm as Dennis moved through DeFeo's lies and distortions to get at the truth, to know, as much as any outsider could, what happened in that house where jack-o-lantern windows grinned above St. Joseph and the Christ child, and a barmaid drove by on a darkened street. Almost as if he were back in the file room, Rafferty recounted the back and forth between him and the murder suspect, and DeFeo's stories tumbled after one another like scribbage cubes. The break came when Butch said he heard two shots and hid in his room. Then he said he heard several shots and checked his parents. Next, he admitted he checked the children. He saw the rifle in Dawn's room and knew he had to get rid of everything and filled the pillowcase and drove to Brooklyn.

That was incredible, Rafferty told him. Butch had to have seen or heard something more. At which point, DeFeo invented the Falini story. Louis Falini and another man committed the murders. The pace of Rafferty's testimony quickened as he described what came next. "I said, 'Tell me what this unknown guy looks like. What does he look like?' He said, 'I don't know.' I said, 'Well, is he six foot tall?' He said, 'I don't know.' 'Is he five-five?' 'I don't know.' 'Is he five foot?' 'I don't know.' 'What color hair does he have?' 'I don't know.' 'Blond, brown, black?' 'I don't know.' 'What color eyes? Blue, green, brown?' 'I don't know.' He didn't know. The man was completely nondescriptive.

"I had said to him, 'This must have been a terrible thing for you to see.' He said, 'Yeah. That Falini loved it. He loved it . . .' He said the gun was smoking and the barrel was hot. And I wondered why he thought the barrel was hot."

Weber objected, and Judge Stark cautioned Rafferty not to include his thoughts in his testimony. But the jurors heard.

"He said the barrel was hot on the gun," Rafferty continued. The jurors were leaning forward, and the next few sentences would stick in the mind of at least one of them, Rosemary Konrad, the supermarket clerk who had known the night before her selection that she would be picked. "He said to me, 'You asked me before about the dog.' And I quote him. He said, 'The fucking dog was screaming while this was going on.' He said, 'The dog was screaming.'"

DeFeo changed his story again after Dunn said the others must have made him a part of the crime to prevent his testifying against them. Butch cried, and admitted shooting his father and Mark.

How could that have happened, Rafferty asked him. It didn't make sense that the murderers would have him shoot the first victim and then, the fourth or fifth after they had killed the others.

"'Butch, tell me what happened,'" Rafferty recalled asking. The courtroom had been still. It seemed even quieter as he repeated the terrible answer.

"'It all started so fast. Once I started, I just couldn't stop. It went so fast.'"

There was not much Weber could do with Rafferty on cross-examination. He pushed and bullied, but Dennis never budged. Soon into the examination, Weber tried to make it seem that Rafferty had not gone to the office on his own that day, but had been summoned to homicide to question Butch.

"So you were called down to interview Ronald DeFeo?"

"No, Sir. That's incorrect."

"Did Lieutenant Richmond tell you any other thing except interview DeFeo?"

"He briefly apprised me of the case."

"Did he tell you to do anything other than interview DeFeo?"

"No, Sir."

"So, you were called in by Detective Lieutenant Richmond to interview DeFeo?"

"No, Sir. That's incorrect."

Minutes later, Judge Stark was admonishing Weber for trying to put answers in Rafferty's mouth. Weber bristled, and Judge Stark sat on him.

"Counselor, will you not argue with me, Sir?"

Most lawyers would have been squelched, but Bill Weber wasn't backing down from anyone, including His Honor. "I don't want to be accused of putting answers in his mouth," Bill said.

What happened next was almost historic. "All right," said Judge Stark, "I take back my accusation." Then he told the witness to continue.

"I apologize to the court," said Weber, and I was almost sorry he did. I was that impressed by his tenacity.

Later, Weber tried to foreshadow the insanity defense. He referred to DeFeo's comment that Falini "loved it." "Was he talking as a rational person in your opinion?" asked the defense lawyer.

"A rational person that had committed murder. Yes, Sir."

"Did you believe he was under an emotional stress at that time?" Weber asked.

"He appeared to me just like every other murder suspect we have had in there," Rafferty replied. "Just about the same type thing. Many of them cry. He cried. They are quiet. He was speaking quietly. He appeared to me to be a very normal murder defendant."

Bobby Dunn reinforced Rafferty. When he told about walking out on the interrogation, I asked where he had gone. "There were a number of desks in the outer room," he said. "I think I sat down in a chair for a couple of minutes. I didn't speak to anyone. I probably remained there five or ten minutes. I went to my office. There was no one there. I sat there for a while, and I went home."

With the confession on record, I tied up loose ends relating to the murder weapon and the other evidence. My first witness in

252

this effort was Patrolman Melvin Berger, the Nassau diver who found the Marlin thirty feet off the dock at the end of Ocean Avenue. I thought his testimony would be perfunctory; it came close to being disastrous.

I had myself to blame. And the bureaucrats in the Nassau Police Department didn't help either. Apparently, a mass-murder case wasn't an important enough reason to pay Berger overtime to come in for pretrial preparation. We never got together. I spent fifteen minutes with him before I put him on the stand, and I thought it would be enough. It wasn't.

The source of confusion was that Butch DeFeo had made two diagrams showing where he dumped the rifle. He drew the first for Rafferty and Dunn, and it was right on target. Later on, however, in an apparent attempt to mislead detectives, DeFeo made a second diagram, changing the location to the canal behind his home. This was the spot at which divers first searched for the weapon. Berger had seen the second map, but he had never seen the correct one. What I didn't know was that he had never been clear on why the search location had been changed.

We went back and forth with Berger on the subject of diagrams. By his last go-around, Weber was trying to cast doubt on the authenticity of all diagrams attributed to DeFeo. "Again, I ask you, Officer, on that day did you see any other diagram other than the diagram you have in front of you, People's Exhibit 91 for identification only?" (The inaccurate sketch.)

"There were other diagrams drawn, but I didn't see them," said Berger.

"Thank you," said Weber.

But Berger was still remembering, and he had an after-thought. "They were drawing them," he said, "but I didn't look at them."

What I wanted most was for the courtroom floor to open up and swallow me. Weber caught it just as quickly. "What did you say?" he asked.

"I said they were drawing them, but I didn't look at them."

Weber made the hole a little larger. "They were drawing them at the scene?"

"They were drawing them on the Suffolk County marine boat."

"You specifically recall that?"

"I think they did," Berger said. "It seemed to me that's what they were doing. Yes."

"Thank you very much, Patrolman," Weber said. This time, Berger had nothing to add. For the moment, neither did I.

"I have no further questions," I said.

It was 4:27 P.M., and we recessed for the day. I tried to avoid Bill Weber's grin as I hurried out of the courtroom and fled to my office. A few sentences from a routine witness and we were in trouble. Our credibility was on the line. The jurors had good reason to think that detectives had been making diagrams as they went along, and that they were lying about DeFeo having drawn the ones attributed to him. From there, it was a quick step to deciding that if the cops were capable of producing phony diagrams, why believe anything else they said? And it was my fault. I knew the diagrams were genuine, but I was equally sure Berger had been telling the truth, that he had, in fact, been extra-conscientious about it. There was an answer, and I hadn't even spent enough time with him to know there was a question.

Tom Spota and I made some quick phone calls and found the explanation. The diagrams being made on the police boat were grid maps, which chartered each area as it was searched so that divers wouldn't explore the same territory more than once. We needed somebody to certify the authenticity of DeFeo's diagrams in open court, and the higher up he was, the better. Our choice was James Caples, deputy chief of the organized crime bureau—a bright, square-jawed cop who had taken personal charge of the command post at the crime scene and had been on top of all the searches.

254

Caples was in my office at 7:30 the next morning, and we spent two hours going over his testimony. Jim commanded one hundred detectives, and I think every one of them respected him. It seemed to me that the jury felt the same way when he began to testify. Caples stated that he was holding a photostat of the correct diagram, People's Exhibit 86, when Berger broke the surface with the rifle over his head, and that the diagram was dated and initialed by Ronnie DeFeo.

"On that morning at the time that you observed the police officer in the water with the rifle," I asked, "did you have occasion to compare his location with anything shown on People's Exhibit 86 in evidence?"

"Yes, Sir."

"All right. And what was the result of the comparison?"

"The result of the comparison," answered Caples, "was that it was the exact location—approximate location—where the weapon was found, and it was described in People's Exhibit 86."

The deputy chief's testimony more than rectified the damage. He came through cross-examination like a pro. So why did I see beads of sweat on his forehead when he left the stand? He told me later that he hadn't testified in more than five years, and he had stayed awake the night before, worrying about whether he still knew how. And I think it mattered to James Caples that he was testifying about his own village—he had lived in Amityville for many years. People in the community knew Caples; he was an usher at St. Martin of Tours, where the DeFeo family had been mentioned in masses for a great many Sundays. For months after the murders, fellow parishioners would ask him about the case, and he would shrug them off with innocuous answers. When people in the village heard about the insanity defense, many of them became concerned. They told Jimmy Caples they were afraid that Ronnie DeFeo would beat the murder charge by pleading insanity.

After Caples testified, I brought back Gozaloff and Della

Penna. Gozaloff described going over a Hagstrom *Atlas* with DeFeo and following the latter's instructions to the storm drain, where he found the rifle scabbard, cartridge casings, ammunition and clothing. It was after Gozaloff returned to homicide and DeFeo initialed the recovered items, that the accused killer asked if he could collect the insurance on his slain family. "I told him I didn't know, that I didn't think so," Gozaloff testified, "but that if he was crazy, that he might be able to collect it. And at that time, he changed his expression, so I said, 'Well, not responsible for your actions.'"

The murder weapon dominated Della Penna's return to the witness chair. With the expertise of a concert pianist demonstrating a Steinway, he explained the Marlin's operation. At first, he pointed to the various parts. When we got to the way in which the spent cartridge casing was ejected, the ballistics expert asked if he could show the jury. "It may be more graphic," he said.

"Make sure it's safe first," I told him. We both knew what we were doing; this phase of Della Penna's testimony was about as theatrical as the prosecution would get. The jurors sat up a little straighter as Della Penna demonstrated how the cartridge was kicked to the right and behind the shooter.

Della Penna said that he washed the rifle with tap water and kerosene, tested it and found it operative. He used a microscope with a dual eyepiece to examine test-fired bullets with those found in the house, as well as with the bullet unearthed in the crawl space at Steve Hicks's home. In all cases, the striations on the bullets matched up. To show how well, we produced photographic blow-ups of the comparisons.

The ballistics expert explained that even expended casings have identifying marks, some of which come from the breech—the flat section at the rear of the rifle, which the casing is forced against as the bullet moves forward.

"Could you see that area?" I asked.

"I could point out the breech face section of the rifle, yes,"

Della Penna answered, and he was grand. "In order to do it, I have to aim the rifle in the direction of the jury. I prefer not to."

"Is it easier to do this down in front of the jury?" asked Judge Stark.

"Possibly, Your Honor," Della Penna answered, and he received permission to step down. The jurors stared at the rifle that had taken six lives.

On cross-examination, Weber repeated my question about how the used cartridges were expended. To the right and the rear, Della Penna answered. In the next minute, at Judge Stark's request, he loaded the magazine. The sound of small metal parts working against one another was audible through the courtroom.

There was no way to discredit Della Penna's testimony, but Weber made a deft move in another direction by asking about the noise the Marlin made when the ballistics sergeant test-fired it. He was getting at one of the questions that would never be explained—the fact that no one had reported hearing the death shots.

"Loud," Della Penna replied. "I don't know what else to say."

"Loud?"

"It's a very loud report. It's a thirty-five-caliber. It has a loud report to it."

Weber had no more questions. Neither did I. Instead, I followed Della Penna with Lt. Vincent Sullivan, director of the police laboratory, and Detective Nicholas Severino, a serologist. Sullivan educated the jury in one of his specialties, high-speed blood spatterings, which he described as "the study of the trajectory and resultant stains caused by blood traveling at varying speeds through space and hitting various types of objects at different angles." He said photographs of the spatterings on Louise DeFeo's sheet showed that her body had been raised three to six inches off the mattress at an angle of less than forty-five degrees. Severino reported on the bloodstains

257

found on the right leg of the trousers recovered from the Brooklyn storm drain, and inside the sleeve of the denim jacket DeFeo was wearing the day after the murders. Both stains were type "A," which was the blood type of all the DeFeos except Louise, who had type "O." Butch had told police he picked up a cartridge from a pool of Allison's blood and wiped his hand on his right trouser leg. Although we had no such direct link to the jacket stain, there was a possibility that he might have worn the garment during the crime.

Severino added another detail to my circumstantial case against DeFeo. The serologist's duties included the examination of hair samples, fibers and fingernail scrapings. He had put the hair samples from the sheepdog and the shed under a microscope. They came from the same dog.

I called one other witness as part of my direct case, but my purpose was outside the effort to pin DeFeo to the what and how of the crime. I was playing chess; setting up a defense against an expected ploy. The witness was Butch DeFeo's aunt, Phyllis Procita.

I knew that Mrs. Procita would not turn against her nephew. More than any other member of the family, she had expressed sympathy for him—making the trip to Riverhead at least once a month and looking at him through a window while they talked by telephone. I also knew that she would tell the truth. And that was all I wanted. I was looking ahead to the psychiatric phase of the trial when both Dr. Zolan and Dr. Schwartz, the defense's expert, would describe DeFeo's latest and wildest account of the crime—that Dawn and someone else were involved, that his sister stood over him with black hands, that he was an agent of God. When he took the stand, Butch would probably go through the same harangue himself.

But he had not gone through it with his aunt. Phyllis Procita had visited Butch nine times at the jail, and he had given her several different versions of what happened. But he never told Mrs. Procita what he told the psychiatrists. Her testimony could be important in impeaching his credibility. The jurors might be suspicious about the intentions of police witnesses, but they had to believe DeFeo's own aunt. Especially if they watched DeFeo during her testimony. He glared at her more than at any other witness, and I wondered if he felt that somehow she was betraying him.

Mrs. Procita was forthright as I questioned her about the jail visits. On January 30th, Butch discussed the crime. He said he hid in the crawl space in his room when he was awakened by gunshots, and stayed there until the killers left. "After they left," the aunt testified, "he went and he looked around and it was a mess. He said his sisters were hit bad. He said to me it was just awful; he was scared. And he asked me if I ever heard the sound of screaming children." Mrs. Procita said Butch didn't answer when she asked him why he hadn't brought Dawn into his hiding place from her nearby room. When she asked why he didn't telephone for help, he said the phones were dead.

On February 24th, Butch told another story. In this one, a friend of his came to the house late at night, and they went to the TV room. His friend got high, apparently on drugs, and fell asleep. Butch couldn't rouse him. He had to leave, and he told Dawn to wake his friend in the morning. When he came home, he discovered the murders. "And when I would question him— that didn't make sense, like—he wouldn't answer," said Mrs. Procita.

A month later, DeFeo tried the Falini story on his aunt. "He said that Falini did it, that Falini wanted to kill his father, and I said, 'Why should Falini want to kill your father?' And he told me that I didn't know what was going on in that house. He said my brother was no angel; he talked to people in organized crime; his mother had a boyfriend. I said, 'Why wouldn't Falini just kill your father on his way to work? He could do that.' And he said that he always went to work with his father."

There were additional stories over later visits, testified Mrs.

Procita. He named a buddy as the killer and told his aunt not to trust this person and to keep her children out of Amityville. He blamed an older man, whom he described as "a real tough guy." And he tried to bring in Dawn: "I asked him another time if he would cover up for somebody and take the rap himself, and he said, 'Why not?' And he says, 'What makes you think I'm not covering for someone in the family?' His sister, Dawn. And I thought that was just ridiculous. And I thought—I said, 'I don't know why Dawn didn't just fight for her life. She was big enough to give anybody a good beating. . . .'"

Throughout these conversations, said Mrs. Procita, her nephew maintained his innocence. "He would say to me that he was no angel and he was involved in different things, but he said he never killed his family."

Or, at least, I thought, Butch could never look his aunt in the face and tell her he committed the slaughter. My last question was whether there was anything else she could remember of the conversations. "I asked him many times if he did it," she answered, "and he said that I would never hear him say he did it."

Weber's cross-examination of Mrs. Procita showed that the DeFeos tried to keep Butch's troubles to themselves. "I suspected he had a drug problem," the aunt testified.

"Well, are you telling us that his family never really talked about it?" asked Weber.

"Right."

The defense lawyer reached for Ronald DeFeo, Sr.'s religious revival. He referred to previous testimony that the elder DeFeo had been turned on to religion a few years before his death by a Canadian priest, with whom he exchanged gifts and letters. According to Mrs. Procita, this occurred when her brother went on vacation in Canada and visited a place called St. Joseph's Oratory. On his return home, Ronald, Sr., read the life of the oratory's founder, Brother André, and was sufficiently inspired to send his first contribution.

"And was there an event in Brother André's life where he was saved by a miracle?" Weber asked. I couldn't see the connection, and Judge Stark called us to the bench. Out of earshot of the jury, Weber said that Ronald, Sr.'s religious rebirth began shortly after the family quarrel in which Butch clicked a rifle at him and the gun failed to go off. According to Weber, the elder DeFeo decided he was similar to Brother André, because both had been saved by miracles. When Judge Stark asked how this related to the case, Weber said he would produce evidence of insanity in his client, and then show "that the ancestors were—his father also had acts of insanity. And we are going to show this man believed he had ESP."

"Wait a minute," asked the judge. "What man?"

"The father—Senior," Weber explained. I couldn't believe what I was hearing. Six murders, and now miracles and ESP. The next thing I knew, somebody would try to drag in demons. But I was relieved when Weber agreed to question Mrs. Procita about her brother's religious fervor at a later time. I preferred to wait until we got to the psychiatric testimony before exposing the jury to arguments that Butch inherited insanity from his father. Tom Spota saw another construction. As we left the bench conference, he kidded that we were no longer facing an insanity defense. "Now, it's a miracle defense," Tom said.

"If he can't sell insanity, it'll take one big miracle to beat six murder raps," I answered.

But as I sat down, I saw the look of grief on Phyllis Procita's face. There was nothing funny to her, and I felt guilty about our levity. Nevertheless, Spota and I kept up the joke for the rest of the trial, referring on and off to the new legal defense the case had given birth to—the defense of miracle. It was black humor, and I'm not defending it. But I can't say it wouldn't happen again. Black humor is an acquired reflex with prosecutors—part of the cynicism that helps shield them from becoming too personally involved in other people's tragedies.

Further into his cross-examination, Weber misfired by asking

Mrs. Procita if she knew prior to the murders why Butch had been rejected by the Army. "The actual reason, no," she said. "I didn't question it."

Bill was trying to infer that DeFeo was a Section Eight. I knew something else, and I was delighted at the chance to get it on record. I examined Mrs. Procita again, and asked if she had ever discussed the Army rejection with DeFeo during her jail visits.

"He mentioned something to me about—I'm trying to think how he put it—about why he didn't go in the Army," said the aunt, "or they got his records that he was insane—on his records that there is insanity, something like that. And I said to him, 'You know why you were not in the Army? Your father or Mr. Brigante paid to keep you out of the Army.'"

"Would you tell this jury now the circumstances that you became aware of as to why he did not serve in the Army?"

Phyllis Procita gave me exactly what I was looking for. It was pure hearsay, and it was beautiful. I couldn't have gotten it into evidence if Weber hadn't opened the door. "At the wake," said Mrs. Procita, "I was introduced to a man by Michael Brigante, Jr., and the man said to me that he was paid five thousand dollars to keep my nephew out of the Army."

21

THE JURORS SAW HIM DAILY at the defense table; his mustache still neatly clipped, his natty appearance unchanged. They watched him stroke his mustache, stare at women spectators, freeze the muscles of his face. That was one view of Butch DeFeo, and it was constant, as permanent as the flags flanking the judge's bench. But there was another view that was almost cinematic in its motion.

The jurors could see him growing, moving in the minds of the defense witnesses—friends and relatives who described him in many parts. He was his father's namesake in a family that could rake leaves one moment and fight the next. He was an abused two-year-old, a son and brother alternating between love and hate, a thief, a big spender, a raging assailant. And if the jurors accepted Bill Weber's dominant theme, he was insane. In some form, Weber asked each person who knew Butch the same question: "Would you describe those acts as

263

being rational or irrational?" "Irrational," the witness would reply. Before he rested the defense, Weber would build a mountain of acts committed by DeFeo that were arguably insane. By itself, each act could be handled as an isolated incident. But the cumulative effect was something else, and it worried me. We were dealing with a lay jury likely to distrust psychiatrists. Sometimes, the testimony of nonexperts telling what they perceived about someone they knew could do more to make a jury buy legal insanity than a battery of Viennese psychoanalysts.

Even I found out things about Butch DeFeo that I hadn't known before. But I didn't see insanity. I saw anger, willfulness, a spoiled kid's need to get his way, suburbia's child exploding in the nuclear family, what Dr. Zolan called the antisocial personality. I saw an heir apparent getting ready to kill. And as I cross-examined the defense witnesses, I tried to sharpen that view for the men and women in the jury box.

I had the most success with Bobby Kelske. The first witness called by Weber, Kelske was as helpful to the prosecution as to the defense, if not more so.

Weber tried to contend that DeFeo and Kelske were both prime suspects before the investigation was three hours old. The attempt foundered; Kelske's testimony was not specific enough to be admissible. And he came off as a wise guy. He repelled the jury when Weber questioned him about a conversation Kelske had with a detective whom he was unable to identify.

"Well, yes, after he said something to you," Weber asked, "then what did you say to him?"

Kelske seemed to be enjoying his answer. "I told him to go fuck himself," he said.

But when the examination turned to Kelske's knowledge of Butch DeFeo and his family, the jurors listened. They seemed hungry for that kind of information. They learned that Butch and Kelske put up most of the statues at 112 Ocean Avenue, that Ronald DeFeo, Sr., threw a silver pitcher at his son because he disparaged a police officer, that the family argued but was "close-knit." And that Butch, for no apparent reason, pointed a rifle at his friend in the DeFeo home the summer before the killings. "I saw his eyes," Kelske testified. "They were like on fire, like."

I cross-examined Kelske for an hour, and I owed my success to the information George Harrison had gotten from him over the past month. Harrison's information enabled me to defuse testimony that I suspected would come from other witnesses, including the prosecution psychiatrist and DeFeo himself. Most important was Butch's claim that he passed out in the auto agency because he had been poisoned in a bar the night before.

I asked Kelske if DeFeo had ever said that any member of his family was trying to kill him. No, Kelske answered. Then I asked if DeFeo ever said that other people were after him.

"He didn't name a name," Kelske said. "But supposedly they found him on the floor of the Buick place and they put him in a hospital or something, I don't know, and he said somebody tried to poison him. About last year, in '74."

"Did he later tell you what actually happened?" I asked.

"He said he drank too much whiskey," Kelske testified, "and ate some pills or something."

"Did he tell you that he thought that somebody really tried to poison him?"

"At that time, he didn't know. He said he just made that up."

I dealt with the sanity issue by asking for Kelske's opinion about the rationality or irrationality of Butch's conduct.

"A lot of times he would get very irrational, you know," Kelske said.

I wanted him to dig the trap a little deeper. "I'm sorry?"

"A lot of times he was, you know, very irrational."

"Very irrational?"

"Right."

"A lot of times?"

"Yes."

"Bobby, would you examine this document?" As I would with other witnesses, I showed Kelske the sworn statement he had made to police less than two weeks before. He confirmed that it was his statement, and I quoted him: "Ronnie's personality would change after he had a few drinks and that would bring out the aggressiveness in him. I would describe Ronnie as a rational person and the type of guy that liked to impress people."

I asked if Kelske had witnessed other aggressive actions by DeFeo. "Another time at the bar," he answered, "we had an argument. It was around eleven o'clock at night, and he had been drinking. He went home and came back with a shotgun. He was threatening he was going to shoot me again, and I ran out to the car and I grabbed the gun out of the car. And a New York City cop was off-duty. He grabbed the gun and broke it up and threw it on the roof."

I underscored what Kelske had already made plain. "Now, had he been drinking on that occasion?"

"Yes."

The cross-examination drew an unexpected bonus. Prior to jury selection, Judge Stark had ruled that I could not question DeFeo about his complicity in the Brooklyn holdup. In my opening statement, I had made a vague reference to the robbery, saying we would offer evidence about "an event which occurred in Brooklyn some ten days earlier that proved to be the final catalyst" in Ronnie's decision to commit murder. In the light of Stark's prohibition, even that had been risky—the problem was to get the holdup into evidence without causing a mistrial. Kelske did it for me. He supplied Butch's admission of guilt and linked the holdup to DeFeo's final quarrel with his father. I never had to go to the mat on admissibility, and I obtained a more credible account than I could have gotten from DeFeo.

The sequence began with my asking if Butch had ever

discussed any problems he was having with his father a month or two before the murders. Kelske revealed a major problem—the DeFeos wanted to throw Butch out of the house.

I asked why, and his answer brought me up short. "Well, there were a lot of reasons. The reason I thought the most was about the holdup."

"Wait a minute," I said. "Just what did he tell you about the reasons?"

"About the phony holdup that was in the city there."

I asked for details, and Kelske tried to remember. He thought he heard about the robbery from Butch on a Friday night. "He came home, he said somebody held up the Buick dealership, you know, where he worked at, held him up and, you know, stole twenty thousand dollars, something like that. I don't know. And then he later on told me that, you know, that he did the job himself."

"Did he tell you—"

"That was about a week and a half, two weeks later. I know his father was putting a lot of pressure on him about it because he didn't believe him, you know, because they had a fight that Saturday. I was over there one day and they had an argument about it."

"What did he tell you about that incident?" I asked.

"You mean about the holdup?"

"No, about the argument."

"That he went out and bought a lot of clothes, and his father knew he didn't have that much money left. I think he went out and bought around five or six hundred dollars' worth of clothes or something. He came home that Saturday, and his father knew he had a limited amount of cash. He knew (sic) where could he get the money to buy the clothes. And that's when I think he started suspecting."

"Do you recall the date that Butch told you that that happened, that argument with respect to the clothes?"

"The date?"

"Yes, the date that it happened."

"The holdup, you mean, or the argument?"

"No, the date that the argument occurred with respect to the clothes and his father knowing that he didn't have that much money."

"Well, it was on a Saturday," Kelske answered. "It was exactly three days before, because I stopped off there and they were all raking leaves outside, the whole family. And then later on I think he came home with the clothes."

"Three days before what, Mr. Kelske?" I asked.

"Before, you know, everything happened; they were found killed."

Weber took Kelske again, trying to restore the image of Butch DeFeo as a lunatic in waiting. Aggressive behavior triggered by booze didn't fit the picture. Besides what Kelske had told the court, Weber asked, were there any other instances where he had observed DeFeo being irrational?

I felt as if Kelske were my witness rather than Weber's. "When he was drinking, there were a few times," he said. "Just the things he told me. You know, what I told you about before. Those are the only ones I remember."

But Weber had the ball and he kept running. If he lost yardage on Kelske, he ripped off gains with other witnesses. John Carswell, a twenty-five-year-old Air Force veteran, told about taking a gun away from Butch after the latter shot it off outside the bar from which Sherry Klein had been fired. Chuck Tewksbury remembered driving Butch's car in September, 1974, when county police pulled them over and asked for registration. Butch started screaming at the cops. "Why are you always bothering me?" he shouted. And Tewksbury described how Butch became excited when a particular song was played on the juke box where they were drinking or on a car radio. Butch would bang on the bar, or turn up the radio, and start going wild. The name of the song was "I Shot the Sheriff."

Steve Hicks added to the mountain with an incident involv-

ing DeFeo and his mother. In the summer of 1968, he said, the
DeFeos gave Butch his first car, a used Buick Special. Butch,
Steve and another friend, Frank Davidge, pulled into the DeFeo
driveway and Mrs. DeFeo berated her son for going joyriding
when there were chores to be done at the house. Butch lunged
at his mother, screaming that he wanted to kill her. Davidge
and Hicks wrestled him to the ground and calmed him down.

Hicks talked about Butch's attack on Barry Springer with the
chowder clam, but his version differed from the one DeFeo had
given Dr. Zolan. In DeFeo's story, he jumped into the bay and
saved Barry. But Hicks said he grabbed Springer before the
latter went overboard. He upbraided DeFeo, who said nothing.
"His eyes had a glazed look, a stoned look," Hicks testified.
Later, Butch said he didn't remember hitting Springer with the
clam. Nor had he remembered the tantrum with his mother.

Hicks told about going to the hospital with Butch, Tewksbury, Springer and Sherry Klein the day Mark DeFeo was hurt
in a football game. At the emergency entrance, they ran into
Butch's father. The elder DeFeo told Butch he didn't want to
see him. "'You guys,'" Hicks quoted Ronald, Sr., as saying,
"'I'm leaving it in your hands. If you got to break every bone in
his body, I don't care what you do to him, but just get him out of
here.'" During a second visit, he said, Butch started to cry in
Mark's room, and his mother told him to leave. When they got
out of the elevator, a security guard said something Hicks
couldn't hear. Butch tried to hit the guard.

I tried to chip pieces off the mountain. Or, sometimes, not to
enlarge it. For instance, I didn't touch the hospital story. But I
did go after the incident involving Mrs. DeFeo, eliciting the fact
that she wasn't hurt or knocked off her feet, that Butch never
got his hands on her throat. "Did he touch his mother in any
way?" I asked.

"I can't say that I saw a hand brush, you know, part of her
body," Hicks said. "It's possible."

I asked several of the witnesses to define what they meant by irrational behavior. I hoped the jurors realized that the answers were vague and rarely the same. Whenever possible, I used the witnesses to reinforce the prosecution's case. Hicks was a good example; I had him describe the incident in which the Marlin went off accidentally in his home. And I used the one tool I had in reserve—the signed statements in which some of the witnesses had described Ronnie as a rational person. In Tewksbury's case, Weber tried to get him off the hook by asking him which statement was the truth, the one he gave Harrison or the one he gave the court?

"Well, I don't know how to answer," Tewksbury said. "They are both kind of right. You know, he did irrational things and he did irrational things while drinking."

When Sherry Klein took the stand, I tried another approach, one that drew more headlines the next day than Sherry's direct testimony.

In answer to Weber's questions, Sherry said she had known DeFeo—whom she called "Ronnie"—for five months before his arrest, and recited her own chapter and verse of violent times. Two were incidents that DeFeo had lumped together in his sessions with Dr. Zolan. In the summer of 1974, Butch brought several drinking buddies to her apartment, started a fight and had to be restrained after he shoved Sherry across the floor and slammed a chair into the ceiling. A month or two later, he forced her to go out one night by taking her car keys. He drove 60-to-70 MPH in a 30 MPH zone, and when he stopped at a bar, she left and got his father. At 1 A.M., they found Ronnie in front of the bar. DeFeo pushed Sherry to the ground, and his father grabbed him and told him to apologize. Instead, he broke free and ran. He didn't attempt to hit his father.

Sherry claimed that DeFeo loved his brothers and sisters. She had eaten at the DeFeo home, and Ronnie had gone to dinner with her family at a local diner. "He was a perfect gentleman," she said, "quiet, reserved, polite."

After she testified about one of DeFeo's bad moments, Weber

270

asked about her feelings. "Sherry, at the time, were you in love with Ronnie?"

"I liked him," Sherry Klein said.

Sherry Klein was articulate, attractive, not at all flashy. I felt she was making a good impression on the jury, and it was important to attack her credibility. On cross-examination, I asked if she had spoken to some of DeFeo's buddies at the murder scene. "Did you tell any of these people, Sherry, that if he had given you the gun, you would have hidden it for him?" I asked.

"I don't recall that at all, Sir."

"Well," I insisted, "do you recall saying it or definitely not saying it, or do you have no recollection?"

"No recollection," she answered.

I established that she had a string of barmaid jobs to her credit, and asked if she could distinguish between a drunk and someone who was high on drugs. Sherry conceded that she wasn't sure how a person under the influence of drugs might act.

Soon, I was ready. I specified a bar, and asked if a customer there had complimented her on her figure.

"I have been complimented before," Sherry said.

"Miss Klein," I asked as politely as I could, "do you recall an incident where, after such compliment, you exposed your breasts to this individual?"

In the lexicon of Batman and Robin, Ka-Pow! "Your Honor—" Weber began, but before he could object, Sherry Klein broke in. "I resent that absolutely!" she said.

We approached the bench. Weber demanded a hearing on my good faith in asking the question, and the judge had the jury removed from the courtroom. The rule that controlled this kind of cross-examination required that I be able to show a reasonable basis for believing that she had engaged in such conduct. Weber could call me on it, and I had to prove my good faith.

I called George Harrison. George had told me about the incident but didn't know I would use it. Now, he testified that over the past five weeks, he had interviewed bar workers and patrons and had questioned several people about Sherry Klein. "As a result of talking to these individuals that you just named," I asked, "were any specific acts Sherry Klein engaged in related to you?"

"Not that I can recall, Sir," George said, totally unprepared for what was happening.

Weber objected that I was leading the witness. I retorted that he had been doing his own leading earlier in the day. But Bill came right back. "I never accused anyone in this courtroom of exposing their breasts," he said. He had a point. However, Judge Stark said that we were not in front of the jury and he was permitting me to lead the witness.

In a physical sense, the word "lead" was an understatement. I was staring at Harrison, thrusting myself forward with my hands cupped in the vicinity of my upper chest.

"Did there come a time," I asked, "when you discussed a specific act that Sherry Klein engaged in with one or more of the people that you have named?"

Detective Harrison was worried about every detective's nightmare—a mistrial. He didn't really believe I was asking the question, and he echoed my cupped-hands gesture. I nodded my head. "I can only comment on one act," he said. "I hesitate to state it. If it took place at the (he named the bar), if that's what you are talking about, Sir."

I nodded some more. "Proceed," I said.

But Weber demanded the name of the person who gave him the information. Harrison named two of DeFeo's pals, but said he couldn't swear to either one. I told him to go ahead with the story, and he still hesitated. "And if I may," he said, "is this the act in which she revealed herself that we are talking about?"

I nodded vigorously. "That's what I'm asking you about, Detective Harrison."

"Yes, Sir," George said. "Someone commented to Miss Klein in the terms that were related to me—I'll repeat them almost exactly—'You have a nice pair of tits.' At that point, Miss Klein revealed them."

When the jury returned, I had the court reporter read back my original question.

"No," Sherry answered. "Absolutely not. And I still resent the question."

Another young woman who testified was more damaging. Nineteen-year-old Grace Fagan had been a best friend and classmate of Dawn DeFeo. She felt close to the family—she was at 112 Ocean Avenue seven days a week. And she gave a sympathetic picture of Butch DeFeo. On September 26th, she said, she helped the family celebrate Butch's birthday. There was a cake and presents, and Butch blew out the candles and walked around the table, thanking everybody. I was sure the jurors shared my thought—it was less than two months before the murders. The family that fought together celebrated birthdays together. Why not? I thought. But I wondered how that struck the jury.

Fagan also recalled a summer day that year when Butch walked into the kitchen, where she was sitting with his brothers and sisters. In response to something that was said—Fagan wasn't sure exactly what it was—he told the younger children to emulate Dawn, who was taking classes at Katharine Gibbs Business School. "He told them not to look up to him, that to look up to Dawn because Dawn was going to school and Dawn was going to make it in this world, and not to take after his example."

Grace Fagan also gave some examples of what she considered irrational behavior on Butch's part—including one night in October when she and Dawn were going out, and he told them to stay away from his hangouts, not to go in any place where they saw his car "because we would just get in trouble because they probably wouldn't let us in because they didn't like him."

I dealt with this on cross-examination by asking the witness to explain the difference between rational and irrational. "Well, if you're rational," she answered, "you think it out, you know, before you just go and do something. If you do something irrational, you just do it and then you say, 'Oh, why did I do it?'"

"Have you ever done irrational things?" I asked.

"Yes."

"When you do things on the spur of the moment?"

"Yes."

"And you are excited?"

"Yes."

"Okay. Would you tell us that most people at one time or another do irrational things?"

"Most people do," she answered.

Weber called only two relatives of DeFeo—using them to supplement the testimony given by his friends and to cover the Wyssling issue. They were Butch's maternal grandfather, Michael Brigante, Sr., and the latter's son, Michael, Jr. The Brigantes had about as much character similarity as the North Pole and Tahiti. Michael, Jr., who was thirty-nine, single and lived with his parents, was as mild as his father was excitable. But he became upset before his cross-examination was over.

Weber used Michael, Jr., to show erratic behavior on the part of Ronald DeFeo, Sr. He asked about an incident that occurred when Butch was two years old. "I believe we were all sitting down in the basement, watching TV," Michael, Jr., testified, "and I don't know, the boy had did something, and all of a sudden he stood up, the father, and just pushed the boy this way into the wall, and the boy banged his head or part of his shoulder or something."

Young Brigante also testified that the day before the murders, Ronald, Sr., left work because he felt his family was threatened with death. He didn't say why, Michael said, "he just emphasized that he was afraid they were all in danger of being killed."

274

On cross-examination, I asked if DeFeo, Sr., seemed excited when he said this. Michael, Jr., said he seemed very composed.

"Did you tell him to call the police?" I asked.

"I don't think so," Michael said, and he added a second later, "if you knew Ronald DeFeo, Sr., you couldn't tell him anything. Without me being disrespectful, don't misunderstand."

I kept at him. Did he call the police? Did he tell anyone else in the Buick Agency to call the police? Did he call DeFeo, Sr., later at home to find out how the family was? The answers were all "No."

"You did nothing," I said.

"No."

"And isn't it true that you did nothing because he didn't say that?"

That was when Michael Brigante, Jr., lost his composure. "Mr. Sullivan," he said, "I can only repeat—I'm under oath and I am a Catholic—what I have heard. If I may say something, Mr. Sullivan. Please don't think I am trying to tell you that I heard something that I did not. I'm very perturbed now the way it is. And I am being slandered and my father is being slandered by testimony that father and I are part of organized crime and we have associations. I have never been arrested. I was in the Armed Services for eight years. I don't understand that people won't talk to me because they saw articles that I'm associated with—I have strong criminal links to the underworld. I don't understand what's going on. Are you trying to slander me as an individual? I don't know what's happening."

"Have you finished?" I asked.

"I've finished."

Weber took him back again, asking why he did nothing.

"Because Ronnie a lot of times used to personally feel that the way he used to feel that things were going to happen that they didn't happen," said Michael, Jr. "And I thought it was just a figment of his imagination that someone would feel or know that their family was going to be killed, because they wouldn't

275

be in there in the first place if they felt or knew that."

Michael Brigante, Sr., followed his son. His testimony centered on the Wyssling issue, but there were some new details. The most important was that he saw Wyssling hand his card to police.

The show started when I asked if Brigante had mentioned a card at the pretrial hearing. "I don't recall whether I did or not," said the witness. "And the reason why I was so tense that day, I'll tell you what it is. Every morning, I take a red pill for my blood, a lasix pill for water in my system, a Valium pill, ten milligrams, for my tension, and an acid pill, uric acid pill. And of course I was in duress, such duress—under duress here that half of the questions that were put to me, I didn't even understand half of them. And I didn't want to make an idiot of myself. And I stood my ground as a man. I was busting inside to get to the bathroom and I didn't do it. I said, 'No, Your Honor, I'll stay here until I die, if I have to die.' That's why I didn't say it."

Judge Stark asked Brigante if he needed a recess. "I feel fine," replied the witness. "Thank you very much, Your Honor, I appreciate it very much. As a matter of fact, to be truthful, I didn't take a lasix pill this morning purposely not to run to the bathroom and stay here."

The judge asked Brigante to limit his answers, but it was like trying to dam the Pacific. "Some of the questions he don't ask me, Your Honor," Michael, Sr., explained. "I'd like to answer some of these questions. I'd like to answer some of mine."

I broke in, asking that the judge direct the jury to disregard Brigante's last remark.

"Yes, ladies and gentlemen," said Judge Stark, "do not pay attention to remarks of a witness which are not responsive to a question."

Brigante wasn't through. "I belong in a nut house," he said.

I wished he were somewhere else besides in front of a jury. For all the comic relief some of his answers may have engendered, the bereaved grandfather was a tragic figure. And he was not frugal with his emotions. He hosed the court with them when I asked why he had tried to get into the house the night the murders were discovered.

Brigante insisted that he wanted to embrace the victims. "And don't try to trick me," he said, "because you are not going to trick me. I wanted to hug them. The C.O. said to me, 'You don't want to hug them. It's a disgraceful scene.' I want to see every picture of my daughter and grandchildren and my daughter's son and daughter. I'm not ashamed of holding them with their blood. I wanted to kiss and hug them, the whole six of them, that's what I wanted to do. . . ."

I asked if he would lie to protect his flesh and blood, if he would color the truth. "I never lied in my life, Mr. Sullivan," he said. "I'm a decent-living Catholic person receiving Holy Communion once a month."

At the end of Brigante's cross-examination, I decided that it would be better to leave the jurors smiling, rather than crying. "All right, Mr. Brigante," I said, "if I have caused you any discomfort, I'd like to apologize."

"No, Mr. Sullivan," he answered, "you are perfectly right, and you are an assistant district attorney. I know a lot of district attorneys, assistant district attorneys. You did a nice job."

"Thank you very much," I said.

At the pretrial hearing, Richard Wyssling had been the star witness. At the trial he was a bit-player; the star was the emotionless young man at the defense table. Ostensibly, the jurors knew nothing about the hearing—that had been one of the criteria for their selection. And they were pledged not to read newspaper accounts of the trial, which at this point were referring to the hearing and to Judge Stark's finding that Wyssling's testimony was unworthy of belief. What they actually knew, I can't say.

I do know that Wyssling was no more impressive at the trial

than he had been at the hearing. There were a few minor changes, but his basic story was the same—he had identified himself as a lawyer, and he had been kept from seeing DeFeo. I cross-examined him as I had at the hearing, with similar results. When I asked questions about his indictment, he took the Fifth again. The only difference was that this time Wyssling had his own lawyer with him in the courtroom.

As October ended, and the trial went into its fifth week, I think that we were all waiting. I had called twenty witnesses in my direct case. Weber had already called eighteen—friends of DeFeo, relatives, neighbors, even a physician associate at the county jail, who testified that Butch had bruises on his shin and stomach when he was admitted. (I established that both bruises were four to seven days old, which meant they were at least two days old when DeFeo was questioned by detectives.) Weber had made some moves in the direction of police brutality and violation of DeFeo's civil rights, but his major effort had been in laying the groundwork for legal insanity. Witness after witness had described the defendant as a Jekyll and Hyde in denims; the jurors had to be curious about what went on inside Butch DeFeo's head. Or what he would say went on.

We were waiting for DeFeo, all of us. A twenty-four-year-old dropout who took drugs and came alive in bars had become a center of attention by slaughtering his family. He was why we were in that teak-paneled courtroom on the third floor of the bright, white building within sight of the county jail.

Weber called him on November 5th, but not until the afternoon. He used the morning to set the stage with an ex-friend of Ronnie's, a twenty-four-year-old plumber named Frank Davidge, or as he told Weber, a man nicknamed "Remus." "Who gave you that nickname?" Weber asked. "Ronnie," Davidge answered.

If Weber were building a mountain, Davidge was his last ridge. He recited a series of incidents that went back to 1972. They showed Butch at his deadliest:

• In the summer of 1972, Davidge and DeFeo went on a double-date in Butch's car. They took in a movie and got something to eat in a diner. They dropped off Davidge's date first. When they took Butch's girl home, he got out and Davidge waited in the back seat. After a minute or two, Butch returned and grabbed a gun from under the front seat. Davidge jumped out and saw the girl bent over the trunk of the car, and DeFeo pointing the rifle at her head and yelling. Davidge pulled the gun out of Butch's hands and threw it in the back seat. "Let's go," he said. "We have to leave." He flung Butch back into the car, and they left.

• In November, 1972, Davidge, Butch and two other friends went on a hunting trip, upstate. They walked into the woods in pairs; Davidge and Butch were partners. Butch moved ahead, and kept going when Davidge called to him to slow down. Then Davidge saw Butch looking in his direction. He wasn't actually aiming his gun, but it was pointing at Davidge. Frank stepped behind a tree and heard three shots, evenly spaced about two or three seconds apart. One of them went by close enough for him to see tree branches falling down. He looked out and saw Butch staring at the ground with his gun pointed downward. Davidge ran screaming at Ronnie. "What's the matter with you?" he hollered. DeFeo stared downward for another fifteen seconds. Then he looked up. "What's the matter, Remus?" he said. "Why are you so excited? Relax." He said they should keep hunting. Davidge turned and left. Butch went on by himself.

• In the spring of 1973, Davidge called for his friend around 7 P.M. one night. Mrs. DeFeo answered the door. She was crying and told him Ronnie was on the rampage. Davidge saw three or four guns bunched together on the kitchen floor. Her husband wouldn't be home that night, Mrs. DeFeo said. Would Frank please stay over? Davidge went upstairs and found Butch lounging on his bed, watching television. They talked about things in general, and Davidge went downstairs and brought up some food. When they turned in, Butch used the bed and

Davidge took a pillow and stretched out in front of the door on the shag rug. Three times during the night, Butch woke up angry and dove for the door. Davidge stopped him each time and held him down on the floor until his breathing slowed and he relaxed and said he was all right. In the morning, they went downstairs. Mrs. DeFeo made them a big breakfast.

Two weeks after spending the night at the DeFeo home, Davidge stopped by to ask if Butch could get a particular part for his mother's Buick. Mrs. DeFeo said Butch was upstairs, and Davidge knocked on his buddy's door. Butch asked who was there. "It's Remus," Davidge said, and Butch told him to come in. As soon as Davidge turned around, Butch had a shotgun pointed at his head; the barrel only two feet away. DeFeo pulled the trigger, and the gun made a click. It happened so fast Davidge didn't even have time to be afraid. In the next instant, Butch threw the gun on the bed and walked out of the room. Davidge picked up the shotgun, and pumped it twice, and a shell fell on the floor. He wondered why it hadn't gone off, and he went downstairs to the kitchen, where Ronnie was getting something to eat out of the refrigerator. Davidge addressed himself to Mrs. DeFeo. "Ronnie almost shot me with a gun," he said. "I've had it with him. I don't want to be his friend any more. I won't be around here any more at all." As he left the house, Mrs. DeFeo followed him. "Frankie," she yelled, "come back." After the incident, Butch would try to talk to Davidge whenever they ran into one another. "No, Ronnie," Davidge would say, "I'm going." And he would leave.

Davidge had one more story to tell. It was as frightening as the others, except that the central figure was Ronald DeFeo, Sr.

The incident took place sometime in 1973. It was 7:30 or 8 P.M. Davidge had just arrived, and Mr. DeFeo and Butch were eating dinner. Mrs. DeFeo was in the kitchen, and she invited Davidge to join Butch and his father. While they were eating, she did the laundry. The children were screaming, and Mrs. DeFeo yelled at them. Several times, Mr. DeFeo asked his wife to be quiet so that he could eat in peace. But the noise continued. DeFeo, Sr., left the table and went to the stairs, where his wife was coming from the basement with a basketful of laundry. She was at the top step when he punched her with a closed fist. Davidge heard her falling down the stairs. DeFeo, Sr., slammed the basement door shut. "Now we'll get some peace and quiet while we eat," he said.

Mr. DeFeo returned to the table, and Butch started shouting at him. Butch hollered that he didn't like his father hitting his mother, and he didn't want his friend to see it. But he ran upstairs to his room instead of going to his mother's aid. "He'll get over it soon," Mr. DeFeo told Davidge, and they finished dinner.

I figured that DeFeo's drug usage contributed to some of the incidents Davidge had described. But it was powerful testimony, and I didn't want to prolong it. I had no questions.

I would have a great many for Butch DeFeo.

22

Q: Ronnie, do you have a nickname?
A: Yes, Sir. "Butch," they call me.

SO IT BEGAN. A moment before, as he took the stand, quiet had gripped the courtroom. Now the jurors stared at him, and Ronald DeFeo, Jr., preened, smirking in their gaze.

He would spend three days in the witness chair, more than half of it under cross-examination, and the smirk never left his face. During his direct examination, I watched the jurors as much as I watched DeFeo, and I felt that they were viscerally affected by him, especially the younger women. If one can swagger while sitting, Butch was doing it. He sat there, playing macho—his eyes glittering, his shirt open, his chest hair showing, and I wondered if what I call the super-bad-guy syndrome was at work. James Cagney as Public Enemy

Number One, Al Pacino as Michael Coreleone, Ronnie DeFeo as himself.

On direct examination, he was cool, under control, but the sneer clung to his face and the arrogance came through. Weber tried to present him as a pathetic young man in whom childhood abuse triggered insanity. DeFeo took his cues from his questioner and responded in kind. He shrugged in answer to some of Weber's questions and played the victim whenever possible. Burn his father's boat? Never. And he didn't even know the house next door was robbed. And he loved his parents; he never hit either one. And that was despite what went on in his home.

"How far back do you remember in your childhood?" Weber asked.

"I was twelve," DeFeo answered. "Somewhere around there." The memory was of the day he was thrown out of St. Jerome's Parochial School in Brooklyn. He went home and told his father, who was quickly nasty. "He said to me that I wasn't even his son," DeFeo testified, "that he had to marry my mother when she was pregnant with me, he had to marry her six months early . . . and then he started with my mother." Butch said the argument escalated into a fight, and his mother went after his father with a knife. "My father picked up a chair and threw it. I got hit with it and it knocked all the teeth out of the front of my mouth. That's why I remember that incident because the teeth in front of my mouth are all caps."

A few minutes later, Weber showed his client People's Exhibit 38, the picture of Louise DeFeo as she lay murdered in bed in the room with the mirrored wall. DeFeo said the furniture looked familiar, but not the body. "I never saw this person before in my life," he said.

"Ronnie, that's your mother, isn't it?" Weber asked.

"No, Sir," came the answer. "I told you before and I'll say it again. I never saw this person before in my life. I don't know who this person is." DeFeo sneered as he looked at the photo. I glanced at the jurors. Several were shaking their heads. Either they were overwhelmed by this kind of evil, I thought, or they were buying the insanity act.

Under Weber's direction, Butch paraded his childhood in front of the jury—trotting out one violent episode after another. Fights in school, blow-ups at home. At St. Jerome's, he got into a fight with two classmates and was stabbed in the back. At home, he watched his father beat Mark so badly that the child's head had to be sewn. Once, he called his maternal grandfather a fuck and Brigante chased him through the house and Butch ran into Dawn and started beating her brains out. He saw the psychiatrist in Brooklyn for a year and a half after that. He stopped the visits when he was fifteen or sixteen. "It was a crazy house," he said of his home. "I couldn't take it. I couldn't take it back then; I couldn't take it before this happened."

Weber was piling it on for the jury. A hundred reasons to feel sorry for Ronnie DeFeo. All that trouble, and drugs, too. DeFeo's story was that he took drugs to escape life at home. By 1968, when he was seventeen, he got into speed, using crystal Methedrine almost daily for close to two years. "Sometimes I snorted it," he explained to the jurors. "Sometimes I put it in a drink, Coke or a Pepsi, to kill the taste. Once in a while I would shoot it, put it in my arm and shoot it up." He described what it was like. "You move around fast, you talk a lot, you are always awake, you couldn't sleep, you couldn't eat. You had to force yourself to close your eyes."

I wondered how much of the sad sell the jury was buying. There was too much bravado in DeFeo's manner, too much hate waiting in the back of his eyes. In 1970, he said, a doctor in Brooklyn prescribed Thorazine to get him off speed. During that period, he brought a girl home drunk with her clothing ripped. Her uncle phoned his home and threatened to kill him. Butch went to see the uncle with a loaded shotgun, but his father and his friends jumped out of the bushes and disarmed him. For a while after that, he stuck to liquor but in 1972, he turned to heroin because his family was giving him a hard time again.

The most lethal family quarrel DeFeo described was the one in which he pointed a rifle at his father and pulled the trigger. Butch said his father thought it was a miracle that the gun had failed to go off. The family had to share Ronald, Sr.'s burst of religion: "Next thing I know is he had myself and my mother and everybody hanging pictures up of Christ all over the house. Had me and Robert Kelske putting statues up on the front lawn, in the backyard, all over the place. Statues of St. Joseph and Jesus Christ, the Holy Family. . . . He got very, very religious. Started saying the Rosary every Sunday."

Then Weber showed DeFeo a photo of his father's body, and Butch said he didn't recognize it. Weber looked at hi. "Butch," he asked suddenly, "did you kill your father?"

"Did I kill him?" DeFeo echoed. "I killed them all. Yes, Sir. I killed them all in self-defense."

"Anybody help you, Ronnie?"

"No, Sir."

I glanced at the jurors. Several had their hands to their mouths as if they were trying to suppress gasps. I was suppressing jubilation. The son of a bitch had admitted it. Whatever worries I had relating to the confession seemed irrelevant. DeFeo had admitted the crime on the stand.

The next day he supplied details. But instead of opting for truth, he went for insanity—giving the macabre version of the murders in which he implicated Dawn. He went through the whole thing, from Dawn hovering over him with black hands to the mysterious figure running across the Ireland lawn. As he finished the story, he looked expectantly at Weber. "Whether or not it's my imagination or my mind is playing tricks on me, I don't know," he said. "You told me it was my imagination."

DeFeo was reveling in the attention. It seemed to me that his sneer widened as Weber asked him why he had killed. "As far as I'm concerned," Butch answered, "if I didn't kill my family,

285

they were going to kill me. And as far as I'm concerned, what I did was self-defense and there was nothing wrong with it."

"Had there been other people who have been threats to your life?" Weber asked.

"There has been a lot of people who have been threats to my life," came the answer. "I tried to find them and kill them. And if I couldn't find them and kill them, I couldn't do anything about it. I might have killed a dozen people before this. I don't know."

"Are you telling us, Ronnie, that you may have killed others besides your family?"

I thought about the unsolved drowning death as DeFeo answered. "It's quite possible," he said, and he was almost pompous. "When I got a gun in my hand, there's no doubt in my mind who I am. I am God."

Weber asked if anyone in the courtroom was a threat to DeFeo's life. Butch said there were two people. He named one; his aunt, Phyllis Procita. He didn't name the other person. It was November 6th. At 1:16 P.M., I began my cross-examination.

I moved to the lectern, meeting DeFeo's stare. There's a piece of you up there for me, I thought, and I'm going to have it. I'm going to cut it off. I wanted to hype up his super-bad-guy image for the jury; I wanted him to bristle and sneer and shout with rage. I wanted the jury to get a good look at the antisocial personality that Dr. Zolan was going to describe. I knew DeFeo hated me; I wanted him to show it on the stand. The more aggressive he acted, the more antisocial, the better. Get angry, Ronnie, I thought. Get furious. Let everybody see. Let them see the smirking punk who could slaughter his family without having the slightest remorse.

From the start, I went after DeFeo; ripping at his credibility, hitting him with discrepancies between the testimony he had just given and statements he had made to Dr. Zolan and police, and at the pretrial hearing. "I don't know," he would answer. "I'm not sure." I could sense the growing anger.

I questioned him about the murders; I pressed for details of the aftermath. There was a small crack when I asked about the blood on his hands. DeFeo said he didn't touch any of the bodies, but that the blood might have come from the pool on Allison's floor. "Why in God's name would you have put your hand in the pool of your sister's blood?" I asked. DeFeo couldn't hold back his arrogance. "I don't know," he said. "Maybe I like blood."

I kept pressuring, pushing, even asking questions with built-in accusations. I referred to his visit to Junie Reimer's house before reporting the murders. "Mr. DeFeo," I asked, "it's a fact, is it not, that you went there to purchase heroin to shoot into your veins to fortify you for the sham you were about to go through, isn't that true?"

"No, Sir."

The crack widened when I asked about the phone calls he had made to his home after the murders. Why did he mention them to the people in Henry's Bar? "You were setting up a bunch of people who were going to be able to tell the police later that Ronnie had said that he called his house and got no answer and he couldn't understand it," I said. "Isn't that a fact?"

"No, Sir. I wanted somebody to come back with me."

"Why, Mr. DeFeo, did you tell people that day that you had called your house and couldn't understand why you had gotten no answer. Why did you do that?"

DeFeo shouted his reply. "I wasn't sure if they were all dead. I wasn't even sure if I killed them. I ain't even sure if they are dead right now. One of them might come walking in here any minute, then we'll see who the laugh is on."

"Is that your answer?"

"Yeah, that's my answer."

I moved on to other areas. DeFeo admitted that he knew about the hiding place in the master bedroom; he identified the metal box. But he denied stealing from the box—claiming that he was allowed to go into it. DeFeo was vague on dates but said he took twenty-five-hundred dollars about a week before the killings. Some time after that, he emptied the box at his father's direction, removing eight-to-ten thousand dollars and bringing it to Ronald, Sr., in Brooklyn. When I asked where the money came from, he said Brigante-Karl Buick. "My father used to rip my grandfather off a lot," he said.

"Did you help him?"

"I was involved. Yes, Sir."

"Tell us what happened," I said. "Tell us how you and your father ripped Brigante-Karl Buick off for the cash."

DeFeo was boasting. "The body shop next door, it was our building. But this guy from the street was in there. He used to do all our work. And my father would tell him how much like to charge the company. Like, say, if the job was five hundred, he'd charge maybe eight hundred, a thousand, and that extra three or four hundred would go into my father's pocket. He'd send me over there to get the checks from the body shop, and I'd take the checks down the street to the loansharks and I'd cash the checks, and they would take so much out. There was that body shop. There was another body shop off of Coney Island Avenue. Those two. And there was some other work they did on the stolen cars."

I asked who worked on stolen cars, and he said the people in the body shop. "Did you and your father get a percentage of that, too?" I asked.

"My father was the one that was running the show, Mr. Sullivan."

"Okay. Well, you were a partner with him, weren't you?"

"I was his son. Yes, Sir," Ronnie said.

We got to the phony holdup, and I tried to foreshadow Burt Borkan's testimony. On Friday, November 8, I asked, "Did you tell your father at Brigante-Karl Buick, 'I will kill you, you fat prick'?"

"I'm not sure," DeFeo said.

"You mean you could have, you just don't remember?"

"That's what I'm trying to say. Yes, Sir."

He said both he and his father knew who committed the holdup, and he named an employee. But he admitted that he refused to look at mug shots, and I put him in a corner. As a result of his refusal, didn't the Brooklyn police tell his father the holdup was a phony?

"I don't know what they told my father, Mr. Sullivan."

"And on Tuesday, prior to the murder, your father came home and had a confrontation with you about it. Isn't that true?"

"No, Sir."

"As a result, you took a gun and shot him dead, didn't you?"

DeFeo barrelled out of the corner and tripped on his own arrogance. "No, Sir, I did not. I'm not going to take somebody's life for two thousand dollars."

"Would you take it for more than that?"

"I wouldn't kill anybody for money," he explained. "If I wanted money, I'd rob a bank."

I switched to his account of the murders, checking it against evidence that had been presented to the jury. He was vague as to whether his mother moved when he shot her, he didn't remember killing Allison, he hadn't been concerned about the source of the shots he heard in the television room.

But he was definite about his feelings. He couldn't remember whether he shot his father or mother first, but he knew how he felt afterwards.

"You felt good at that time?" I said.

"Yes, Sir, I believe I felt very good."

"Is that because you knew they were dead, because you had given them each two shots?"

"I don't know why. I can't answer that honestly."

"Do you remember being glad?"

"I don't remember being glad. I remember feeling very good. Good."

I drew more denials. He never told police he watched John's

foot twitch after he shot him, and he never put the dog outside.

"Was the dog barking during the time these things were happening in the house?" I asked.

"I don't remember hearing the dog barking, Mr. Sullivan. That I can remember."

The jurors had heard John Nemeth; they had heard Deborah Cosentino. When DeFeo denied putting on the lights after the murders, I drew anger. "Can you explain to this jury, how at 3:30 to 3:45 on that morning every floor in your house appeared to be lit up?"

"I can't explain it to them," he retorted. "And I did not put a light on in my house. And if you ask me, them people that come here to testify that the lights were on is just a few more of the people that are in this conspiracy that are out to get me."

A conspiracy? DeFeo said yes, and I took advantage of the opening. "Incidentally, Mr. DeFeo, who is the other person in the courtroom today who you feel is going to kill you?"

"The other person?"

"Yes." Come on, I thought, say it.

DeFeo sneered. "You."

"How am I going to do it?"

"I don't know how you're going to do it," he answered. "I tell you what, as long as you're in this courtroom and I'm in here, I'm keeping my eyes on you all the time."

We stared at each other. He was like a wolf, straining against a rope. Before the day ended, I made him bare his fangs twice.

The first time occurred when I questioned him about the psychiatrist his family had tricked him into seeing in the city. The psychiatrist had said he was dangerous to his family. Had DeFeo told John Carswell that what the psychiatrist said was funny?

"What the psychiatrist said. Yes, Sir. I'm still laughing at the psychiatrist."

"Even though now, twelve months later, you murdered six people in your family, you are still laughing at the psychiatrist?"

"You are goddamned right I'm still laughing at that," DeFeo replied. "I think they're all crazy. Furthermore, I think I'm the only sane man in this courtroom."

I punctuated the outburst for the jury's benefit. "Are you finished?"

"I'm finished."

But he wasn't. Had he felt since his arrest that people were out to get him? Yes, DeFeo answered, and he cited his relatives.

"What relatives?" I asked.

"Well, Michael Brigante, Senior. If I walked out of here now, I'd kill him and his son, Michael Brigante, Junior, and Phyllis Procita and Vincent Procita and Rocky DeFeo and Pete DeFeo, Mr. Falini, Mr. Lee. A lot of other people, too; I don't want to start getting into their names."

DeFeo and his maternal grandfather had embraced during the trial as they had at the hearing. "Is that the same Mr. Brigante that not more than a week or so ago you embraced in this courtroom?" I asked.

"Yes, Sir," DeFeo said. "That is correct. I could kill him just as quick."

I didn't doubt it. At 4:20 P.M., Judge Stark recessed the trial. I couldn't wait to resume.

The next morning, I felt as if I could reach out and touch the hate dripping off Ronnie DeFeo's answers. I was glad my wife, Betty, wasn't in the courtroom. She had attended DeFeo's first day on the stand and been unmoved. That had been direct testimony, and she had left in the early afternoon before the girls came home from school. She had seen DeFeo's sneer, but she hadn't seen his hate.

The hate boiled over as I reviewed his direct testimony, comparing it to what he had told Dr. Zolan. I was reading from the transcript, intermittently coming off the lectern, moving toward the witness, even making challenging gestures. DeFeo asked if I was quoting from the first interview. I said I was, and he lost control. "If I was you," he snapped, "I'd take that report and throw it in the garbage can, because you know the story behind that."

"Well, why is that, Mr. DeFeo?"

His answer was a tirade. "Because you are the district attorney, you were over there with some strange woman with Mr. Weber and myself. And furthermore, you're trying to put me in prison for the rest of my life, which I couldn't give a shit less about, and you and that doctor and that woman were in there giving me these strange looks, asking me these crazy questions. And you expect me to answer them with you sitting there?"

He paused for breath and went on. I made no effort to stop him. "And then you've got the nerve to get up and leave the room with that woman when the doctor and Mr. Weber went to the bathroom, and that woman said maybe he was flipped out on LSD. And you said to the woman, no, I think he did it for another reason and I did it without other people. That's what you said to the woman. And you are just as bad as the rest of the people that are talking about me. And I'll tell you something else, I couldn't give a shit what these people find me, guilty or innocent. It doesn't make no difference. I either go to the prison for the rest of my life or a mental institution. What's the big thing? And you keep harping on me."

You know it, I thought. I harped some more. "Let me ask you a question, Mr. DeFeo. You remember talking about that, going to a mental institution, with James DeVito, with the correction officer in the jail?"

"I remember him telling me that you're better off going to a prison than a mental institution. I remember him telling me that. Yes, Sir."

"Do you remember, Mr. DeFeo, telling him no, you're better off at a mental institution because you will be out in two years?"

"No, Sir."

"And you've got the money waiting for you when you get out?"

"No, Sir. I ain't got no money waiting for me when I get out."

With any other judge, there might have been a free-for-all as Bill Weber interrupted. He demanded that Stark call a mistrial or tell the jury that he would send DeFeo to a mental institution for life if he were found insane. "And this bit about two years was highly out of order by this district attorney, who knows better," Weber added.

Judge Stark denied the motion, pointing out that the law prohibited him from discussing the effect of any verdict with the jury. But Weber was angry. "How could you possibly allow him to tell this jury that he is going to stay in a mental institution for two years, Your Honor, when you know it's not true?"

Stark said Weber hadn't listened to the question. Weber said he had. "I know exactly what he said, and you know what he said."

"All right. I have ruled on it."

Bill wouldn't stop. "And you let him get away with it."

It was my turn; I wasn't giving up turf. Weber should make such statements at the bench or the side bar, I said.

He came right back. "You should have mentioned two years at the side bar, not in front of the jury." I really did admire the guy's tenacity.

Judge Stark said he would retire the jury if Weber kept it up, and the defense lawyer subsided. I returned to DeFeo. He couldn't remember the last part of the question, and I repeated it. "Isn't it a fact that you told James DeVito that it would be better if you did go to a mental hospital because within two years you'd be back on the street and you'd be able to get the money?"

"No, Sir. I did not."

"Your Honor, he did that again," Weber broke in.

Now Stark was annoyed. "And I have ruled it is proper. Will you not interrupt, Sir, when there is a ruling being made?"

If Weber was angry, his client was angrier. I pushed harder. "Is it your testimony that everything you told Dr. Zolan on that occasion was a lie?"

"No, I wouldn't say it was all a lie," he answered. "There's some things I didn't tell him and a lot of things I felt I shouldn't tell him at that time, Mr. Sullivan, because you were sitting in the room."

"Is it your testimony, Mr. DeFeo, that the things that you did tell him were lies?"

"Not all of them, Mr. Sullivan. There's a lot of things I didn't tell him, which you told me in this courtroom in front of the judge and Mr. Weber."

DeFeo's face was getting red; I wasn't about to let him go. "Were some of the things that you told him lies?"

"I don't believe they were lies, Mr. Sullivan. I believe I just didn't tell the whole story."

"Why?"

"Because you were sitting in there, Mr. Sullivan."

The hate burst out at me like heat from an open oven. "Okay," I said.

But DeFeo had already cracked. "You think I'm playing," he shouted. "If I had any sense, which I don't, I'd come down there and kill you now."

Atta boy, Ronnie, I thought. Come on down. He got to his feet; then the court officers moved forward and he sat back. The explosion was over in seconds. But it was enough. The jurors had seen Butch DeFeo.

They saw him again as I finished the cross-examination. I was pointing out a series of inconsistencies between his testimony and the Zolan transcript. "'My own family were the only people that were with me,'" I read.

"You told Dr. Zolan that, didn't you?" I asked.

"Yes, Sir. I did."

"And despite the fact that you were ultimately telling him the truth, you said nothing about your family being out to get you, did you?"

"I don't believe so at that time," he answered.

"Because it's a big lie," I said. "Isn't that true?"

"It is not a lie!"

DeFeo's voice was rising; he was losing control. "I have no further questions," I said, cutting him off, and Judge Stark told Weber he could conduct redirect examination. But DeFeo overrode both of us. "I tell you, you're going to see what kind of lie it is when I kill another person," he shouted. "I want to see what you tell the next twelve when we pick them. What are you going to tell them, it's another act? Well, you're going to be hooked up for a fucking conspiracy."

As Weber questioned him, DeFeo calmed down. Weber read from DeFeo's second interview with Dr. Zolan, and contended that it matched his client's direct testimony. Then he gave him a last chance to play insane. "Now, yesterday you said that there were two people in the courtroom that you thought were threats to your life?"

"Yes, Sir," DeFeo answered. "I was wrong. There was three."

"Who was the third person in the courtroom that was a threat to you?" Weber asked.

"You are," DeFeo said.

Judge Stark had something he wanted to clarify. "When you shot any members of your family," he asked, "did you realize at the time that you were firing your rifle directly at their bodies and that your shots could kill them?"

"No, Sir. When I fired the gun, the gun didn't make no noise, Your Honor. I didn't hear anything when I fired the gun, that's what I believe."

"And you did not believe in your own mind when you shot the gun at all that this was wrong?"

"No, Sir. I didn't think it was wrong. I still don't think it's wrong."

"Did you shoot the gun at any member of your family with the purpose or intention of killing them?"

"You see, I can't answer that, Your Honor," DeFeo said, "because I don't remember the gun making noise. That's what I'm trying to say."

I didn't believe the jury would buy it. I felt I had cut off a big piece of Butch DeFeo. It was 11:07 A.M., and Dr. Daniel W. Schwartz, the defense psychiatrist, was the next witness. No matter what else they heard, I was sure the jurors wouldn't forget what they had just seen.

The next day, *Newsday* ran a five-column headline: "DEFEO THREATENS LIFE OF PROSECUTOR." Betty was upset by the story. She was concerned for me; she was concerned about our family. She wanted to know if there was any chance of DeFeo escaping custody. I told her not to worry. He could never break out, I said. And, in any case, the threats against me were a lot of chest-beating.

I don't know that I believed it. And I didn't tell Betty what was really on my mind. She was worried about DeFeo escaping from jail; I was more concerned as to what might happen if he were acquitted on grounds of insanity. In that case, he could win his release as soon as doctors decided that he was no longer dangerous. He could be out on the street in a couple of years. And that worried me. I wasn't thinking of myself as much as my family. Butch DeFeo was a demonstrated child-killer. He had murdered four young people—two of them less than twelve years old. In a few years, when DeFeo was likely to get out if he were found legally insane, my oldest daughter would be the same age as his youngest victim. I thought about that, but I couldn't say it. I couldn't give Betty that kind of pain.

Instead, I told her that I was certain he would never get loose. I knew there was only one way to keep Butch DeFeo in jail—if not permanently, at least for a long, long time. I had to convict him.

23

IN APRIL, 1969, a six-foot, eight-inch giant named James Farley tore a woman to pieces in a Queens alleyway. Farley pleaded insanity, but was convicted of murder. The defense psychiatrist was Dr. Daniel W. Schwartz. The DeFeo case was perhaps the one hundred and fiftieth in which he had been retained to determine the defendant's criminal responsibility. The Farley case was the first.

By the time I cross-examined Dr. Schwartz, I had a well-thumbed copy of the Farley trial transcript on the lectern. I had been doing homework on Dr. Schwartz since the pretrial hearing seven weeks before when Bill Weber announced his designation. Dr. Schwartz—who would heighten his public aura years later by deciding that "Son of Sam" killer David Berkowitz was crazy—was director of the forensic psychiatry service at Kings County Hospital and an associate professor at Downstate Medical College. Although he had never testified in

Suffolk, he had figured in big-time cases in Nassau and New York City. He and Dr. Zolan were as aware of each other as Macy's and Gimbel's. Or, on occasion, as Lord and Taylor. In three or four cases, Dr. Zolan and Dr. Schwartz had worked together. In several others, they had been on opposite sides. Just months before, both men had testified for the prosecution in the trial of Joanne Brown, who shot her law-clerk lover to death in his Nassau Supreme Court office. (Despite their combined firepower, Brown was found not guilty by reason of insanity.)

The day I learned that Dr. Schwartz would call psychoses for the opposition, I started phoning prosecutors in New York, Nassau and Westchester who had dealt with him. Steve Scaring, the Nassau assistant district attorney who prosecuted Joanne Brown, not only gave me a scouting report but loaned me transcripts of Schwartz's testimony in two murder trials. Two more transcripts, including the Farley case, came from the office of then-Queens District Attorney Thomas Mackell, whose aides treated me like a member of their staff. It helped that I had roomed with Tom Mackell, Jr., at Seton Hall, and had met some of the Queens assistants through my friendships with the family.

When I was through researching, I knew enough about Dr. Daniel W. Schwartz to write a profile for *Time, Life* or *Psychology Today*. His first advantage as a witness was that he fit the image of a movie psychiatrist. Dr. Schwartz was about five-eight, dark-haired with dark glasses, a neat mustache and a small, spade-shaped beard. His second advantage was that he knew his way around a courtroom. He was expert on the rules of evidence, effective with juries and difficult to cut down on cross-examination. Whenever an opposing attorney had him on the brink of a damaging statement, Schwartz would argue phraseology or smother the issue in a welter of multisyllables. And he was a competitor—according to my sources, Dr. Schwartz rated himself by whether his side won or lost the case. He didn't like losing, and he was quick to carry the attack to the cross-examiner by zinging him any time he saw an opening.

Finally, my scouts agreed that as a forensic psychiatrist, Dr. Schwartz was an autocrat. He sought dominance not just in the witness chair, but in determining strategy for the lawyers who retained him. I doubted this would go down with Weber, who didn't let anyone dictate to him. At that, I wondered whose decision it was to call Schwartz to the witness chair on Ronnie DeFeo's heels. I would have reversed the order. If Schwartz had gone first and testified that DeFeo was criminally insane, the jurors might have seen Butch differently. They would have been more likely to excuse his hate, sneers and threats as symptoms of what the psychiatrist had described.

If I didn't want Schwartz to sell insanity to the jury, I had to discredit his testimony. But not on his grounds—there was no way I could fault his expertise. I could, however, attack his knowledge of Ronald DeFeo, Jr. I could convince the jurors that they knew a great deal more about DeFeo than the doctor. The jurors had been learning about DeFeo and his murders for almost two months. They had listened to his lies and vituperation for days. Dr. Schwartz had only talked to him for hours. I would show that the psychiatrist didn't know the real Butch DeFeo.

The contest started a few minutes into Dr. Schwartz's direct testimony. After listing his qualifications and explaining that he had appeared in various courts as both a defense and a prosecution witness, he tried to get in a gratuitous reference to his impartiality. I never let him finish the sentence and Judge Stark upheld my objection. Schwartz looked sheepish.

Weber came quickly to the central question: "Doctor, having conducted your examination of Ronald Joseph DeFeo, Jr., and having looked at all the reports and papers you have told us about, do you have an opinion as to whether or not Ronald Joseph DeFeo, Jr., on November 13th, 1974, lacked substantial

capacity to know or appreciate either the nature and consequence of his conduct, or that such conduct was wrong?"

"Yes."

"Doctor, what is that opinion?"

"It is my opinion," replied Dr. Schwartz, "that as a result of
mental disease the defendant at that particular time lacked
substantial capacity to appreciate the wrongfulness of his acts."

"Doctor, will you tell us the basis of your opinion?"

It was as if Weber had tight-wound the rubber band on a
balsa-wood plane and let it fly. Instead of giving his testimony
by way of questions and answers, Dr. Schwartz looked straight
at the jury and delivered a fifteen-minute lecture. I wondered
who had chosen the technique, Schwartz or Weber. There was
no questioning its effectiveness. The jurors not only listened
intently, but a few of them began to glance back and forth from
the psychiatrist to the defendant.

Almost as if he were a screenwriter presenting a scenario, Dr.
Schwartz started with DeFeo's childhood—painting a picture of
a boy raised in violence, a boy who developed an explosive
temper. But a boy who never struck at his father. "As wild as he
could be with others," said the psychiatrist, "he could not
respond in kind to his father. But the anger had to go
somewhere. . . . His came out, among other ways, at most of
his teachers and school authorities, who for many children
quite naturally stand as parent figures."

At the same time, Dr. Schwartz testified, Ronnie was
indulged—given most of what he wanted, including money.
The result was a short-fused youth, afraid of his own violence.
He tried to remove himself from dangerous situations by
running away from home. He tried to escape through drugs.
But neither effort was successful. "In fact," Schwartz testified,
"things reached a culmination, really."

Dr. Schwartz cited the incident in which Butch aimed a gun
at his father in 1973. He said the incident intensified DeFeo's
love-hate feelings toward Ronald, Sr. Torn by these feelings,

Butch gave in to paranoid delusions that diverted his preoc-
cupations away from his family. He began to believe that people
were after him wherever he went—people he met in bars, police
who pulled him over for speeding. "He began to get the feeling
that—and the belief that—there were people who were going to
kill him, that his only recourse was to kill them first."

DeFeo had developed these delusions to turn his anger away
from his father, said Schwartz. But they swung back. His father
became his chief enemy. Yet, he continued to love his father.
"There was a birthday party held for him, and he went around
at the party and kissed all of his family and felt love for them. At
the same time, the delusions were eating at him, that these
people were going to kill him."

Dr. Schwartz retraced the night of the murder; his series of
events paralleling those given by DeFeo. He said Ronnie's
conflicts were aggravated by a fight between his father and
Dawn, and that he was influenced by the movie he watched
before falling asleep in the TV room. The psychiatrist said he
had seen the movie, *Castle Keep,* and offered a description: "It's
a movie about—presumably about our Army in Europe in World
War II. And the culmination of it is that our troops are forced or
ordered to defend a hopeless position, and amidst incredible
violence and explosion, every one of our soldiers are killed. The
defendant, the patient, told me that he was moved by the
bloodshed and the violence in the picture. It's also clear to me
that the picture had other meanings to him, too. There is a
significant theme in the picture of some soldiers who have
renounced violence and who walk through this town in Europe
preaching religious nonviolence, but it's to no avail. Religion,
peacefulness, has no effect in this movie. The violence will out.
And I think this was a significant message to the defendant,
that nothing he did was going to prevent this final showdown.

"I'm not saying that the movie caused the actual killings," Dr.
Schwartz told the jury. "I am saying that it was the straw that
broke the camel's back. It was the final thing that he could no

longer cope with. And now in a paranoid psychotic state of mind, he proceeded to do what he thought was the only thing he could do, namely, kill those who were out to kill him."

At this point, Weber interrupted the narrative. He was anticipating my cross-examination. Did Dr. Schwartz consider that Butch might have been malingering or faking in their interview?

It was a remote possibility, said the psychiatrist, so remote that "I don't consider it as having any likelihood in this case." His reason was based on dissociation, which he defined as a person divorcing himself "from a certain sensory perception of reality." DeFeo had told Schwartz that he didn't hear the gun during the murders but that he heard a tremendous roaring in his ears the following day. "I don't believe that someone with his limited education and sophistication and lack of familiarity with psychiatry could have invented this particular symptom of dissociation," Schwartz said.

The rest of the doctor's answer exemplified what I had been told to expect. He spoon-fed psychiatry to the jury in language that was more pulp than science. "The other thing that comes through with such striking strangeness in this case is his calmness throughout the killings," Schwartz alliterated. He said that if DeFeo had killed in anger, there should have been bodies riddled with bullets, a house in shambles. But not a bullet was wasted. "Every one of them was fired with an almost eerie accuracy. This was the act of an absolutely calm, cold person who had no feelings at all at the time. This is exactly how he coped with his feelings. He just turned them off. I don't mean intentionally. Psychologically, unconsciously, without his awareness, all his feelings were turned off completely; and now in an eerie, calm, machinelike way he goes about executing the closest people in the world to him, but the same people who he believes are the greatest threat to his life."

A few minutes later, Weber surprised me. "Thank you very much, Doctor," he said. It was like expecting a shore dinner and stopping at the chowder. The direct examination was over. For a moment, I thought about looking contemptuous and announcing, "No questions." But it would have been too great a gamble—the jurors who had been impressed by Schwartz were likely to misinterpret my action.

I asked two questions—had Dr. Schwartz taken notes of his interviews with DeFeo, and could I examine them at the noon recess? Then I asked for the recess. I did not simply want to go over the defense psychiatrist's notes. I wanted to consult with Dr. Harold Zolan, who had arranged to be available at his office phone.

In the lobby, Tom Spota and I ran into Dr. Schwartz, and we greeted each other like football players at a pregame show. The doctor told us that he was an opera buff, that he lived in Nassau and that he wasn't wild about traveling to Riverhead to testify. He said he was used to the faster pace of city courts. He also talked about the trial—referring to the fuss over defense witnesses quoting DeFeo's boast that he could plead insanity and get out of a mental institution in two years. Actually, the defendant in such a case would be entitled to release as soon as he was found to no longer be a danger to himself or others. Schwartz said Weber should have asked for his prognosis—he'd have stated that DeFeo would have to be confined for a prolonged period. No way, I said. I'd have climbed all over him with objections. Schwartz's comeback was that he would have slipped in the statement before I had a chance to say a word. Okay, Doctor, I thought. I'm on guard.

Before court reconvened, I spent close to an hour on the phone with Harold Zolan, going over strategy in the light of Schwartz's testimony. My opening remained unchanged—the old "give-the-witness-something-to-worry-about" gambit. In this case, let him know just how well I had done my homework.

In his direct testimony, Schwartz said he had examined more than eight thousand criminal defendants. I ascertained that the vast majority of these tests were to determine capability to stand trial. In how many cases had he been asked to determine criminal responsibility? "Possibly one hundred," he said. "One hundred fifty."

"Okay," I asked, "when was the first one?"

"I believe the first time was, the first trial that I can recall probably was in sixty-nine."

"James Farley?" I said.

"Yes."

I felt good. "Did you testify in April of 1969 in Queens Supreme Court in that case?"

"I can't remember the exact date," he answered, "but obviously you know it. Yes."

I picked up the Farley transcript, suitably dog-eared and indexed, and carried it to the lectern. Schwartz watched as I put it down in front of him.

With the transcript at hand, I asked what method Schwartz used in deciding if a defendant was malingering, or fabricating answers. He said he used his knowledge and experience. When I tried to hold him to this, he began a lecture on psychotic symptoms. I cut him down immediately, telling him to confine himself to the question.

"Do you remember the question, Doctor?"

"Yes. And I was trying to explain how I reached this decision."

"I asked you whether or not this decision is based upon an intellectual judgment, which is based upon your experience and your background."

"Okay," Schwartz said.

"And the answer is yes or no."

"It's based upon my professional opinion as a forensic psychiatrist."

I flipped the transcript open to a carefully marked page. I did it noisily.

Had Dr. Schwartz been asked a similar question in the Farley case?

"I don't remember what questions exactly Mr. Mosely [the prosecutor] asked me."

I was only too glad to jog his memory. The prosecutor had asked how he determined whether a patient was lying, hallucinating or telling the truth. I read Schwartz's answer: "I can tell you it is more a sense of feel than anything else. I can't spell it out for you. I mean, you have a feeling about a person as to whether or not they are being truthful, and if you think they are not, you, of course, try to confront them with contradictions."

"Did you tell Mr. Mosely that?" I asked.

"I honestly don't remember, Mr. Sullivan, but I don't doubt the authenticity of your records there."

I'll bet you don't, I thought. I didn't want to give him any room to maneuver and I switched to other topics. Fifteen minutes later, I came back to Farley. In determining whether a person was malingering, were there any other tools he could use? "Isn't there one thing you could have done in this case, Doctor?"

I started flipping pages again. Schwartz stared at me. "You have something in mind, Mr. Sullivan. I don't know what."

I grinned at him. "What makes you think I have something in mind?"

Some other people were grinning. Schwartz wasn't. His face remained set when I asked my next question. In his profession, did he use sodium amytal?

"Yes," he said, "it's used usually when there's amnesia or alleged amnesia." He said that although sodium amytal was known among laymen as truth serum, it was not used for that purpose.

I had him. "Do you remember testifying in James Farley, in the James Farley case?"

"In James Farley," answered the doctor. "Yes, as a matter of fact, we did use it on him."

"Why?"

"I thought at the time it would be helpful."

"To get at the truth?"

"That was six years ago."

"Has it changed within six years, Doctor?"

"I have become—what shall I say? I put less stock in it."

But he had used sodium amytal with Farley. Had he thought of using it with DeFeo? No, he said. I brought up Butch's story about Dawn taking part in the murders, and his professed doubts about it. Would sodium amytal have resolved these doubts?

"I don't know," Schwartz said.

"Would you consider using it?"

"Would I now or did I?"

"Did you then?"

"No, I told you before I didn't."

"Would you now?"

He was in a corner. "I don't know," he said.

A few questions later, he tried to wriggle free. I asked if he was saying that he didn't know whether sodium amytal would have helped with DeFeo. "I don't think I need any help from sodium amytal," he said.

"Has something happened within the past two minutes to change your feelings on the subject?"

"Oh, no. My opinion that he was not responsible was clear this morning, Mr. Sullivan. That's the question before us, whether he's criminally responsible. Sodium amytal won't help to add to that opinion in my own mind."

The man was tough. I tried to match him. "Nevertheless, Doctor, you tell us that it is a drug that you have used in the past to get to what the person's actual recollections were at the time of an event in the past?"

"Mr. Sullivan, in the thousands of—or hundreds of cases that I have examined for this question, I think I have used it four times."

"Would you now answer the question, Doctor?"

"I answered it specifically," Dr. Schwartz said, but he couldn't escape. "Yes."

I did not get very far asking if there could have been some basis for DeFeo's animosity toward police, and whether his drug usage could have accounted for paranoid thinking. Then I asked about DeFeo's account of being fired from various jobs because of fighting, and I got what I wanted. Schwartz's answers made it clear that he had accepted the stories as fact. I would show beyond any doubt that they were lies—my rebuttal roster included five of DeFeo's ex-bosses, none of whom had been aware of any such incidents. More proof that Daniel Schwartz did not know the real Ronnie DeFeo.

We took a twenty-five-minute recess in the afternoon, and I came back careless—overemphasizing the obvious and getting slapped down. Had Dr. Schwartz ever examined anyone with more reason to lie than DeFeo? I asked. The doctor said he had, but couldn't give me names. Well, had he ever examined anyone who stood accused under one indictment of six separate murders? No, he said.

"With that in mind, Doctor," I said, "who in the course of your career has had the greatest motive to lie and fabricate to you?"

And Schwartz zapped me. "You can only do life in prison once," he said. "It doesn't matter if there was six people killed or one person killed. Every man I have seen—and there have been plenty—who feared life imprisonment have had good reason to lie."

"Is it your testimony that the fact that this defendant stands accused of killing six is no different than somebody who is standing accused of killing one insofar as the motive to lie?"

"I think this man has less motive to lie because this crime itself shows that there is something wrong with him."

"Is that your answer?"

He zapped me some more. "I think the man who kills only

one person in the course of a felony crime . . . that person has loads of reasons to lie. Because there you have before you a common, well-recognized motive for killing. That man is in bad trouble. I have seen loads—not loads. I have seen men who have killed policemen; they have good reason to lie. Every effort in the country is going to be directed against them. I have seen men who have killed people in public where there were scores of witnesses, factual witnesses, against them, in whom the only evidence was not their confession. Lord, they had good reason to lie."

I'd given him room, and Dr. Schwartz had romped. I was angry at myself, and I wasn't alone. One look at Tom Spota's face was all I needed to know I had company.

It didn't happen again. Near the end of the cross-examination, I even was able to ridicule Schwartz's talent for dramatic psychology. The opportunity came as I forced him to go over all of DeFeo's actions in gathering and hiding evidence, which Harold Zolan and I saw as graphic proof that Butch understood the wrongfulness of this crime. I had gotten to DeFeo's taking a shower and tossing the towel in the pillowcase. "Is this not indicative of a person who has gone to very careful lengths to remove evidence of the crime, that would connect him to that crime, out of that house?" I asked.

"It's evidence of somebody who is trying to remove evidence from himself, too, that he has done this," Schwartz answered. "We are now speculating as to the motive for the cleaning up. If you are familiar with Lady Macbeth's complaint—'What, will these hands never be clean?'—she's not hiding a murder from anyone, but she can't live with the imagined blood on her hands."

Baloney, I thought. I had put a key question to the defense's medical expert, the chief of forensic psychiatry at a leading hospital, and I got Shakespeare in return. We weren't staging a play at Stratford, we were in a courtroom, trying a murder case. I strode to the rail in front of him and slammed my hand on it.

"Doctor," I said, "is that your considered psychiatric opinion?"

Now Schwartz was angry. I turned and walked away, shaking my head. "My considered psychiatric opinion, Counselor," he snapped, talking to my receding back, "is that he's not hiding this crime from anybody by picking up the shells. The bodies are there. The bullets are in the people. You don't use the shells to prove the origin of bullets. You use the bullets themselves. He knows this. The cleaning up is some kind of neurotic, inappropriate act on his part. It's not a concealing of a crime."

It was weak, very weak. I showed the jury how weak in my follow-up questions. "Did you assume that he didn't know the cartridge casings could be connected to his gun?"

"I assume that he knew the shells in the victims could be connected with the gun."

"Doctor, he couldn't get them very well, could he?"

"No, Sir."

"Everything that he could get that would connect him with the crime, he removed from the house, didn't he?"

Schwartz made a mistake. "What you are talking about is trivia compared to the six bodies," he said.

I was blazing. "Trivia that he removed the evidence out of that house that would connect him to the crime, trivia that has nothing to do with whether he thought that the crime was wrong?"

Weber objected to what he called badgering. I apologized, but now it was Schwartz who couldn't stop. "The evidence is there in the victims," he said.

I pressed him about the evidence in the Brooklyn storm drain. Again, he used the word "neurotic" to describe DeFeo's actions. He said DeFeo could have burned the clothing, and scattered the cartridge casings. "Why in one location?" he said. "Why all together?"

I radiated disbelief. "So it's your testimony, as I understand it, Dr. Schwartz, that the fact that it wasn't too bright to throw everything in that sewer drain all together in one location is significant of the fact that it was neurotic that he did this?"

His answer was that it was not consistent with the picture of someone who was knowledgeable about guns and wanted to cover his tracks. Dr. Schwartz was reaching, and I suggested we check his notes. What reason did DeFeo give for throwing the gun into the drain?

Schwartz's annoyance showed. "Perhaps you could expedite things by giving me the page you have in mind?" he said.

I got annoyed back. "I don't find it as easy to read your notes as you do, Doctor."

Schwartz found the place. I repeated the question. "Now, what did he tell you about why he threw the evidence in that storm drain in Brooklyn?"

"He said, 'The place was a mess. I'm not a pig. I wasn't trying to hide nothing. Just put the stuff in storage until I decided what to do.'"

"Do you believe that?" I asked.

"I don't think that he had any one clear purpose in mind at the time. I think that the overall picture of uncertainty was the best explanation of why he did this."

"Did he tell you about not wanting to leave clues for the police?" I rubbed it in by giving him the place. "Top of page fourteen."

Schwartz looked at his notes. "I asked him about the casings, and he said he didn't want to leave the police any clues as to what kind of gun it had been. He was not a friend of the cops, and he didn't want to help them."

"Okay," I said, and I was derisive. "Now you know why he removed the casings, don't you?"

Schwartz sounded petulant. "I know one of the reasons. There are others."

If I looked arrogant, it was deliberate. "I have no further questions."

It was after 5 P.M. Weber's redirect examination lasted less than a half-hour, and did not change anything. I watched the jurors. They were glancing more at the clock in the back of the room than at the witness.

I was ebullient when we left the courtroom. Dan Schwartz wasn't going out on a stretcher, but he was hurting. We weren't.

In the lobby, we shook hands. The doctor smiled. "Where the hell did you dig up James Farley from?" he asked.

"The Farley transcript was easy," I told him. "It was more trouble to dig up your medical school exams."

I was kidding, but for a second Schwartz looked as if he wasn't sure. Then he grinned.

"We country boys do our homework," I said.

Schwartz said good night. He told me he was going home to listen to some opera. As I got in the elevator, I had a last word. "You should read some Shakespeare. Brush up on *Hamlet* for your next trial."

I have to give the doctor credit. He was laughing as the elevator doors closed.

24

BY PUNCHING HOLES in Dan Schwartz's diagnosis, I had demonstrated that Ronald DeFeo, Jr., might not have been psychotic when he murdered his family. That was not quite the same as proving that he was legally sane. And in dealing with Dr. Schwartz, I was not at all sure that I had resolved what Tom Spota called the "he-killed-all-those-people-so-he-must-be-crazy" syndrome. My rebuttal witnesses had to wipe out doubt. It was, at that moment, a case for Harold Zolan.

Dr. Zolan took the stand at 9:45 A.M. on Wednesday, November 12th. The day before had been Veteran's Day, and court had been recessed. It would have been a nice day for rediscovering my family, but that was out of the question. I couldn't even stay home. Tom Spota and I drove to Dr. Zolan's office in Massapequa Park, and spent the day reviewing his testimony.

There was not much small talk; we had to map out our direct

testimony and anticipate Weber's lines of attack. One of the few outside topics we discussed was a murder that had occurred the night before on Suffolk's North Shore. An unknown assailant had bashed a young woman's head in outside a Smithtown bar. At lunchtime, Spota and I went across the street for pizza. Dr. Zolan passed. I wondered afterwards if he would have caught anything unusual in the counterman's behavior. We didn't. But eight hours later, the man who served our pizza would be arrested for the killing in Smithtown. Even the evidence was nearby; he had taken his bloodstained T-shirt, spattered it with spaghetti sauce and tossed it in the dumpster behind the restaurant.

On Wednesday morning, we sent a detective to chauffeur Zolan to Riverhead. The ride took over an hour, and I wanted my star witness fresh and authoritative. The doctor didn't disappoint me; he was dapper and dignified in a gray tweed jacket and matching gray slacks. His silver hair glistened; the morning light burnished the green stone on his ring. "Make sure there's plenty of water," he told me. In court, Harold Zolan's water-consumption could be measured by the pitcher rather than the paper cup. I suspected that the practice aided his system in terms of forensics as well as health—his sipping style allowed him time to mull his answers. I had stung Dr. Schwartz, but I doubted that Bill Weber would be able to do the same thing with Dr. Zolan. Our man was as imperturbable as he was deliberate.

My direct examination lasted almost four hours; three more than Bill Weber had spent with Dan Schwartz. The psychiatrists had opposite styles. Schwartz was most effective when he could expound for five or ten minutes at a time; Zolan's measured speech suited the brief-question-and-answer form. And I wanted to go slowly for the jury's sake. At this point, the jurors had been pelted with psychiatry—almost as if someone had lectured on the split T offense without first explaining the forward pass. I wanted Dr. Zolan to provide some basic concepts of psychiatry, which would help the jurors understand the points at issue. At the outset of his testimony, I asked him to define a psychosis. He described it as "a form of mental illness in which the patient has lost the capacity to deal with reality, to distinguish between reality and fantasy." He added that such patients may develop delusions and hallucinations, but that someone could be psychotic without having these symptoms.

"Now, are there some forms of mental disorders, Doctor," I asked, "which are not as grave or serious as a psychosis?"

"Yes."

I was setting up. "And is antisocial personality one of those?"

"Antisocial personality is a personality disorder, as opposed to a mental illness," he answered.

Soon, we recited the litany that established Dr. Zolan's opinion as to the defendant's sanity at the time of the crime. He testified that Ronald DeFeo, Jr., had substantial capacity to know and appreciate the nature and consequences of his acts and that they were wrong. Based on his examinations, I asked, did he have a diagnosis?

"My diagnosis was that of an antisocial personality," he answered.

I established that DeFeo was not suffering from a psychosis when Dr. Zolan examined him or during the murders. Then I returned to antisocial personality. What were its characteristics?

"The antisocial personality runs a fairly wide gamut," said Dr. Zolan, "including people who appear different but actually basically are the same. And that gamut extends from a smooth, persuasive con artist to the aggressive, destructive, rather obviously criminal activity that we are more apt to identify as an antisocial personality. The characteristics, the basic characteristics of all antisocial personalities are that they are people who have not been socialized into the society in which they live. They pretty much have a code of their own. They are people who are grossly selfish and callous, who are extremely egocentric, who have no capacity to experience or to feel guilt. They have a low frustration tolerance. They are easily aroused and at times often explosive. And their main purpose in life is self-gratification, generally regardless of what the cost to others."

He took a sip of water. "I should add one other important thing, and that is that the antisocial personality fails to benefit from experience or punishment, and therefore is found to repeat antisocial acts despite the fact that they have been punished or warned or admonished. They probably constitute one of the largest groups of recidivists in our penal institutions."

"Now, Dr. Zolan, can you tell us how these or any of these characteristics of antisocial personality affect the ability or capacity of one to know and appreciate the wrongfulness of his conduct?"

"They do not affect it in any way at all," he said.

With the diagnosis in hand, I had Dr. Zolan review the examinations he conducted with DeFeo. He explained how DeFeo's consuming need to get his way in school indicated antisocial personality, and he discussed Butch's drug usage. I asked what happened when a user came off speed. Dr. Zolan said the result could be either deep depression or, less common, a period of paranoid thinking. He said DeFeo's violent episodes at that time could have resulted from his withdrawal.

I wanted to spotlight the malingering issue, and I spent an hour having Zolan read portions of the first examination, in which DeFeo was fabricating. Then we went back to basics. "Now, Dr. Zolan," I asked, "can you tell us what malingering is?"

"Malingering," he said, "is defined as feigning disease, pretending to have a disease."

At any point during his examinations, did he consider whether DeFeo was malingering?

"I came to the conclusion that there was no mental illness," the psychiatrist answered, "and that the symptoms that were

315

being presented as a form of mental illness constituted a form of malingering."

He elaborated. To start with, Butch was too easily deterred. He told Zolan he went to a bar with hand grenades to get even with someone who poisoned him. But he did nothing because police were there. A person suffering from a paranoid delusion would not have held back for anyone—including police. Secondly, DeFeo had too many symptoms. "I don't mean to be facetious," said Dr. Zolan, "but I would say that he was too psychotic. He had everything. He was hearing voices all the time. Now, even psychotic people don't hear voices all the time. Everybody was against him—everybody. Even people with paranoid delusions don't believe that everybody is against them."

We moved to the second examination, and I had Zolan read the questions and answers relating to the murders. Generally, the responses followed the testimony DeFeo had given a few days before. I asked Zolan to comment on each statement by DeFeo that was clearly fabrication. My fear was that jurors might buy the whole mishmash no matter what—I was dealing with the he-must-be-crazy syndrome

Dr. Zolan emphasized the following implausibilities:

• DeFeo said he watched television and fell asleep after he heard his family plotting to kill him. A normal person would try to stay awake after hearing something like that. A paranoid person would try even harder.

• DeFeo said that after shooting his parents, he left the loaded rifle in the television room, where Dawn was able to grab it. This made no sense. Especially since Dawn supposedly told him that she intended to kill everybody.

• DeFeo said he ran upstairs after Dawn and caught her as she was reloading the gun. "He would certainly not go up to her room unarmed," Dr. Zolan said. "I would suggest he would either arm himself, or if he couldn't, he would get out of the house."

316

• The whole business of not hearing shots when he pulled the trigger. Dr. Schwartz had described this as dissociation, and contended that DeFeo lacked sufficient education or sophistication to make up the symptom. Dr. Zolan asserted that such fabrication had nothing to do with education, but would be influenced by motivation and shrewdness. Butch DeFeo was more than shrewd enough to come up with it. I asked him to assume that Butch actually had experienced a dissociative reaction. What would that mean? Dr. Zolan said that would only strengthen his belief that Butch knew he had done wrong. Such blocking out was triggered by guilt. And the awareness of guilt implied wrongfulness. Finally, there was another consideration: people who were not mentally ill suffered dissociative reactions under stress. Dr. Schwartz had based his belief that DeFeo wasn't faking on his not hearing the shots. Nonsense, I thought. We had given the jury three alternatives to show that either DeFeo was malingering or the symptom had nothing to do with insanity—and everything to do with guilt.

Next, I attended to a loose end. Weber had given no indication that he might try for a verdict of extreme emotional disturbance, which would call for a manslaughter conviction rather than a murder conviction. But I was afraid that he might go for it on a catchall basis; that at the last minute, he might ask Judge Stark to include extreme emotional disturbance in his charge to the jury. I had seen juries deadlocked in murder trials compromise on manslaughter. It had little to do with evidence; it had a great deal to do with people. "Now, Doctor," I asked, "do you have an opinion as to whether or not the crime occurred as part of a frenzy as a result of an extreme emotional disturbance?"

"Yes, Sir, I have such an opinion."

"What is your opinion?"

"I do not believe that it occurred as part of a frenzy or an extreme emotional disturbance."

Zolan's reason was that the murders and the elimination of

317

evidence were too systematic. A crime committed under great stress did not fit the carefulness demonstrated by DeFeo.

From there, it was a hop, skip and small jump to one of the strongest segments of Harold Zolan's testimony—the manner in which DeFeo's attempts to establish an alibi proved that he understood the nature of his act and its wrongfulness. "He told me that he went from room to room and picked up the shell casings," Zolan testified. "I think he had to crawl under some piece of furniture to get one of them. He then piled them in the hallway, along with the gun and with, I believe, other objects. I think they were a box of shells, an empty box which had contained some shells, and perhaps some other items which I don't remember, and then he proceeded to take a shower and left the house."

"All right," I asked, "now can you tell us, Doctor, what significance, if any, that conduct played in your opinion, particularly with respect to his ability to know and appreciate the wrongfulness of his conduct?"

"Well, in my opinion, these acts—and I did leave out one item. He, as I recall, mentioned that he subsequently put these in a pillowcase. The gathering of all this material, which would have been identifiable with the gun that he owned and with which the crime was committed, demonstrated the awareness of and appreciation of the wrongfulness of the act."

"In what way?" I asked. "How is that demonstrated?"

"Well, by eliminating your connection with a crime, you—or in order to consider eliminating your connection with a crime—you must first be aware that it is a wrongful act or there would be no purpose in eliminating evidence. So when evidence of a crime is removed, in my opinion, it is removed, provided it is removed by the perpetrator, for the purpose of dissociating himself or herself from the crime."

Zolan spoke slowly, authoritatively, even bluntly. Butch had told him he threw the rifle into the water instead of giving it to police because he wanted to be able to attend to his family's burial. I asked Dr. Zolan what he thought of the excuse. "I didn't believe it," he said. Or there were Butch's phone calls to his house. What did Dr. Zolan think about them?

"My opinion is that he was setting up an alibi," the psychiatrist answered.

Zolan was equally cynical about DeFeo's carryings-on at Henry's and the murder scene. "In my opinion, all of this was an act that was being put on for the purpose of furthering the alibi that he was setting up for himself; that here he had come upon this tragic scene and now he was overwhelmed and wanted the emotional support and, of course, also the physical presence of these people."

Nor did the doctor hesitate when I asked about DeFeo's visit to Junie Reimer before going home. Zolan said DeFeo knew what he was going to find in his house. "Even an antisocial personality is going to have some reaction to finding six dead bodies. And, in my opinion, he did what he did at the Reimers to fortify himself against that ordeal."

By now, Dr. Zolan's water pitcher had been replenished. He poured another cup as we returned to the antisocial personality. The psychiatrist discussed DeFeo's need to blame other people for his troubles, and went into Butch's relationship with his father. "In my opinion, this defendant was attempting to build himself up into a big man. . . . You know, the macho image, the man of great strength and virility. This is an image which is very understandably diminished and even prevented from developing when your father can reach out and pull you back each time you make an effort to become independent of him."

As DeFeo became older, his father controlled him through money. "He is fully aware of the value of money, of his own lack of any real capacity to earn money, because he's held many jobs and he's never been able to keep a job, and the only source of money is his father, who doles it out and doles it out very, very generously. But there is always a string attached. And it's that string which ultimately becomes strangulating to this defendant."

Eventually, even DeFeo's sexual potency became affected. "And this, I think," said Dr. Zolan, "played perhaps not a key part, but certainly an important enough part in having the defendant reach a point where he just had to be his own man and be free of all restraint, and that any restraint that he had, most of which was exerted by his father, would result, among other things, in his impotence. Although he was not consciously aware of this . . . not consciously aware of his sexual impotence. He certainly was aware of impotence in another way. He was really not at all a free agent. There was only one way that a personality type like this could resolve this problem, and that is to eliminate the source of these restraints, which he proceeded to do."

I decided to bring the discussion right up against the jurors; I wanted them to feel what we were talking about. They had watched Ronnie DeFeo sneer and swagger on the stand. Dr. Zolan had read the transcript of DeFeo's testimony. Had he found any evidence in it of what he called the macho syndrome?

"Well," Zolan answered, "it is my recollection that during his testimony, the defendant indulged in a number of bravado outbursts in the courtroom, indicating his contempt for the proceedings . . . and then even stated parenthetically or words to the effect that I would come down there and kill you, meaning yourself. All of this adds up to the strong individual, the individual who cares about nothing, is afraid of nothing. In fact, he repeatedly states in his statement to me . . . that he's not afraid of anything. He has no fear. And this is essentially what he was trying to convey in the courtroom."

I had a final area to explore that was extra-satisfying. Under *People* v. *Sugden*, we were able to offer into evidence records that Weber had turned over to Dr. Zolan just before the latter's first examination of DeFeo. They were the notes of a psychiatrist—whom I shall refer to as Dr. Y.—who saw DeFeo between March, 1966, and March, 1967. Weber objected, but was overruled. I couldn't blame him, but I enjoyed his annoyance—we were using his material to bolster our case.

Primarily, Dr. Y. had concerned himself with Butch's school problems. The records indicated that some of what DeFeo had told Dr. Zolan about school was not true—or at least exaggerated. Dr. Y described the fourteen-year-old DeFeo as a withdrawn child who bought protection from hostile peers and got other kids to throw his snowballs. His mother told the doctor that "Ronald used to ask me if I loved him." His father wanted the boy to be more aggressive. According to a psychological report included in the records, the family needed counseling. Dr. Zolan read from the report: "Impression is that Ronald's problems serve family needs, preserving a familial balance, albeit maladjusted. Father projects hostility re: authority figures who mistreat Ronald. Enables father to project, and yet vindicate himself via his beneficent efforts for Ronald. Parents see Ronald as problem; they have, by their attitudes toward him, written out a script for him to follow. Which he does, playing the role of the bewilderingly bad boy."

Dr. Zolan said that Dr. Y.'s records provided him with a clue to DeFeo's development as an antisocial personality. I asked him to explain. His response was the closest he came to a lecture, but it held the jury: "The antisocial personality, as I have mentioned before, has a wide spectrum. But there are some psychiatrists—and I happen to agree with them—who believe that actually there are two types of antisocial personalities. There is the antisocial personality who is just born that way, and then there is the other who becomes that way based on the factors in his environment which produce certain pressures and stresses on him.

"Now this defendant was seen by a psychiatrist and a psychologist when he was somewhere between the ages of fourteen and fifteen. He is noted to be a passive-aggressive individual. A passive-aggressive individual is an individual who never manifests overtly aggressive behavior, but feels aggressive, never expresses it directly, gets other people to do it for him. . . . Now, on the other hand, this passive-aggressive individual is being urged to assert himself. His father tells the doctor, 'Dr. Y., I wish he could become more aggressive.' I have no doubt that this father told this not only to the doctor but to the defendant as well. And not only that, but displayed a perfect model for aggressive behavior. And this defendant began to follow this aggressive model which was provided for him, and he began to assert himself; he began to be aggressive. But of course, always with the awareness, always with the knowledge, that there was one figure in the background that could prevent all of this from continuing. . . ."

Zolan took a long sip and set down the cup. "So the father was saying to him, 'Be aggressive, but don't be aggressive.' Nonetheless, despite his father's attempts at suppression, this defendant did become more and more aggressive, attempting to make impressions on people that he was a big man, an important man and that the various things that he did to start fights to produce the image of the macho were all for the purpose of attempting to overcome what started out as a passive-aggressive individual and now is becoming more and more overtly aggresive to the point where he finally reached a point of aggression where he committed the ultimate crime."

I had been as intent on Dr. Zolan's words as any member of the jury. He had just filled in the evolution of a mass-murderer. To my mind, it was a much more believable sequence than the one given by Dr. Schwartz. And a more frightening one. Dr. Schwartz had described a psychotic. Hell, we know all about them; the movies are full of them. But Dr. Zolan had described a sociopath. A shy kid who wanted to be a big man. A teenager who had everything and could never get enough because he also had nothing. A killer who came from the new America. A killer who could have lived next door to anybody in Amityville, Long Island, or Shaker Heights, Ohio.

A killer who could grow on my street. It always came back to that. Butch DeFeo was suburbia's child.

For right now, a killer who wasn't crazy. I had one last question: "Now, Doctor, in any event, beginning with the early indications of his personality disorder as reflected in Dr. Y.'s reports and in the later history of this defendant's life as you have heard it from various sources, including the defendant, do you find any indication that would support a psychosis?"

"None whatsoever," replied Dr. Zolan.

Weber went after Dr. Zolan for a hour and a half with little effect. It was close to 5 P.M. and Judge Stark excused the jury while we argued over whether to continue the session. Weber wanted to stop, and resume his cross-examination in the morning. However, Dr. Zolan said that would be almost impossible for him. He had patients who needed him, and he had put their appointments over a day. And on Friday, he was scheduled to testify in Nassau County. Judge Stark settled the issue. We would recess for dinner, and return at 7:25 P.M.

At dinner in a Riverhead restaurant, Tom Spota, Harold Zolan and I talked about the doctor's testimony and about the crime itself. We also talked about the date. In a matter of hours it would be the first anniversary of what had occurred at 112 Ocean Avenue, Amityville, on November 13, 1974. The jurors were eating somewhere else in Riverhead, and I figured that they, too, had made the connection. I wondered about DeFeo and what he was thinking.

When we returned, Weber bulldogged Dr. Zolan for another hour and a half. I felt that he was not able to detract from Zolan's diagnosis. But by keeping Zolan on the defensive, he showed that the psychiatrist was partisan. Dr. Zolan was for the prosecution as much as Dr. Schwartz was for the defense. And at 9 P.M., Weber pulled a tactical move I had to admire. "Your

Honor," he said, "I have another portion to go through, but I feel it's going to take me too long, and I respectfully request we adjourn."

Judge Stark compromised. "We will take a short recess," he said. He turned to the jury. "All right, ten minutes, ladies and gentlemen. You will be retired to the jury room, ladies and gentlemen."

Weber tried to break in. "Your Honor—" he started.

"Retire the jury, please," said Judge Stark.

Bang! "I have no further questions of this witness, Your Honor," said Weber.

"You completed your cross-examination?"

"I can't conduct it until twelve o'clock, midnight, Your Honor, and I will not conduct it."

Judge Stark was not giving in this time. "I'll tell you how long you should proceed, Sir."

"Your Honor, I will not participate in a trial that's going to go until twelve o'clock, midnight, under these conditions."

The jurors were still in the room. "I think the jury should be retired," I said.

The jurors left, and Judge Stark looked at Weber the way junior high principals look at kids who throw sandwiches in the lunch room. "Mr. Weber," he said, "I do not appreciate such expressions of petulance. We will take the ten-minute recess, and you may conduct such cross-examination as you choose, Sir."

The irresistible force had met the immovable object. "Your Honor," Weber said, "I have advised the court I have no further questions. I will not conduct a cross-examination until twelve o'clock, midnight."

"All right," Judge Stark said. "Ten minutes, gentlemen."

I was scared stiff. I was positive Bill Weber was thinking ahead to an appeal. All an appellate court had to do was decide that Weber's right to cross-examine a key witness had been abridged, and we were in deep trouble. If we got a conviction, it would be wiped out on appeal. An appellate court would not be overly concerned with Dr. Zolan's professional obligations. It would be very concerned with the defense's rights. It would be difficult to justify continuing a cross-examination into the night after almost two months of trial.

During the recess, I communicated my worry to Zolan, and he volunteered a solution. There was no way he could come back the next day without endangering two of his patients. But he could testify Friday afternoon, following his Nassau appearance.

We returned to court, and I announced that we would send a police car for Zolan on Friday as soon as he was finished in Nassau. I glanced at Weber. My gut feeling was that he was bluffing, that he really didn't have much cross-examination left. If he wanted to play poker, I could do that, too. I called. "I would ask counsel that if he seriously intends to further cross-examine substantively, that he pursue this opportunity. If not, why if he has only a few more questions, that he pursue it this evening."

Bill didn't exactly raise, but he saw me. "I appreciate the offer, Your Honor. I will accept it. I do have at least two hours of further cross-examination."

As it turned out, Dr. Zolan's Nassau trial was rescheduled and he was able to appear in the morning on Friday. But Weber had been bluffing after all. Or he was a poor judge of time. His projected two hours actually took only a half-hour. Again, he was effective in identifying Zolan as a member of our team. In a statement-within-a-question, Weber claimed that the doctor examined a defendant for the Nassau district attorney's office before the man had been arrested. The inference was that the pyschiatrist sometimes functioned as an auxiliary detective. Zolan remembered the case, and said he assumed the arrest had already been made when he was called in. On redirect examination, I asked if he had ever been retained to obtain a confession. "Never, under any circumstances," he said.

I took advantage of Dr. Zolan's presence, and spent an hour reinforcing his testimony. He said that DeFeo had never discussed *Castle Keep* with him or attributed his actions to the movie. And the doctor testified that he believed Butch's story about trying to shoot his father in 1973. According to Dr. Zolan, the incident fit the picture of an antisocial personality. He said that if DeFeo really was stopping a fight, he could have found another way. "But the use of a gun, a gun such as the defendant used—I believe it was a shotgun—to stop this is typical of the threatening, menacing attitude that the antisocial personality will often take to intimidate people. This is characteristic of the antisocial personality, who is a callous individual, who is one who intimidates other people, or at least attempts to intimidate other people."

The next day, Dr. Zolan flew to Florida for a two-week vacation at his condominium in Palm Beach. I figured we had added to the comfort of his time in the sun—he would send us a bill for three thousand dollars.

It's easy to sound cavalier about money that doesn't come out of your own pocket, I suppose, but I had never been as willing to authorize a payment. Win, lose or deadlock, the people of Suffolk County—at least the ones included in *The People* v. *Ronald DeFeo, Jr.*—had gotten their money's worth from Harold Zolan.

25

I MADE SURE John Donahue wore his school uniform to court. John was two months away from his tenth birthday. He had blond hair, blue eyes and a high clear voice. "How did you know John DeFeo?" I asked him.

"We were friends from the first grade," he answered. Sitting up straight in the witness chair in his white shirt and plaid tie, he evoked the slain boy.

Although Dr. Zolan was my key rebuttal witness, I attended to other phases of the case. I called John Donahue to squash the brutality issue.

"John," I asked, "do you remember the last time you saw John DeFeo?"

"Yes."

"When was that?"

"On Monday."

"What Monday was that?"

"I don't remember."

"Was it the Monday before the things happened at their house?"

"Yes."

"Was it the Monday before he died?"

"Yes."

At the hearing, I had to ask several questions to get a full description of the fight the child had witnessed between Butch and his father in the DeFeo basement. This time, it came out in a breathless swoop. "His [John Defeo's] brother asked for some more money and he wanted a new car. Then his father said no, and his brother punched him, and then he punched him back, and then we went upstairs." John Donahue pointed to his mouth to show where the elder DeFeo had struck Butch. If Ronald DeFeo, Jr., had a bruised lip at his arraignment, it came from a fistfight with his father.

I was putting finishing touches on the picture of a liar. A good enough liar to con the psychiatrist who testified in his defense. Dr. Schwartz had accepted DeFeo's stories about losing jobs because of fights. I called five of his former bosses, and all told similar stories. He had been dismissed from Fairchild because of absenteeism, he had quit his uncle's pharmacy after shortages were discovered. But he had never been fired for fighting. As far as the five witnesses knew, Butch had never even been involved in any fights.

The liar put on charades. I called James DeVito to critique DeFeo's prison performance. DeVito was a useful witness, but hardly as central as I had thought he would be when Tom Spota called him to my attention three months before. The corrections officer testified that Butch launched the crazy act after an article about the murders appeared in a national magazine. Butch read it and asked DeVito if the jailer thought he would reach the same status as mass-murderer Charles Manson. "Yeah," DeVito recalled answering, "I think you are going to be as big as Manson."

"'Mr. D.,'" Butch told him, "'I wish you could come to my trial.

You are going to see a show like you never saw before.'"

DeVito gave a synopsis of the show DeFeo staged in jail—he described Butch taking off his clothes, climbing the cell bars, acting forgetful, setting things on fire. And practicing a deranged laugh. "I would come down the hall," testified DeVito. "I would say, 'Okay, Ronnie, let's hear it,' and he would start the laugh. And he would say, 'How is that, Mr. D?' I said, 'Bad, Ronnie, very bad.'"

Two other corrections officers, Emil Ross and Vincent D'Augusta, backed up DeVito. But nobody was as effective in exposing DeFeo's jailhouse dramatics as John Arthur Kramer, the gap-toothed felon whose police record included a conviction for committing arson to an outhouse.

I wanted Kramer to feel important, and, the weekend before his testimony, I had George Harrison and Dennis Rafferty bring him to our office in Riverhead. I ushered him into District Attorney Henry O'Brien's deserted inner-sanctum, which oozed first-class accommodations in the form of thick new carpets, teak-paneled walls and a well-polished walnut desk. Within minutes, Kramer was leaning back in O'Brien's large leather chair, with his feet propped up on the desk. As he talked, he chainsmoked Rafferty's cigarettes.

By the end of the day, John Kramer had come to think of himself as our star witness. And I think he saw himself as performing a public duty because he never asked for a deal. A large part of the day had passed when I realized this, and I began to worry. Kramer had put no conditions on his testimony. Weber was certain to ask Kramer what he was getting in return for taking the stand. Suppose Kramer said he wasn't getting a thing? The jurors were knowledgeable citizens who watched television, went to movies and read newspapers. They knew a convict never turned state's witness unless he got a deal. They would be suspicious of Kramer to begin with. They would be even more suspicious if he said he was testifying out of public spirit. It would never do.

I made an offer. If Kramer testified truthfully, I would

recommend that he get two to four years instead of three-and-a-half to seven on his upcoming sentencing for third-degree burglary. Further, I would ask that he be allowed to serve the time upstate in protective custody. Since he hadn't asked for anything, Kramer was as delighted as a teenage girl with a free pair of designer jeans. As for me, I couldn't see where I was defeating justice—the crime for which I would recommend a minimal sentence was the theft of twenty dollars from the woman he claimed had invited him home from a bar.

Kramer did have one request. He wanted to look like an important witness, which was difficult in prison clothes. He insisted that we arrange for his father to deliver a suit he could wear.

On Monday, I called John Arthur Kramer to the stand. His entrance called for a marching band, or at least a good kazoo player. He strode to the witness chair with Rafferty on one side of him and Harrison on the other. If his escort had not attracted notice, his outfit would have. It was a nice suit, but it was two sizes too large.

He could have been wearing pajamas. John Kramer was a powerhouse witness. He had been locked in the slammer with Butch DeFeo, and he was telling Butch's story the way Butch had told it to him. Butch had told him plenty. Butch had told him about the phony holdup, about the fights with his father and about his plan to beat the rap by pleading insanity and getting out in two or three years. "Ronnie had admitted to me that he had done the killings," Kramer testified. "Ronnie said that he will beat it by reason of insanity. I said, 'Ronnie'—I just told him, I says, 'Ronnie, I can't see how you are going to beat it by reason of insanity.'"

His testimony went beyond DeFeo's conduct in jail. John Kramer helped us prove that DeFeo's motive was made of money, not madness. I asked if Butch had told him about a hiding place for money in the DeFeo home. "Yes," Kramer answered, "in the bottom—in the floor, like."

"He took the money out the night before," Kramer added, "and he buried it."

"All right. The night before what, Mr. Kramer?"

"The night before the killings."

"How much money did he say that he removed?"

"He said there was about two hundred thousand dollars or more in cash, and there was a couple of hundred thousand dollars in jewelry."

"What did he say that he did with that?"

"He said that he buried it. . . . He said that he removed the money because he was going to take off with his girlfriend and that he needed the money, and that he needed money for her. . . . And he was just going to take off with the money and everything, and just leave, and that his father had found out that he was taking some money. Then it led to a big argument, fight and everything."

When it came to cross-examination, Kramer shone; he was used to being grilled. Several times, DeFeo whispered to his counsel. But each time Weber asked a question after one of these huddles, Kramer shot it down.

Weber went after Kramer's debriefing by Rafferty. What did he tell the detective at their first meeting? The question backfired when Kramer mentioned telling Rafferty about running into DeFeo in the courthouse. DeFeo asked him to testify for the defense, and he refused. "I said, 'Ronnie, no, I would not,' because that would be perjury and I would not lie for him. I didn't want to get involved in it."

"Because Ronnie couldn't promise you anything," Weber pressed. "Is that right?"

"Ronnie offered me money," Kramer said.

"He did?"

"Yes, he did."

"How much?"

It was like watching a counter-puncher. "Ronnie offered me one thousand dollars to testify for him," Kramer said.

"Did you think that he had the money to pay you?"

"Did I think so? Yes, I thought he did."

The cross-examination reached a peak when Weber asked if Kramer had coached DeFeo in his crazy act.

"I told him to do stupid things," Kramer answered.

"Like what?"

Kramer responded with pride. "Scream. Yell. Bang on the wall. Hit the wall with your head. I told him to sit up on the shelf. I told him to go under your bed, do anything. I admit it. Yes, I did."

The Stanislavski of sickbay, I thought. I felt like applauding. As a self-confessed drama coach, Kramer was proof positive that DeFeo's lunatic behavior in prison was a well-planned act.

I took a second turn with Kramer. With a specific purpose in mind, I asked for everything he could remember about meeting Butch in the courthouse.

He gave me what I was after. "I went to court one day, and I seen Mr. DeFeo. You know, I was asking him how his case was going along. He says, 'Not too bad.' He says, 'Don't worry. I'll take it.' I said, 'Ronnie, you know, it doesn't look good for you.' Then I had seen him another time and I had went to court again. And he said, 'Do you know that Mr. DeVito is going to testify?' I said, 'No, I did not know.' He says well if I get to see Mr. DeVito, tell him he's got a nice wife and he's got a nice daughter. He says, 'If he testifies, tell him I'll do something.' So I had went to the dentist. And I saw Mr. DeVito and I told Mr. DeVito what Mr. DeFeo had said. And then, from then, I saw Detective Rafferty . . ."

Shortly before 10 A.M. on November 17, I called the witness I had saved for last. He was Burt Borkan, the beseiged cop we had turned up just a few weeks before. The man who had heard Butch DeFeo threaten to kill his father.

Quickly, I elicited Borkan's close relationship with the De-

Feos, his long friendship with Ronald, Sr., the fact that he was Allison's godfather. Then I asked about the scene he had witnessed at the Buick agency the Friday before the murders. It was between 5 and 5:30 P.M., he said, and Butch and his father were arguing.

"Mr. Borkan," I asked, "can you tell the court and jury what, if anything, you heard Ronald DeFeo, Sr., say?"

"That he had the devil on his shoulder and he got to get rid of the devil."

"Can you describe the voice in which he said this?"

"A very harsh voice."

"Now, at that point in time, what was he doing with respect to Ronald DeFeo, Jr.?"

"He was practically face-to-face or leaning in on Ronald, Jr."

"Mr. Borkan, can you tell us what, if anything, you heard Ronald DeFeo, Jr., say to his father?" I asked.

"He told—he called him a fat prick and something. He said, 'I'll kill you.'"

"And upon his saying that, what, if anything else, did he do?"

"He ran to his car and got in his car and left."

The threat was what I wanted the jury to hear. The threat to kill that preceded the murders by a few days. The threat that showed premeditation. Then I asked about the following Wednesday, when blood and bodies scarred 112 Ocean Avenue, and Burt Borkan hailed Butch DeFeo at the Buick agency. "I asked Ronald, Jr., to tell his father to call me."

"Did he say anything to you in reply?"

"Just looked at me and he took off."

The family friend was within arm's length of Ronnie and saw his face. It was two days after Butch and his father had fought in the basement. "He had a bruise on the right side of his lip," Borkan testified.

On cross-examination, Weber did what I would have done. He attacked Borkan's credibility by accenting his troubles in

Brooklyn. Borkan invoked the Fifth Amendment eleven times. Then Weber asked about Borkan's deal with the Brooklyn district attorney's office. Had he come to an understanding with them? Yes, Borkan answered.

"And part of that understanding permits you to remain on the job under the public payroll, is that correct?" Weber was in high gear. "Is that correct?"

"I take the Fifth Amendment on that," Borkan said.

I had already emphasized that Burt Borkan had nothing to gain by appearing in the DeFeo case. He wanted to. I rested my case. After that, Weber called his rebuttal witnesses. It was the last day of testimony.

The defense tried to discredit John Kramer by calling two county jail inmates, Robert A. Luongo, Jr., and Vito Coscia. Luongo testified that Kramer's reputation for telling the truth was "very bad." What I tried to demonstrate was that his was even worse. I made it clear that Mr. Luongo had been extradited from Sweden for embezzling hundreds of thousands of dollars from Suffolk investors in a Ponzi scheme. On cross-examination, he took the Fifth eight times.

Coscia was the child-murderer I had been prosecuting when I took over the DeFeo case. I never even had to cross-examine Coscia. He pleaded the Fifth the minute Weber asked his first question, which was whether he was presently incarcerated in the Suffolk jail.

Shortly before the day ended, Weber recalled Ronald DeFeo, Jr. DeFeo took his curtain call in character, slouching and sneering at a courtroom packed with high school law classes. His testimony consisted of denials. He never divulged anything to Kramer because Kramer was a rat who testified against other inmates. He never said anything to DeVito, who kept bothering him. He never even saw Burt Borkan at the Buick agency the

Friday before the murders. He never in his life heard his father say anything about having a devil on his shoulders. And the day he was supposed to have had a fistfight with his father, he never got home until 7 or 7:30 P.M. And he never hated his family. "I didn't have hatred for any of them," he told Weber. "I loved them all."

The denials continued as I cross-examined him for the last time. DeFeo denied that he had a physical confrontation with his father the week of the murders; he denied that he performed a monkey act in sickbay; he denied that he sat on the shelf in his cell.

"You never sat up on the shelf in the sickbay area?" I asked.

"No, Sir. I had no reason to do anything like that."

"No reason at all, right?" I said.

"To do something like that?"

"Yes."

"I can't see why, Mr. Sullivan."

I hated Ronald DeFeo, Jr. But the hate was ice instead of fire, and I let him feel the chill. "The fact that the rest of your life depends upon this defense is no reason at all. Is that correct, Mr. DeFeo?"

"Mr. Sullivan," DeFeo answered, "I couldn't care less what happens in this courtroom."

He repeated the statement to Weber. It made headlines in the next day's newspapers, but I didn't think anyone in the courtroom believed it. Weber and I were down to our summations. If there were any more questions, they would have to come from the jury.

26

BILL WEBER'S SUMMATION took up the morning; mine filled the afternoon. They both came down to the insanity defense.

"Justice doesn't dictate convictions in all cases," Weber said. "Sometimes, justice dictates psychiatric treatment, even in the face of six murders, even in the face of what we are dealing with today."

Weber called for a verdict of not guilty by reason of mental disease, and he strummed the "must-be-crazy" syndrome: "What more proof of the defense of disease of the mind could there be than the mere fact that Ronald DeFeo, Jr., stands accused of the crime of murdering all six members of his family? . . . Isn't there some feeling—I know there is in my mind and my gut—that were anybody to do this, he's got to have a diseased mind, he's got to be sick? There is a psychiatrist who bolsters that gut feeling—Dr. Schwartz. Are we going to disbelieve him? There are witnesses who bolster the develop-

ment of Ronald DeFeo's stormy mind. Are we going to disbelieve them? . . . There is reason to believe in this case more
than just a mere doubt. There is reason to believe that Ronald
DeFeo, at the time he committed this act, was acting under a
diseased mind, incapable of understanding that what he was
doing was wrong."

I tried not to overdramatize the facts. I said the murders were
planned and premeditated, methodical rather than impas-
sioned. I stressed the deliberate manner in which DeFeo
operated—putting the dog outside, removing the evidence,
setting up an alibi. And I discussed motive. DeFeo killed for
what he told John Kramer was "not just a few bucks, but big
money, between one hundred and two hundred thousand
dollars."

I did not say that DeFeo was normal. "There is no question,"
I said, pointing at him, "but the fact that there sits an abnormal
person. Normal people do not kill other people. If we are to
determine that normalcy is the test, then let us unlock the
jailhouse doors. Normal people don't commit crimes, and
normal people don't kill six people.

"Bear in mind," I said, "that we don't say that he did not
suffer from some abnormality. . . . Ronald DeFeo, if you will,
was sick, sick with an antisocial personality, but in no way and
not for one minute that night—and I think you good people at
this point in this case are prepared to accept it—not for one
minute did he believe that what he was doing was right."

Not to hold DeFeo criminally responsible for his acts because
of their venal nature, I argued, was to condone what he had
done. I told the jurors to look for the motives. "Consider the
evidence that he did it out of his warped character and
antisocial personality anyway and didn't feel one bit of guilt
about it. He didn't display it for one minute in this courtroom in
three days of testimony. And that's how he was capable of doing
it, and that's how he found himself able to sit up there on that
stand for three days and to revel in telling you about it.

"Ultimately, members of the jury," I said, "you have got to accept, you have got to conclude that there are people in this world capable of extreme and hateful evil. One of them has sat just a few feet from you during seven weeks of trial. Now, I ask you in your verdict, that you come back here and identify him as such a person. I ask you to find him guilty of six counts of murder in the second-degree, because that, members of the jury, is what he did."

27————

JUDGE Stark INSTRUCTED THE JURY on Wednesday, November 19. He had begun working on the two-hour charge on Veteran's Day, writing with a black pen on lined, white paper, underlining with a red pencil and using his own shorthand, which included a triangle to denote the defendant. After covering all aspects of the case and the law, the judge explained that DeFeo faced six counts of second-degree murder, one for each victim, and that there were four possible verdicts on each count—guilty as charged, guilty of manslaughter in the first-degree, not guilty by reason of mental disease or defect, or not guilty, period. He asked for verdicts "which are at the same time fair to the defendant, Ronald DeFeo, and fair to the People of the State of New York."

And he gave me something to worry about. In his summation, Weber charged that I had been obligated to call Lieutenant David Menzies, who had been in charge of the Fourth

Precinct when Wyssling came in seeking DeFeo. The lieutenant had been a lackluster witness at the hearing, and I had not thought it worth bringing him back from his Florida retirement for the trial. I felt as if Judge Stark had pointed out my mistake with red arrows. "If you find that the People have failed to give a reasonable explanation for not calling Menzies as a witness on this issue," he told the jury, "then you may infer or conclude that his testimony would not have been contrary to that of Richard Wyssling."

At 12:45 P.M., the jury was retired and the waiting began. We waited for three days. I had a great deal of work backed up, but I didn't get much done. I took long lunches, hoped for a verdict and agonized. Several times, I was called to the courtroom for read-backs—requests by the jury for the repeat of specific testimony.

On Thursday, Henry O'Brien took Rafferty, Harrison, Spota and me to dinner at a pub in Westhampton. O'Brien had not been around during the trial, but now he was showing a lot of interest. I was dubious about the sudden attention, but I appreciated the dinner. I didn't know how much I needed the break. I had a few drinks, and they hit me right away. When a Westhampton Village cop came in looking for "District Attorney Sullivan," I was extremely relaxed. Unfortunately, I was wanted in court.

Rafferty drove me back. I don't know if Judge Stark could tell I was sloshed, but Bill Weber had a big grin on his face. Rafferty, Harrison and Spota splashed water on my face, buttoned my jacket and straightened my tie. They stayed close to me in the courtroom, and I did my best to concentrate.

The jury had asked for read-backs. My concentration improved when I realized that one juror was leaning forward intently, and the others were all watching her. She was Rosemary Konrad, the supermarket cashier. It was a telltale sign that she had asked for the read-back. Or worse—that she was holding out.

340

One of the read-backs concerned Phyllis Procita's account of her visit to DeFeo in jail, when he tried to involve Dawn. The other request was worded as follows in the note handed to Judge Stark: "Testimony during interrogation of DeFeo by detectives concerning the dog screaming at the time of the commission of the crime. Rafferty's testimony?"

The read-back showed that Rafferty had quoted DeFeo as talking about the barking dog a few minutes before he confessed: "He said to me, 'You asked me before about the dog.' And I quote him. He said, 'The fucking dog was screaming while this was going on.' He said, 'The dog was screaming.'"

The dog, I thought. That afternoon, before we went to dinner, the jurors had asked Judge Stark to reinstruct them on the insanity defense, and for Dr. Zolan's testimony about dissociation. I wondered what was going on in Rosemary Konrad's mind. DeFeo claimed he hadn't heard the shots when he killed his parents. But he had told Rafferty he heard the dog. If he heard one, he should have heard the other. I hoped Mrs. Konrad was thinking along those lines. All it took was one person to hang a jury.

On Friday, I drove to work in a steady rain. The rain kept on through the day, shrouding the court building like a curtain of gray beads. It was cold, wet, the kind of day that chills from the inside out. At 11:30 A.M., we were called into the courtroom. The jury wanted Rafferty's testimony again, including the moment when DeFeo put his head on the detective's shoulder and said, "Once I started, I just couldn't stop. . . ."

The jurors had been sent to their hotel at 11:55 P.M. the night before, and they all looked haggard. Rosemary Konrad was still leaning forward. Watching her, I was positive she wanted to hear about the dog. "The dog was screaming," Butch DeFeo had told Rafferty. Apparently, Bill Weber had similar thoughts. Rafferty was standing near him after the read-back. "If I lose this case because of a fucking barking dog. . . ." he heard Weber say.

341

At 12:05 P.M., we were called back again. The jury was coming in. The courtroom was crowded. Detectives, court buffs, people from our office, Henry O'Brien, the press, and children and spouses of some of the jurors. We took our seats. Tom Spota and I glanced at each other and then at the jurors.

John Roberts, the court clerk, had been around a long time. But I heard a tremor in his voice. "Case on trial, *People* versus *Ronald DeFeo, Jr.*," he said. "Jury, defendant and counsel are present, Your Honor."

Judge Stark's voice was as resonant as when the trial began. "Ladies and gentlemen, I have just received the following note from you: 'The jury has reached a verdict.' I will now direct Mr. Roberts, the Clerk of the Court, to proceed with the taking of the jury's verdicts."

Roberts turned to Mary Astromovich. "Madame Forelady, has the jury agreed upon a verdict?"

"Yes, we have," Mrs. Astromovich answered.

Long after the trial was over, I was able to form a picture of the give-and-take inside the jury room. Each morning when the jurors got to court, someone would bring in the coffee. They were not allowed to have newspapers, but someone else would bring in a crossword puzzle and the jumble puzzle from the *New York Daily News*. Usually, Rosemary Konrad was in charge of the crossword. The jury's deliberations were secret, but years later, Mrs. Konrad told us some of what happened.

Not long after retiring, the jury took its first vote, and the result was ten-to-two for conviction. It was a secret ballot, but Mrs. Konrad and Margaret Giambra identified themselves as the dissenters. Near the end of the day, Mrs. Astromovich called for another vote, and the result was the same. But that night, in the Best Western Motel where Konrad and Giambra were roommates, the younger woman changed her mind. In the morning, the vote was eleven-to-one for conviction. As I suspected, Rosemary Konrad had become the holdout.

As I had waited at my desk for summonses from the judge, I had wondered what was happening in the jury room. According to Mrs. Konrad, the room was filled with cigarette smoke and tension. For weeks, Mrs. Konrad said, she had been enjoying the group dynamic—"These were people that I got along with. We had lunch together every day. We had a ball." But now the ball was over, and she felt like a loner. At the start of deliberations, she had sat in the middle along one side of the table. As her holdout continued, she took a chair at the end of the table near the window. "'I have children home to take care of,'" she quoted someone as telling her. "'Weren't you listening?'" someone else said. "'Were you there for the whole trial?'"

Near the beginning of her holdout, Mrs. Konrad told us, she went to the bathroom and cried. She hadn't thought they would vote that quickly; she wanted more discussion. Mrs. Konrad said she never questioned DeFeo's guilt, but she wasn't sure of his sanity. She knew she wouldn't stay on the fence forever, but she had to be sure before she made her decision.

Mrs. Konrad began searching for something, and she found it in the read-backs. She wanted to hear testimony about the dog. It was as I had thought. She was thinking about Dr. Schwartz's dissociation theory, about DeFeo saying he never heard the shots. But it seemed to her that DeFeo had told someone that he heard the dog. And when she listened to Rafferty's testimony, she knew that she was right. You said it yourself, she would remember thinking about DeFeo. You said you heard the dog.

After the last read-back, Mrs. Konrad was positive. The jurors returned to the deliberation room and sat at the imitation wood table. "Are you satisfied now?" someone asked. "Can we take a vote?"

"Yes," Rosemary Konrad would remember saying. "Go ahead."

"Will the defendant rise and face the jury?" asked John

Roberts. "Madam Forelady, please rise. In the trial of the *People* versus *Ronald DeFeo, Jr.*, how do you find as to the first count charging the murder of Ronald DeFeo, Sr.?"

"Guilty as charged," answered Mary Astromovich.

Behind me a murmuring. Slapping noises; detectives congratulating each other. I looked at the jurors. Some were crying. I had craved the moment, fantasized about it. I had expected elation, but it wasn't like that. I looked at the jurors, and it wasn't like that at all.

Now the clerk was asking for the verdict on each count. "Guilty as charged," Mrs. Astromovich said five more times. Then Weber asked that the jury be polled. John Roberts went over the six counts with each of the six men and six women. "Juror number one, is that your verdict as to the first count?" "Yes, it is," came the answer. Roberts went down the line, and the litany continued for several minutes. When it ended, Judge Stark thanked the jurors, telling them that, to his knowledge, the trial was the longest ever conducted in the history of Suffolk County. Through all of this, as the outside world closed in front of him, Butch DeFeo smirked. Occasionally, his hands went to his mustache.

The jurors were leaving the room as the clerk took DeFeo's pedigree. His name, date of birth, status as a citizen. John Roberts was going by rote as he asked the fourth question: "Are your parents living?"

Ronald DeFeo, Jr., sneered. His voice held the hint of a chuckle. "No, Sir," he said.

A minute later, Weber asked if his client could make two telephone calls. DeFeo had done that after court throughout the trial. Usually, he called the Brigantes, and his aunt, Phyllis Procita.

Court was recessed at 12:17 P.M. People were congratulating me, but I wanted to go back and thank the jurors. Reporters and photographers were pressing against us, looking for jurors. Henry O'Brien was talking to the press. He was the district attorney, and I couldn't resent his making a statement. I would have my turn later.

I went back to the jury room. Judge Stark was in the hallway, still wearing his robes. Inside the room, the smell of dead cigarettes was overpowering. Rosemary Konrad had thrown up violently in the bathroom, and Margaret Giambra was crying. Several jurors were leaving with their suitcases. A few were going out the front way, while a court attendant was getting ready to take Rosemary Konrad, Margaret Giambra and three men out the rear entrance to a staff elevator. All I could do was shake a few hands.

I found a phone and called Betty. I phoned Dr. Zolan's secretary, and answered a call from CBS radio. The lobby was still crowded, and I talked to reporters, praising the jury in my statement. It was close to 3 P.M. when Spota and I and the detectives who had worked on the case went out to celebrate. We had a lavish dinner; I had expected to stay late. But two hours later, I was excusing myself. Suddenly, inexplicably, I felt a sense of loss.

I was like a kid who wanted to go home. Or maybe like an adult. I missed Betty; I missed the children. It was 7 P.M. when I walked in the house.

I couldn't stop talking. I talked about everything except the DeFeo trial.

Epilogue

ON DECEMBER 4, 1975, Ronald Joseph DeFeo, Jr., was sentenced to twenty-five years to life on each of the six counts of second-degree murder for which he had been convicted. Under the law, when the charges stem from one continuous act, the sentences may be served concurrently. DeFeo had already spent a year in jail—he could be eligible for parole in 1999, when he would be forty-eight years old.

Judge Stark could have imposed a lesser sentence of fifteen years to life for second-degree murder, instead of twenty-five. At the time, first-degree murder still carried the death penalty. But first-degree murder could only be invoked for such crimes as the slaying of a police officer or a killing committed by someone already serving a life sentence. In imposing the maximum sentence possible for what he described as the "most heinous· and abhorrent crimes," Judge Stark tried to signal future parole boards against freeing Ronnie DeFeo. "I am of the belief he is a real danger to society in that he may kill again, and the law provides for certain sentences to insure the community's safety," Stark said. Although he could not enforce the recommendation, he asked that the sentences be served consecutively.

Bill Weber asked for clemency. "There is really very little I can say for him," Weber said of his client. "It was an act of insanity. The only proper sentence in this case is that he be confined for life in a mental institution but the court cannot impose that sentence. I would urge some mercy for him because now he is an animal but in ten or fifteen years he may be rehabilitated and possibly make a contribution to society."

Except for Weber, DeFeo was alone in the courtroom—his relatives did not appear. DeFeo remained composed throughout the sentencing, his chest hair showing through his open shirt beneath the plaid jacket. When the judge asked if he had anything to say, DeFeo spoke clearly. "I'm going to appeal this sentence and conviction," he said. "I'll bet I'll be back here in one year." On his way out, he obtained permission to make his two phone calls.

After hanging on in the courts for about two years, DeFeo's appeals failed. He is serving out his sentence in the state correctional facility at Dannemora, New York.

If the drama was over, the curtain stayed up. Several weeks after the DeFeo trial, I appeared at John Kramer's sentencing to recommend leniency. Kramer and I discussed the DeFeo case and got around to the money and jewelry Butch claimed to have hidden. When the subject came up, Kramer's expression changed. "Are you holding something back, John?" I asked.

He didn't answer. "Can anything happen to our agreement?" he asked.

"No," I said. "You've done your part in court."

Kramer nodded and smiled. "What if I knew what Ronnie did with the two hundred grand and the jewelry?"

"Give it up, John," I said. "It won't help you. That's stolen property."

All I could get out of him was that DeFeo said he had buried the money in a park in Amityville. "If you get out of jail and they catch you digging up Amityville," I said, "you'll go back for a long time."

Kramer kept smiling. I never told him that a shovel was found in the trunk of DeFeo's Buick—and that a small park was located less than two blocks from 112 Ocean Avenue.

A year later, we got a report that DeFeo had discussed the buried loot with a fellow inmate in an upstate prison. Coincidentally, the prisoner was the murderer who had served pizza to Tom Spota and me the day we went over Dr. Zolan's testimony. According to an informant, DeFeo told his fellow prisoner that the money was buried about seventy-five feet from where he got rid of the murder weapon. I thought the report was worth looking into, and I sent a memo to police authorities, suggesting that they search the area at the end of Ocean Avenue. As far as I know, the search was never conducted.

In the fall of 1976, I was appointed chief of the newly created major offense bureau, which specialized in the prosecution of homicides and other violent crimes. The following year, Henry O'Brien was defeated in his bid for reelection by Patrick Henry, a former chief assistant. O'Brien knew that I had supported Henry, and felt this represented disloyalty on my part. I had worked for both men and believed that Henry was by far the better man for the district attorney's job. The morning after election, O'Brien fired me. Before the day was over, he hired me back. I was close to trying a gangland killing in which two men had been hit—both found in a car with .38-caliber slugs in their heads. Our star witness was the driver of the getaway car, and we had him under a round-the-clock guard. I had worked for months to establish a rapport with the witness, and he trusted me. Besides which, it was obvious that he wouldn't hang around if the prosecution suddenly ran into a delay.

By the time the case ended in a conviction, O'Brien and I had made our peace. In January, 1978, Pat Henry took office and appointed me chief trial prosecutor. In March, 1980, after ten years in the office of the Suffolk County district attorney, I went into private practice, specializing in criminal defense work. As of this writing, when I read about a major prosecution in Suffolk, I still get homesick. It helps a little when the prosecution is being handled by my successor—Tom Spota.

Recently, I talked to some people in Amityville about Ronnie DeFeo. "There was a lot of relief around here after the conviction," a village cop told me. "People figure he's tucked away for a long time."

A young woman who had reason to be afraid of DeFeo said the same thing. "I was very nervous that he wouldn't be put away," she said.

I still think about the DeFeo case—especially about the children. And I wonder about the questions that were never answered. Did any of the victims wake up? If so, why didn't any of them defend themselves? Why were all six found face-down in death? Why didn't anyone hear the shots?

The house where everything happened has been resold a couple of times. The first purchasers lived there less than a month, and participated in the profits of a book claiming that the house was possessed by evil forces. The book was followed by a movie, and the house became an object of national notoriety.

The house still stands. There are no demons inside, just rooms that once housed a mass-murderer and his victims.

And a barking dog.

Roy

Date Due

SE 3 '81	MY 7 '83	MY 8	
SE 22 '81	AG 1 '83	MY 28	
OC 9 '81	JE 12 '84	SEP. 26 1992	
OC 23 '81	JY 5 '84	JUL 21 '95	
NO 9 '81	JE 1 '85	AUG 22 '95	
NO 24 '81	JY 17 '86	OCT 2 '95	
Dec 7 '81	MR 3 '87	JUN 23 '97	
DE 24 '81	SF 28 '87	21 92	
JA 26 '82	OC 13 '87	NOV 10 97	
FE 8 '82	MR 16 '89	JUN 02	
FE 22 '82	MR 27 '89	JAN 28	
MR 9 '82	JE 29 '89	MAR 19	
JE 28 '82	DEC 18	PR 18	
OC 18 '82	FE 12 '91		
FE 17 '83	JE 11 '91		
MR 24 '83	AG 24 '91		